Reparations to Palestinian Refugees

This book delves into the issue of reparations in relation to Palestinian refugees in their search for a solution to their displacement and dispossession. Highlighting the broad spectrum of reparations available as forms of remedy for a historical injustice, the author probes the reasons behind the failure to reach a reparations agreement till the present day and discusses the significance of issues of apology, recognition and acknowledgement of responsibility.

In its approach, the book departs from traditional and modern perceptions of reparations as featuring in international law, history, politics and philosophy. The analysis is focused on a comparative study of two other cases – the German–Jewish Reparations Agreement of 1952 and the Cypriot conflict – in search of parameters that may constitute a framework to a potential reparations model applicable to the case of Palestinian refugees. When compared to the history of negotiations over reparations in the Israeli–Palestinian case, the findings of the comparison shed light on why reparations are still illusive. The book thus offers an explanation of why reparations to Palestinian refugees have failed, and offers suggestions on how to enhance prospects for reparations to Palestinian displacement and dispossessions.

A unique contribution to the study of the Arab–Israeli peace process, this book will be an important reference for scholars of the Arab–Israeli conflict, and for students and scholars of politics, conflict resolution and history.

Shahira Samy is Jarvis Doctorow Junior Research Fellow in International Relations and Conflict Resolution in the Middle East at St Edmund Hall and the Department of Politics and International Relations at the University of Oxford. Her research interests focus on reparations politics, in addition to refugee issues in the Middle East.

Routledge studies on the Arab–Israeli conflict

Series Editor: Mick Dumper
University of Exeter

The Arab–Israeli conflict continues to be the centre of academic and popular attention. This series brings together the best of the cutting edge work now being undertaken by predominantly new and young scholars. Although largely falling within the field of political science the series also includes interdisciplinary and multidisciplinary contributions.

1. **International Assistance to the Palestinians after Oslo**
Political guilt, wasted money
Anne Le More

2. **Palestinian Political Prisoners**
Identity and community
Esmail Nashif

3. **Understanding the Middle East Peace Process**
Israeli academia and the struggle for identity
Asima A. Ghazi-Bouillon

4. **Palestinian Civil Society**
Foreign donors and the power to promote and exclude
Benoît Challand

5. **The Jewish–Arab City**
Spatio-politics in a mixed community
Haim Yacobi

6. **Zionist Israel and Apartheid South Africa**
Civil society and peace building in ethnic-national states
Amneh Daoud Badran

7. **The Political Right in Israel**
Different faces of Jewish populism
Dani Filc

8. **Reparations to Palestinian Refugees**
A comparative perspective
Shahira Samy

Reparations to Palestinian Refugees

A comparative perspective

Shahira Samy

Routledge
Taylor & Francis Group
LONDON AND NEW YORK

First published 2010
by Routledge
2 Park Square, Milton Park, Abingdon, Oxon OX14 4RN

Simultaneously published in the USA and Canada
by Routledge
711 Third Avenue, New York, NY 10017, USA

Routledge is an imprint of the Taylor & Francis Group, an informa business

Typeset in Sabon by
RefineCatch Limited, Bungay, Suffolk

British Library Cataloguing in Publication Data
A catalogue record for this book is available
from the British Library

Library of Congress Cataloging-in-Publication Data
Samy, Shahira.
Reparations to Palestinian refugees : a comparative perspective / Sharira Samy.
p. cm.—(Routledge studies on the Arab-Israeli conflict)
Includes bibliographical references and index.
1. Refugees, Palestinian Arab. 2. Arab-Israeli conflict—Reparations. 3. Arab-Israeli conflict—Refugees. 4. Reparations for historical injustices. 5. Restorative justice. I. Title.
HV640.5.P36S36 2010
956.04—dc22 2009034686

ISBN10: 0-415-48579-7 (hbk)
ISBN10: 0-203-85703-8 (ebk)

ISBN13: 978-0-415-48579-1 (hbk)
ISBN13: 978-0-203-85703-8 (ebk)

To my nephew, Fouad Samy

And to my niece, Nadine Samy

Should they wish to learn a story
as they make the story of their lives

Contents

Acknowledgements

This book is the product of several years of work in which my educational, professional and intellectual journey has moved from one stage to the other. As this journey took me from Alexandria to Exeter, Cairo and now Oxford, I find myself indebted to many people who have touched my life in so many direct and indirect manners. I only mention some of them here yet remain grateful to a multitude of others scattered across the world.

I wish to thank each and every person who has shared with me an experience of exile and the sharp agony of displacement. To the many Palestinians, Sudanese, Cypriots, Iraqis and all those whose paths have crossed mine, I am touched by how you tried to tell me what displacement is to you and how/if you see an end to it.

Prof. Michael Dumper (University of Exeter) has followed the development of much of this writing project since it started as a burgeoning idea through to encouraging me to make a book out of it. Closely working with Mick for many years as a student and on a number of other projects has made a great impact on my learning process and has taught me to have a critical mind as well as seek precision (at least I try!).

To my friends and colleagues, Leila Hilal (independent legal consultant) and Lena El-Malak (SOAS), I wish to say a big thank you for the time they took to painstakingly read and patiently comment on amorphous drafts of parts of this volume, for the many exchanges of thoughts about reparations and, most importantly, for their moral support throughout. A word of thanks is also due to Prof. Riccardo Bocco (Graduate Institute of International and Development Studies, Geneva) for the many insights and advice he provided since the process of assessing my doctoral thesis. I am equally indebted to my anonymous reviewer, who engaged with my manuscript, helping me with his expertise as he generously offered me one valuable comment after the other. Since my early years as an undergraduate in Alexandria, I have been very fortunate to enjoy the constant professional and friendly support so profusely and kind-heartedly provided by Prof. Laila Morsy (University of Alexandria). I owe her an awful lot.

My sincerest thanks go to Dr Lex Takkenberg (General Counsel and Ethics Officer, UNRWA) for facilitating and supervising an internship at the Damascus field office in 2002–03. The time I spent at UNRWA offered me a firsthand insight into the dynamics of the UN organisation in charge of Palestinian refugees. But mostly, this was a rewarding opportunity to develop direct communication with a large segment of the Palestinian refugee community and to learn through them their perception of their uprooting.

I would also like to thank Badil Resource Center for Palestinian Residency and Refugee Rights in Bethlehem, which I joined for a fact-finding mission to Cyprus in late 2004. The trip offered a unique chance to meet with Cypriots on both sides of the island and be exposed to the various opinions regarding settlement of the conflict. I would particularly like to mention my appreciation of the insightful conversations with Dr Yiouli Taki (Index) throughout the visit. I am also appreciative of the comments provided by Mr George Vassiliou, former President of Cyprus, as well as Mr Mustapha Akinci, former mayor of Nicosia in the Turkish Republic of Northern Cyprus.

The librarians of the Wiener Library in London have been very resourceful in helping me locate relevant material in their collection on the history of the German–Jewish Reparations Agreement. I wish to express my gratitude to them and my appreciation of their assistance.

It is not possible to write any acknowledgements without telling my family what a source of love and support they have always been to me. In my moments of happiness, despair, joy, hope, pain and utter darkness, my mother, Samia Mansour, has constantly been there providing me with love, care and compassion. My brother Sherif Samy, my sister-in-law May El-Sioufy and their children Fouad and Nadine, have tirelessly offered me a shoulder on which to lean, a reason to smile and a push to go on.

Introduction

When Australian Prime Minister Kevin Rudd stood in Parliament in February 2008 to deliver a speech to the Aboriginal population of the country, it was hailed as an 'historic apology' and a 'watershed' in the history of the Australian nation. This gesture of reconciliation for injustices committed over more than a century to Australia's Aborigines had been arduously pursued. Failure to address the injustices done to Australia's indigenous people was 'a great stain' on the nation's soul, Rudd told Parliament, adding, 'We today take this first step by acknowledging the past and laying claim to a future that embraces all Australians.'[1] Equally significant were the events taking place in Chile a few years earlier when Patricio Ailwyn ousted Augusto Pinochet in the presidential elections of 1990. It was not long before the new president went on television and offered a state apology to victims of injustices committed under his predecessor. This symbolic speech crowned a reparations package to victims of human rights violations during the Pinochet era, following the results of an official inquiry into the matter. A similar sense of victory can be detected in the struggle of the Japanese-Americans when their lobbying efforts resulted in a congressional bill requesting the US Government to pay them reparations. A cheque, accompanied by a letter of apology, reached each Japanese-American wrongfully interned by the US Government during the hype of the Second World War. The same cannot be said though about their fellow African-American compatriots. Descendants of the victims of slavery have yet to see their longstanding demands for justice and reparations recognised and redressed by the Government of the United States. Likewise, Korean 'comfort women', victims of injustices committed by the Japanese army during the Second World War, are still assembling every Wednesday in front of the Japanese Embassy in Seoul in objection to the Japanese Government's ongoing refusal to adequately address their plight.[2] International practice and modern history are replete with stories of justice achieved as much as with others where justice is denied. Is there a recipe for success?

On the political map of today's hotspots, the Arab–Israeli conflict maintains a prominent position on the list of the most intractable conflicts of the world. At the heart of this protracted and complex dispute stands a large population of Palestinian refugees calling for a just settlement to their plight. In spite of the various diplomatic endeavours to tackle the refugee issue, the fact remains that almost 60 years on, exile and denial are yet a reality for four generations of Palestinian refugees. Such an impediment brings to the forefront the question of what elements of a solution may conspicuously be lacking.

This book is about why and how injustices are recognised. It is a book about how the international community has come to coin the term 'injustice' itself and find a way to repair it. It is a book about how parties to a conflict attempt to negotiate the terms of justice and the form it takes in an attempt to turn a turbulent past into a more prosperous future.

At the very early stages of writing this study, I spent six weeks among the Palestinian refugee community exiled in Damascus. I arrived with the preconception that the younger the generation, the more 'normal' people's livelihoods would be and the more detached an identity of exile I would find, see and feel. The question was rather the extent to which this conviction of mine would affect perceptions of reparations and terms of justice among this community of displaced Palestinians. As I entered homes, sipped tea, initiated conversations and listened to stories, I was struck by how ubiquitously throbbing and vivid was the pain of exile unrecognised and justice denied among the Palestinians who shared their thoughts with me. It is an observation that was consistently affirmed wherever and whenever I encountered a displaced Palestinian: 'I was born in Damascus and never left Syria in my 50 something years of age. I do not know if I want to live elsewhere. But how can I accept that my story is pushed aside or dismissed?' said a Palestinian refugee who had never fled a home nor felt he had a present one. If exile is so vividly present, can it remain unrecognised? When the collective memory of the Palestinians is shaped by the fateful 1940s marking the birth of their flight, dispersal and denial of their rights, how can this be reconciled with the same historical events marking the birth of the state that the Jewish people emotionally and politically consider a victorious moment in their own collective memory?

When I reached Cyprus a few months after the phenomenal 'No' that the Greek Cypriots flagged in opposition to the Annan Peace Plan in the referendum held in 2004, I was bound to get acquainted with a conflict that had torn the island apart for several decades, displacing and dispossessing one-third of its population. Could the Cypriot experience teach me something about the search for reparations to a displaced and dispossessed population? Crossing the Ledra Palace checkpoint in the heart of Nicosia is a symbol of division as much as is the destruction left intact on both sides of the Green Line I walked through, surrounded by mines, rubble and ghostly remnants of the damage caused by the bloody events of 1974. It was all left intact, a live witness defying the passing of time. Although many Greek Cypriots flock uneventfully to the North as those groups I watched walking along the picturesque bay of Gernse/Kerinia, a significant community of those displaced and dispossessed refuse to cross the artificial borders to visit their properties as long as a settlement remains illusive. Hostilities have certainly stopped since the events of 35 years ago and, to many, Cyprus is associated with an idyllic holiday dream. Yet large-scale photos and graffiti of atrocities committed by each community against the other still adorn the walls of the pedestrian crossing points in Nicosia. If justice has failed and peace plans have faltered, could there still be useful analogies to the Palestinian refugee case? What could various worldwide experiences in transcending conflict have in common and could they illuminate the difficult path the Palestinian refugee issue is treading in the conflict-resolution attempts of the faltering Arab–Israeli negotiations? In this book, I look at Palestinian refugees through other conflicts to probe recognition and redress of 60 years of displacement and dispossession. In this book I delve into intricacies of negotiating displacement and dispossession as a historical injustice.

But first, who are the Palestinian refugees?

Palestinian refugees: a profile

Palestinian refugees presently stand as the largest and most protracted case of displacement in the world. The first massive wave of exodus, displacing about two-thirds of the entire Palestinian population, began in the late 1940s in the context of the establishment of the state of Israel and the first Arab–Israeli War in 1948. Paradoxically, this date, celebrated by Israel as its day of victory and war of independence, is engraved in the Palestinian common memory as *al-nakba*, the catastrophe that caused their displacement from their homeland. The majority of those Palestinians fleeing for their lives headed to the West Bank, the Gaza Strip, Jordan, Syria, Lebanon and also to Egypt. Known as the host countries, the latter remain up to the present day the main geographical locations of the Palestinian refugee population.

Precise figures on how many Palestinians were displaced, what the current total number is and methods of enumeration are but one of the many complex aspects of the Palestinian refugee case. Indicative indeed is the variance of the figures produced at the early stages of the conflict. In 1949, the United Nations Conciliation Commission for Palestine (UNCCP) put the figure at 726,000. A more inflated 957,000 was specified by the United Nations Relief and Works Agency for Palestine Refugees (UNRWA), the organisation purposefully created by the UN for refugees from Palestine. By contrast, the Israeli Government had designated a figure of 520,000, while Palestinian sources offered estimates reaching 850,000 (Palestinian Refugee ResearchNet 2009).

Such was the origin of the Palestinian refugee population, which nevertheless suffered a second wave of major displacement in 1967. A direct repercussion of the Six Days War was an additional 300,000 Palestinians taking flight from the West Bank and Gaza to Jordan, Syria, Egypt and elsewhere. Of these, approximately 180,000 were first-time refugees (dubbed as displaced persons), while the remainder were 1948 refugees uprooted for the second time (Palestinian Refugee ResearchNet 2009). According to UNRWA census covering its areas of operation (West Bank, Gaza, Jordan, Syria and Lebanon), registered Palestinian refugees in June 2008 stand at 4,618,141 (UNRWA 2009) representing approximately 18 per cent of the total number of refugees in the world. UNRWA's figure covers about three-quarters of Palestinian refugees worldwide. The table opposite, based on UNRWA figures (UNRWA 2009), breaks up the Palestinian refugee population in the various host countries.

It is important to note that UNRWA statistics are the official figures quoted for estimations of Palestinian refugees. Nevertheless, these figures should be considered with caution for a number of reasons. Because its mandate covers only the West Bank, Gaza, Syria, Jordan and Lebanon, UNRWA's figures are not all-inclusive and do not account for displaced Palestinians elsewhere. Additionally, compared with the universally accepted definition of a refugee according to the 1951 Convention relating to the Status of Refugees, adopted by the United Nations High Commissioner for Refugees (UNHCR) worldwide, UNRWA operates by a different definition.[3] This matter creates much controversy over the inclusiveness, adequacy and implications of the definition.[4]

From another perspective, unlike the case of the global refugee population registered with UNHCR, UNRWA does not offer full protection to

Location and number of Palestinian refugees

Field of operations	*Total registered refugees*
Jordan	1,930,703
Lebanon	416,608
Syria	456,983
West Bank	754,263
Gaza Strip	1,059,584
Total	4,618,141
Egypt*	50,000–70,000

(Source: UNRWA 2009)

* The Forced Migration Online Research Guide on Palestinian refugees in Egypt puts the figure at 50,000 in 2002. UNHCR 2008 Country Plan for Egypt estimates Palestinian refugees in Egypt to fall between 50,000 and 70,000.

its registered refugees. As the UN agency specifically catering for Palestinian refugees, UNRWA offers considerable assistance to its constituents in the areas of education, health care and other social services. Notwithstanding the essential and vital role played by UNRWA on various levels, the fact remains that the Palestinian refugee population is the only refugee community falling beyond the auspices of UNHCR and the internationally recognised set of legal protection normally offered to refugees.[5]

In such a context, the conditions under which Palestinian refugees reside in the host countries become the bleak reality in which four generations of refugees have plunged.[6] The lack of international protection, coupled with the politicisation of the Palestinian refugee issue by the host states is a stark feature of Palestinians as a refugee community. Various domestic political calculations, intrinsic to each particular host state, reflect on the legal status and aspects of livelihood of Palestinian refugees.

Regionally, the 1965 Protocol for the Treatment of Palestinians in Arab States, known as the Casablanca Protocol, was adopted by the Council of Foreign Ministers of the League of Arab States. Formally, it is the regional instrument acknowledging certain rights for Palestinians by calling upon member states to 'take the necessary measures' to guarantee to Palestinians full residency rights, freedom of movement within and among Arab countries, and the right to work. However, the Casablanca Protocol was not implemented by the various host countries (see El-Abed 2004a). Hence, the legal status and living conditions of Palestinian refugees fluctuate from one host country to the other according to individual political decisions. One of the most significant correlations of this is that about 60 per cent of Palestinian refugees are stateless persons with no recognised citizenship. Palestinians who lost their homes in 1948 and subsequently acquired permanent residency status in Jordan or Israel are the only ones to have collectively acquired citizenship rights since 1948.

The general rationale that the Arab states have tirelessly articulated over the decades is to maintain the national Palestinian identity pending implementation of their right of return to their homes. Accordingly, the initial response of host states to the first flows of Palestinian refugees was to welcome them – temporarily. This implied an adoption of various policies upholding their status as refugees awaiting an imminent return. Over time, some aspects of policies have changed, yet the essence of denying temporary protection to the refugees has persisted, if not intensified, and the problems are largely shouldered on the dynamics of the Israeli–Palestinian peace process. As a result, many Arab governments strongly oppose both resettlement and naturalisation of the refugees.

While standing out as a compelling case of displacement, the multidimensional nature of the Palestinian refugee problem marks it as a matter going far beyond a mere case of displacement. The Palestinian refugee problem is primarily an intrinsic part not only of the Israeli–Palestinian conflict but of the wider Arab–Israeli one as well. The lack of progress in reaching a comprehensive peace agreement, which would include provisions on durable solutions for Palestinian refugees, means that six decades on their status as refugees is yet ongoing. Repatriation of Palestinian refugees is currently not a political option despite its affirmation as an entitled right in international law. It is worth noting here that while voluntary repatriation is the preferred durable solution in UNHCR policies for refugee problems worldwide, Palestinian refugees stand out in the unique position of adamantly demanding their right to return to their homes – a legitimate demand consistently denied by the government of Israel.

The right of return of refugees, resettlement and/or compensation are in fact the options normally put on the table when solutions are proposed for the refugee problem. As mentioned, the right of return to their homes has been a central element of the Palestinian position towards the refugee issue, a position anchored in a number of UN resolutions, particularly United Nations General Assembly Resolution 194 (III) of December 1948 (hereinafter 194). On the other hand, resettlement refers to refugee integration whether in current countries of refuge or in third countries. Because of its opposition to any Palestinian right of return, perceived as a threat to the demographic fabric of the current state of Israel and a destabilising factor to the Jewish character of the state, resettlement and integration in host countries has been an option favoured by successive Israeli governments. By contrast, Palestinian refugees have strongly opposed any resettlement outside of their homeland. Arab host countries have also traditionally rejected the option of resettlement on the premise that refugees have the right to return to their homes (see Palestinian Refugee ResearchNet 2009).

Repatriation and resettlement are undoubtedly central to an eventual settlement of the Palestinian refugee problem; however, this book takes a different approach. It proposes to look at the settlement of the refugee issue from a reparations perspective.

Scope of the book

At the start of this book I posed the question about the perpetuation of the Palestinian–Israeli conflict. The same logic applies to reparations and the reasons lying behind a failure to reach a reparations agreement dealing with Palestinian displacement and dispossession in particular. Some related questions may be formulated as following: is there a model for reparations that could be applicable to the case of Palestinian refugees? And if so, what are the components of such a model and what is its framework? Could other reparations cases in modern international history and practice shed light on the characteristics of such a model? Could other experiences be useful to the Palestinian case?

Two inter-related issues are important to determine at this stage. The first one relates to defining the outcome: what are reparations? The second issue concerns specifying the approach this book will take towards studying reparations. It should be noted that defining reparations and the various approaches to it are the subject matter of Chapter 2. However, far from being exhaustive, some of the questions involved in understanding reparations can be invoked here. For example, is a reparations agreement one that targets an end to refugee status? Are reparations confined to issues of property restitution and payment of compensation, for instance? that devise payment mechanisms? are close-ended? are rights-based? are an element of conflict resolution? are accompanied by repatriation and/or resettlement? are a reconciliation catalyst? are a process culminating in a statement of recognition and apology?

Narrowing down the scope of this multitude of questions would undoubtedly necessitate deciding on what approach to take in tackling the question of reparations. The Palestinian refugee problem and the ongoing search for a solution to it has normally been viewed from various angles ranging from the legal to the economic, the humanitarian, the moral, not to mention the diplomatic. As shall be discussed in the subsequent chapters, the legal approach focuses on studying reparations as a legal concept anchored in a number of international law principles, instruments and resolutions. Reparations is also often the subject of economic analysis, questioning issues related to payment calculations, for instance, devising compensation mechanisms and quantification of losses. From another perspective, standards of welfare, alleviating hardship and living conditions constitute the hub of the humanitarian/developmental approach to reparations. Finally, from a political standpoint, reparations become a conflict-related contentious issue between parties to a conflict. In other words, to what extent do reparations contribute to the search for a settlement of a conflict?

As the reader will learn from Chapter 2, there has been some scholarly interest in the issue of reparations to Palestinian refugees from a legal perspective as well as pondering technical aspects of payment of compensation. The present book takes a different path. Rather than tackling reparations as a legal issue, this book sets out to analyse reparations as a political process. Differentiating between legal and political approaches entails enlarging the context of reparations from a mere legal matter substantiated by rights as enshrined in international law and legal instruments, to a concept of reparations viewed as an evolving process. Each approach has its set of advantages as well as limitations. Enclosure in legalistic frameworks permits to thoroughly evaluate the impact of documents and agreements. However, by neglecting the social forces that influence the exercise of power, legal analysis on its own may be relatively insensitive to other political determinants and hence to the larger political context transcending formal documents. The reverse should also be noted: ignoring the legal significance and characteristics of a reparations agreement within the political context of how a conflict is solved tends to neglect the eventual implications that the structure of an agreement has.

It could also be said that broadening the spectrum – to focus on reparations as a process prone to a game of power and not merely a right or a product of international legal instruments – helps to unravel the circumstances surrounding the agreement: in how many stages and under the pressure of what factors did it take place? How was an agreement negotiated? What kind of obstacles did it face? How did parties to the agreement formulate their demands? Did reparations take a particular form? Such are some of the pertinent issues raised by the international practice and the study of how reparations featured in a multitude of conflicts. However, contrary to the generic literature on reparations and interest in redressing historical injustices, no existing book, to the knowledge of this author, seems to have so far been dedicated to the political dimensions of reparations in the Palestinian refugee case.

Hence, the approach adopted by this volume in looking at reparations as a political process on a macro level implies looking at issues such as how an injustice or a wrongful act is identified and perceived, the form of the remedy to that wrongful act, the parties' perception of reparations and how this affects the form it takes. These are elements that incorporate into the study important themes such as the moral element, the role of apology and acknowledgement of the injustice, for example.

This begs an answer to the question on how to proceed with answering the questions the study proposes to address. How do we go about understanding how and why reparations have failed in the Palestinian case and how do we probe the existence and suitability of a reparations framework? In doing so, this book will rely on a comparative analysis in search of certain parameters that may constitute a framework to potential reparations applicable to the case of Palestinian refugees.

Subjecting an aspect of the Palestinian refugee issue to a comparative analysis may raise some doubts over its suitability for comparison with other conflicts. Comparison in fact refutes the notion of the 'uniqueness' and 'exclusivity' of the Palestinian case, so long dominant in Palestinian circles.[7] In the context of this study, the Palestinian refugee issue is treated as a case of displacement and dispossession resulting from a violent conflict. The latter is the principle common denominator present in the three focal cases of this study, for they all share an occurrence of displacement and dispossession resulting from a violent incident. Comparative analysis thus opens the door for drawing on best-practice observations in other cases.

The first case study this book looks at is the German–Jewish post-World War II Luxembourg Agreement of 1952, signed between Germany, Israel and the Conference on Jewish Material Claims Against Germany (the Claims Conference). Here was one of the most successful reparations cases in history in which the state of Israel, alongside Jewish diaspora organisations united in a representative organisation, successfully negotiated and signed a reparations agreement. Moreover, the intricacies of negotiating reparations, demonstrating how a political will overturns sensitivities surrounding the issue of reparations a few years after the atrocities of the Holocaust, are some factors casting their shadow on this case of reparations. From another perspective, this case study allows for understanding, although in a different context, the early logics of the Israeli negotiators in their approach to reparations.

Cyprus, on its part, represents a conflict characterised by its longevity and its inclusion of several issues interwoven with displacement and dispossession. A future one-state vs. two-states option, power-sharing arrangements between two communities, security concerns and UN involvement are but a few of the issues of concern to the settlement of the conflict and thus closely related to the settlement of the displacement and dispossession dossier. Cyprus also represents failure to reach a reparations agreement despite numerous attempts, rounds of negotiations and several settlement proposals and peace plans put forward by the UN. Although the UN has recently played a less direct role in Israeli–Palestinian affairs in terms of mediation, its experience is no less relevant.

Earlier on I explained that an important aspect of this book is its approach to reparations as a political process on a macro level of analysis. Such a macro level of analysis focuses on looking at what precedes the concrete reparations agreement, what was conducive to it and influencing it. This is reflected in the choice of the comparative elements the book will particularly look at in its analysis of the case studies. Accordingly, the elements the comparison will focus on are the position of each party to the conflict to the issue of reparations, as well as the role played by external involvement. The focus here will be on the interaction of those players in relation to reparations and the resulting effect on the basis and form of the reparations claim. We notice from the diplomatic evolution of the Palestinian refugee issue covered in Chapter 1 that those elements are of paramount importance in the formulation of reparations in the Palestinian–Israeli case. In other words, each of the two case studies analysed in this book is intended to tell a 'story of reparations' through the analysis of the interaction of the conflict parties and the external involvement. Such 'stories of reparations' should distil a certain pattern of how the reparation process has evolved, how the goal was defined and what factors have influenced it. While not suggesting a deterministic correlation, the results of each case, or the 'reading' of each case, suggests points of tension along the way, or refutes – perhaps – the deterministic presence of one of the elements discussed.

Chapter outline

Chapter 1 traces the diplomatic and scholarly evolution of reparations in relation to Palestinian refugees. More specifically, the chapter illustrates how reparations have featured in diplomatic channels concerned with solving the Israeli–Palestinian conflict since the eruption of the 1948 war. In parallel, highlighting scholarly endeavours related to studying the issue of reparations in relation to the Palestinian case complements the overall picture of the evolution of the Palestinian refugee problem over the past decades. Such an outline serves the purpose of gaining a comprehensive understanding of how parties to the conflict approach reparations.

Chapter 2 shifts the focus to the notion of reparations, probing its evolution in international practice and significance in different approaches spanning disciplines as diversified as law, philosophy, politics and history. This exploration paves the way for understanding the elements of reparations, which this study will adopt in its comparative analysis of the various case studies.

Chapter 3 covers the first case subject of the comparative analysis undertaken by this book. The German–Jewish Reparations Agreement – also known as the Luxembourg Agreement – of 1952 was signed by three parties: the Federal Republic of Germany, the state of Israel and the Conference on Jewish Material Claims Against Germany (the Claims Conference). This chapter attempts to answer the broad question posed by the study: how have the comparative elements contributed towards the formulation of the reparations claim in its form and basis?

Likewise, Chapter 4 covers the second case study of this research: that concerning reparations in relation to settlement of the displacement and dispossession component of the Cypriot conflict. It begins with a historical background illustrating the overall evolution of the conflict and the core issues of importance to a settlement. This is followed by two sections depicting each of the two protagonists' positions – the Greek Cypriot and the Turkish Cypriot – regarding the displacement/dispossession issue. The third comparative element dealing with the nature of the external involvement in the conflict is then analysed. It specifically focuses on the role played by the UN in drafting proposals of a settlement, the EU accession dynamics and how they influenced the positions of the parties and finally played a major role in the outcome of the referendum, which the Greek Cypriots voted against while the Turkish Cypriots voted in favour. The final section explores how these factors have shaped the reparations claim in both its basis and form. As its predecessor, the chapter concludes with observations drawn from the case study, which constitute the major characteristics and lessons drawn about reparations.

Finally, Chapter 5 aims to push the argument one step further by exploring the following: what are the prospects for a reparations agreement in the Palestinian case? More precisely, it examines whether the comparison has indicated the presence of a model for reparations in the two case studies. Accordingly, the analysis sheds light on the case of Palestinian refugees in relation to the results of the comparison suggested by the two case studies. To what extent does the Palestinian case, particularly its final rounds of negotiations in Taba in 2001, compare with the findings of the comparison with the two other conflicts? By detailing how the Taba negotiations proceeded and linking that to the pattern revealed by the comparison, an explanation of why Taba has failed – despite the many voices hailing the progress it had achieved – is put forward. The chapter then concludes with a final section outlining a number of themes that may contribute towards enhancing Palestinian prospects for reparations to their displacement and dispossession.

1 Reparations in the Palestinian context

This chapter looks into reparations in relation to Palestinian refugees. More specifically, the analysis will trace how reparations have featured in the diplomatic channels concerned with solving the Israeli–Palestinian conflict since the eruption of the 1948 war. In parallel, highlighting the main scholarly endeavours related to the issue of reparations in relation to the Palestinian case complements the overall picture of the evolution of reparations to the Palestinian refugee problem over the past decades. Accordingly, the chapter looks at the main diplomatic events in the history of the Palestinian–Israeli conflict, beginning with the efforts of the UNCCP and ending with the Road Map, the last document put forward by the international community in relation to the Middle East peace process. Incorporated is a mention of the major studies that have contributed to the scholarship focusing on the various aspects of reparations in relation to Palestinian refugees.

Prior to reviewing the efforts of the UNCCP during the early stages of the conflict, a brief discussion of the causes of the Palestinian displacement and the related issue of responsibility is of importance, as the latter frequently surfaces within the subsequent attempts to propose solutions to the refugee question. What caused the exodus, who is responsible for it and how many refugees fled are but a few issues strongly debated and are highly controversial, whether in diplomatic or academic circles. Delving into the argument of who caused the displacement and what exactly happened during the course of the war is beyond the scope of this book. In other words, this study does not claim to offer a contribution to the exhaustive debate over the historical formation of the Palestinian refugee problem. However, the issue of responsibility linked to the root causes of the refugee problem has been a component of the reparations dossier, frequently featuring in the diplomatic attempts to tackle the refugee question. Therefore, a brief account of the main arguments presented in this context is of relevance and is outlined below.

A deliberate Zionist plan for land seizure involving forced evacuation of Arab inhabitants is one of the strong arguments put forward as a principal cause of the Palestinian refugee problem. According to this argument, such Zionist plans called for a policy of conducting massacres then resorting to psychological warfare to threaten the civilian population, ordering it to leave and finally forcibly expelling the Palestinian Arabs. This exodus – attributed to panic created by fighting, to rumours concerning real or alleged acts of terrorism or to expulsion – was the argument initially advocated by Count Bernadotte, UN mediator for Palestine, in September 1948 in his report to the international organisation (Takkenberg 1998: 14). This in fact is the official position maintained by the Palestinians and is strongly favoured by many Arab and Palestinian historians and scholars (see for example Cattan 1969, Masalha 2003).

The official Israeli position – as well as traditional Israeli historiography – on the other hand proposes a figure as low as 500,000. This position stresses the voluntary departure of the Palestinian Arabs in response to Arab leadership calls promising an imminent victory over the newly established state of Israel and eventual return of Palestinian Arabs to their homes. Eviction plans are denied according to this argument and massacres are considered exceptional acts of extremism carried out by some Irgun troops (see for example Takkenberg 1998: 14, Gelber 2001: 23). The next waves of Palestinian escapees and deportees, according to the same line of thought, were the result of the Israeli Defense Forces' counteroffensive against the invading Arab armies. Another reason for the exodus from the Israeli point of view is the collapse of Arab political institutions, which resulted from the departure of the Arab elite causing the social structure to fragment because of economic hardships and administrative disorganisation (Gelber 2001: 22–23, Takkenberg 1998: 14, Brynen 1998).

A third main school of thought in this regard has emerged since the late 1980s and is represented by the 'New Historians', those Israeli scholars who produced research based on some public as well as private Israeli archives. This scholarship defied the traditional Israeli position regarding the exodus of Palestinian Arabs and attributed responsibility – at least partially – to Israel. Benny Morris, the pioneer of this school, has demonstrated that the flight was due to a complex mixture of factors: military conflict, widespread fear among Palestinians, specific Jewish attacks and atrocities, Arab disorganisation and demoralisation and occasional localised incidents of ethnic cleansing (Morris: 1987).[1] It is worth noting that there have been thriving debates emerging among scholars in the wake of this new scholarship discussing the origins of the exodus.[2] The main contribution of this school is the turning point it created in the historiography of the conflict. There is now an established body of literature and a worldwide acceptance of the revisionist reading of the birth of the Palestinian refugee problem. As Takkenberg points out, it is mainly because of the research of the New Historians that there is at present an increasing recognition of Israel's *shared accountability* (emphasis added) for the flight of the Palestinian Arabs (Takkenberg 1998: 16). This in turn shifts the historical debate over the origins of the refugee problem to a broader struggle over moral and political responsibility for the displacement (Brynen: 1998). By far influential in the present academic circles, Vidal notes the findings of the New Historians are nevertheless solely based on Israeli archives, thus not taking into consideration either Arab archives or oral Palestinian history (Vidal 2002: 34).

In the following pages I wish to turn to the various diplomatic attempts to tackle the refugee problem since its birth in the late 1940s.

Reparations efforts at the early stages of the conflict

In tracing the early international efforts to solve the Palestinian refugee problem since the first waves of displacement in 1948, specifically highlighted are the efforts of the United Nations Compensation Commission for Palestine (UNCCP) in the early 1950s, the Madrid Framework in the 1990s, the Oslo Agreements in 1993, the Camp David II negotiations in 2000, the Taba talks in 2001, the Road Map of 2003 and the Geneva Initiative.

United Nations Compensation Commission for Palestine (UNCCP) and early efforts of identification and evaluation of losses

In the first attempt by the United Nations to deal with the conflict, the General Assembly (GA) in Resolution 194 set up the UNCCP with the general task of assisting the governments and authorities concerned to achieve a final settlement of the Palestine question, to provide protection and promote a durable solution for Palestinian refugees. The Assembly subsequently appointed France, Turkey and the US to the commission. During the 1950s the UNCCP, the US and the Western powers focused on the refugee issue with the premise that its resolution would greatly facilitate a peaceful solution of the Arab–Israeli conflict. It was argued that if the refugees could be resettled and/or repatriated, the major obstacle to a peace settlement would be removed. Thus, proposals for coping with the refugees shifted back and forth between repatriation to Israel or resettlement in the surrounding Arab countries (Peretz 1995: 2, Takkenberg 1998: 25). When little or no progress on repatriation or resettlement was achieved, the UNCCP concentrated on refugee compensation as per Resolution 194 as a means of opening the door to peace talks. The UNCCP ultimately failed to effect any substantial agreement on compensation (Takkenberg 1998: 27, Peretz 1995: 13).

Falling short on making progress on the refugee problem, the GA passed Resolution 512 on 26 January 1952 calling upon the UNCCP to continue its efforts to secure implementation of 194 and to make itself available to the parties. The resolution recognised that it would need to be the parties themselves who made peace. The UNCCP – with its plans, ideas and statistics – could assist, but these ultimately would be mere aids to efforts that the Arabs and Israelis themselves would need to exert. In Fischbach's words, this resolution was 'the final nail in the coffin of the UNCCP as an active mediator in the Arab–Israeli conflict' (Fischbach 2002: 39). This, in his opinion, was encouraged by US delegates, who had been arguing since early January 1950 that the Commission should drop active conciliation efforts and concentrate on secondary issues (Fischbach 2003a: 134). An explanatory factor in this regard was put forward by Rempel in a study of the early efforts of the UNCCP. The internal contradiction of the UNCCP's general mandate to resolve the conflict on the one hand and facilitate repatriation and compensation as refugee-related aspects on the other hand meant that the various rights of the refugees were compromised in favour of the overall politics of the conflict itself (Rempel 2000: 7–9).

However, if the UNCCP has failed in its political mediating endeavours, its principal accomplishments were related to technical matters of identification and evaluation of Arab property and in obtaining the release of some 6,000 Arab refugee accounts blocked in Israeli banks worth approximately 4 million Palestine pounds (for details see Fischbach 2003b; see also Peretz 1995: 2, Takkenberg 1998: 27–28). By 1961, about 450,000 record forms of properties owned by Arab individuals had been prepared. The identification of refugee property was completed in 1964; lists of such property are still maintained by the Commission (Takkenberg 1998: 28). Although since 1964 it made no more substantial contributions towards the implementation of 194, the UNCCP was never formerly abolished.

The above mentioned efforts of the UNCCP are worth detailing here as they are the premise of most of the research undertaken in relation to identification and evaluation of property and are considered to be the backbone of any potential compensation agreement in the future. Moreover, they also represent the efforts of the international community – represented by the UN – in its attempts to deal with the refugee problem during the early phases of the conflict.

The UNCCP established the Refugee Office in 1951. Its chief task was to consult with Israel, the Arab states and UNRWA to develop a practical compensation plan that would include payment to individual refugees and come up with an informal estimate of the overall scope and value of refugee property (Fischbach 2002: 39). However, the Refugee Office was unsuccessful in getting the parties to accept its figures as a starting point for negotiations on compensation, which resulted in the UNCCP's suspension of its efforts to achieve an Arab–Israeli agreement on compensation. Consequently, it shifted its focus instead on the longer term, notably by carrying out detailed 'technical' preparatory work that would be of use if ever a compensation process got under way. Hence, the UNCCP decided to carry out a more thorough evaluation of the refugee property by identifying and establishing a value for each individual plot of refugee land. In part, this was in response to the potential need to compensate individual refugees as opposed to a collective compensation. Accordingly, the UNCCP Technical Office, established in May 1952, drew up what came to be known as the 'refugee property', or R/P1, forms cataloguing individually owned Arab property. These forms include for each individual plot of Arab-owned land within what became Israel such information as the name of the owner, the surface area, the precise location and the estimated value. The Technical Office also compiled an index of the landowners in the forms organised on a village basis (Fischbach 2002: 40–44).[3]

Michael Fischbach presents the most comprehensive and detailed analysis of the efforts of the UNCCP in relation to Palestinian refugee compensation from 1949–1966. In his book, *Records of Dispossession*, Fischbach focuses on the 12-year programme for identifying and evaluating refugee property carried out by the UNCCP's Technical Office. In doing so, the author details the vast land records used and generated by that office and publishes for the first time compensation estimates hitherto buried in the Commission's archives in New York.

Fischbach describes the UNCCP records as being 'invaluable' for determining the scope of individual refugee losses and offers some assistance in assessing individual values. While contending that they do not offer full assistance in assessing collective, communally owned and state-owned land, the R/P1 forms still 'constitute the most complete and reliable record in existence, and as such constitute an invaluable resource for any negotiation' (Fischbach 2002: 44–45). Moreover, the historian thinks that while the methodology and accuracy of the UNCCP figures have been challenged over the years, the Commission's process nevertheless represents 'by far the most exhaustive and "neutral" attempt to qualify refugee losses ever carried out' (Fischbach 2002: 44).

It is worth mentioning that Fischbach's recent research complements earlier efforts of identification and evaluation undertaken by several scholars, such as Sami Hadawi, Atif Kubursi, Yusuf Sayigh and the Arab League.

As the former official land valuer of the Palestine government, with responsibility to maintain a record of land ownership between Arabs and Jews, Sami Hadawi carried out a study on the identification of Arab land ownership. Hadawi attempted to reconstruct the situation as he knows it existed in May 1948, prior to the alterations caused by the Armistice Agreements in 1949 (Hadawi 1988: 113). Since Hadawi claims the *Village Statistics 1945* published by the mandatory government in Palestine to be the most accurate and authoritative source, adjustments on that basis have been made to the findings of the UNCCP's land expert where the figures of the two sources were found to conflict (results appear in details in Hadawi 1988: 224–307). The discrepancy in the results can be explained by the fact that the UNCCP dealt with property of individual Arabs and ignored all other factors. By contrast, Hadawi claims his study covers – in addition to individual land ownership – what the Palestinians believe is the extent of their legitimate property rights and holdings in the total lands of a village, including the communal or common lands registered or recorded as public or state domain, in the name of the mukhtar (headman) or the high commissioner, regardless of category of land tenure or system of taxation[4] (Hadawi 1988: 105–111).

Whereas Hadawi's main contribution was on the identification of property, Atif Kubursi offered a thorough study in the economic assessment of total Palestinian losses in 1948. Kubursi also includes in his assessment of losses the psychological and human suffering, citing the example of Jewish compensation from post-Nazi Germany (Kubursi 1988: 117–118)[5]. Prior to Kubursi's study, there have been several attempts to assess Palestinian losses in 1948, the results of which differed according to what category of losses were covered and what prices were used to express physical property in monetary terms (Kubursi 1988: 123). Kubursi criticises the UNCCP's attempts to assess Palestinian losses for only considering a very small sub-set of these losses. He therefore attempts to re-evaluate those losses, adding to them additional components. In his view, the Commission's first land specialist John Berncastle made his evaluation at short notice without any fieldwork and on the basis of many assumptions that were known to be weak and inapplicable. Moreover, sales data was used to reflect market values: although theoretically correct, these numbers understate by a substantial margin the true value of the land. And finally, as more than 450,000 record forms for properties owned by Arabs were prepared with no computerised facilities, it is difficult to believe they have been processed without significant data management problems (Kubursi 1988: 123–127).

The UNCCP attempt to identify and assess Palestinian losses, however, was not the only one criticised by Kubursi. The study of the Arab League, first published in Cairo in 1955, featured assessments substantially higher than those of the UN and included several additional non-real-estate assets. Nevertheless, Kubursi found that these estimates failed to include lost opportunities of income-generation, the depletion of human capital stock, innumerable public and private assets and private and social psychological damage. While it represented an improvement on the UN land specialist's study, it fell short of computing the full range of losses and used below-market indices in the evaluation of real estate losses (Kubursi 1988: 128–131).

Professor Yusuf Sayigh attempted to redress some of the omissions in the preceding assessments in his book, *The Israeli Economy*, published in 1964. His coverage was deemed more extensive, his indices more realistic and generally in conformity with economic principles; and his analysis was more perceptive and original than all the preceding attempts. Sayigh's estimates, though, did not cover the full range of lost assets and missed opportunities and disregarded psychological damage (Kubursi 1988: 132–136). What Kubursi did, in contrast, was attempt to valuate rural and urban land and buildings by making extensive use of a hitherto neglected set of UN records relating to real estate holdings in Palestine in 1946 and 1947. He also draws on a second rich but neglected source of data relating to all property sales as registered in the official records of the government of Palestine between 1 January 1946 and 19 November 1947 (Kubursi 1988: 161).

Commenting on the various studies mentioned above, Fischbach believes that complaints by Arab states throughout the 1960s concerning the UNCCP's land figures derive mainly from the fact that the documents record only what the technical office could ascertain was individually owned or waqf land. Land that was communally owned by the inhabitants of a village or tribe, public or state land and all but a fraction of the vast, largely Arab-owned Beersheba district were not included in the UNCCP accounts (Fischbach 2002: 44).

It may thus be concluded that the efforts of the UNCCP were born by virtue of the will to implement 194 and a drive to find a solution to the Arab–Israeli conflict. Compensation was never addressed as the first motivation nor did it come in parallel with the others. There were efforts for resettlement, others for repatriation and only when they were not possible was there focus on compensation. Also, the UNCCP found itself focusing its efforts on preparations for compensation, such as the accounts, the valuation of assets and the like. Due to political factors, however, focus became almost confined to compensation. By the middle of the 1950s, even compensation had waned in importance. As Fischbach reveals in his study, UNCCP efforts were doomed from the start by the red lines established by Washington. The US and Israel wanted any compensation scheme to finance the large-scale resettlement of refugees. According to the historian, UNCCP and American archives are replete with evidence revealing the extent to which the Americans ensured that the Commission's policy and initiatives would not cross those lines (Fischbach 2002: 47). Also, Israel's insistence that compensation for the Palestinians be linked to other issues, such as compensation for the property left behind in Arab countries by Jewish emigrants, removed compensation from the realm of the refugees' individual and collective rights and relegated it to merely another dimension of the widening Arab–Israeli conflict.[6] From another perspective, peacemaking efforts were shifting to a land-for-peace formula. This meant that the refugee issue was dwindling in importance on the international level in comparison with the rise of Palestinian national movement in the 1960s. Focus then was on liberating the homeland. This led many Palestinians to equate compensation with abandonment of the national patrimony (Fischbach 2002: 48). As the UNCCP disappeared from an active role on the scene, so did the issue of compensation. Since the 1950s, little attention was given to the question until the launch of the Madrid Peace Process in early 1991, as we shall see below.

Recent efforts for reparations

The multilateral track: the Refugee Working Group (RWG)

The Madrid Peace Process opening on 30 October 1991 envisaged Arab–Israeli peace negotiations on two levels: bilateral negotiations between the direct parties to the conflict as well as multilateral negotiations on those broader issues whose solutions require coordinated action and the international community's support.[7] In that context, the multilateral track was formally initiated in Moscow in January 1992, with the establishment of the RWG and four others.[8] The RWG focuses on seven main themes: databases, family reunification, human resources development, job creation and vocational training, public health, child welfare, and economic and social infrastructure.[9] With the exception of family reunification and the formal declaratory statements of the parties during plenary sessions, the RWG has not discussed, nor addressed, the core political issues involving a prospective solution of the refugee problem and has thus relegated discussion of the issue to a quasi-humanitarian level (Brynen and Tansley 1995, Masalha 2003: 221).

It is worth noting in this regard that although the RWG did not specifically discuss reparations in detail, it is significant to shed light on what the official positions alluded to and the reasons why the first official negotiating venue between the two parties did not tackle the refugee dossier in substantial detail.

To the Palestinians, the RWG was perceived as a forum to address a fundamental issue, such as that of refugees in a multilateral framework that includes supportive Arab states as well as the international community. The Palestinian official position was based on asserting the importance of various UN resolutions, notably 194. While not opposed to the various socio-economic initiatives included in the RWG, Palestinians expressed repeated concern at attempts to separate the political from the humanitarian, fearing that this might jeopardise the refugees' rights (Brynen 1997). Moreover, it is thought that to Palestinian decision-makers, the question of refugees at that stage was of less importance in relation to territorial issues and the mobilisation of political and economic support for the Palestinian leadership. Hence, the Palestinian leadership publicly and rhetorically maintained its traditional positions on the refugee issue for domestic consumption, while devoting relatively little high-level attention or diplomatic resources to the refugee issue (Brynen 1997). Former Palestinian negotiator Salim Tamari believes that the RWG meant the refugee issue was recast not as an exclusive humanitarian issue but as part of restoring the conception of the right to self-determination to the Palestinian people. Palestinians saw in the introduction of the RWG a political dimension not available in the other four groups. It was political in a double sense, for it sent a signal to Palestinian refugees in Jordan, Syria and Lebanon that they were not forgotten in the protracted negotiations of the transitional period. This would give a much needed legitimacy to the impending signing of an Israeli–Palestinian accord, which was bound to be seen as too conciliatory by Palestinians in the diaspora if a refugee component was missing from it (Tamari 1995: 9–10).

By contrast, Israel strongly opposed any attempt to establish 194 as a basis for anything and has emphasised that the RWG should be concerned with humanitarian rather than political issues (Brynen 1997). For Israel, the refugee issue was seen as a highly sensitive one domestically, and an equally low priority in the context of broader Palestinian–Israeli negotiations. Consequently, there was also little incentive to show flexibility or willingness in approaching the RWG and little interest to try to limit RWG engagement to non-controversial areas (Brynen 1997).

Regarding the issue of responsibility, it is worth noting that the Israeli Government has argued that 'refugee movements and exchanges of populations are a common phenomena in world history' and that Israel itself absorbed nearly 600,000 Jews from Arab countries, thereby effectively cancelling out Palestinian claims (Brynen 1998). For Palestinians:

> Israel has been, and continues to be responsible for the process through which the refugee problem was crafted . . . through violence against civilian populations in times of war, and through expropriation of their lands and homes after the war.
>
> (Brynen 1998, Tovy 2003)

Overall, the RWG was an international framework in which certain aspects of the refugee problem were discussed among others. The first negotiating round between the parties to the conflict illustrated differences between the publicly articulated positions of Israel and the Palestinians on the refugee issue, with the former insisting on the resettlement and rehabilitation of refugees, while the latter emphasises the Palestinians' right to compensation and return. These may therefore be considered as differences over both the nature of the refugee issue and thus the level of a solution, the views reflecting a perception of a legal problem vs. a humanitarian one. As Brynen describes the RWG, it was a process of 'quasi-negotiation' characterised by disagreement among the parties as to whether they are negotiating, and what it is they might be negotiating about (Brynen 1997).

Despite those differences, has there been a shift in positions and policies? Some have argued that Israel's approach to the refugee problem remained markedly consistent with its policies of denial of the previous 40 years (Masalha 2003: 223). A counterargument, though, may be that in light of the absence of the discussion on the refugee issue for several decades, the mere mention of it, and the Israeli acquiescence to put it on the negotiation table, may be considered as a variance from the former situation (Tovy 2003).

The eruption of the second Palestinian intifada in September 2000 eventually led to a suspension of all multilateral track activities.[10] Meanwhile, on 3 September 1993, after months of secret Norwegian mediation outside the regular bilateral negotiations of the Madrid Framework, Israel and the Palestinian Liberation Organisation (PLO) signed a Palestinian–Israeli Declaration of Principles (DoP) in Washington, DC, initiating what became known as the Oslo Process.

The Oslo Process

The signing of the DoP was significant in its bypassing of the Madrid Framework and establishing instead the principle of direct bilateral negotiations between Israel and the PLO.[11] In relation to the refugee file, the DoP called for final status negotiations on the refugee issue – among others – to begin by May 1996.[12] The agreement also stipulated the formation of the Palestinian–Israeli–Jordanian–Egyptian Quadripartite Committee dealing with some aspects of the 1967 displaced persons. Oslo in fact meant that the refugee file, together with the other major points of contention between Israelis and Palestinians, were deferred to a later stage of negotiations.[13] Moreover, both the Madrid peace process and the Oslo accords were anchored in Security Council Resolutions 242 and 338, which pose a question mark on the relevance of 194 as a cornerstone of the Palestinian position on the 1948 refugees (Abdul Rahman 2003: 4, Masalha 2003: 226). As called for in the Oslo Agreement, permanent status negotiations between Israel and the Palestinians were formally launched in the spring of 1996. These were interrupted, however, by the election in May of that year of a new Likud-led government in Israel under Prime Minister Benjamin Netanyahu.

In an interview in 1999 about the refugee file within the peace negotiations, Tamari states that, had it not been for Oslo and the RWG, decisions on the fate of Palestinian refugees would have been made by others on behalf of the Palestinians and the refugees. In his opinion, this would have undermined the historical claims of the refugees. Therefore, according to Tamari, these negotiations kept the internationally recognised rights on the agenda (Abowd and Tamari 1999). The Camp David Summit of 2000 was the next negotiations round between Israelis and Palestinians.

The Camp David Summit of 2000

In July 2000, US President Bill Clinton hosted an intensive summit meeting in Camp David between Israeli Prime Minister Ehud Barak and PLO Chairman Yasser Arafat. These talks failed to produce an agreement and little progress was made on the refugee issue in particular.[14] Camp David 2000 was the first organised discussion between the Israeli leadership and the PLO to deal with the refugee question and other subjects in the final settlement. During the course of the summit, it was reported that Israel continued to maintain its position of not accepting any legal or civil responsibility for the Palestinian displacement and would consider the return of about 100,000 refugees on 'humanitarian grounds' in the form of family reunification as its compliance with 194. At most, it was prepared to express its 'regret' for the suffering the Palestinians endured during and after the 1948 war and offered to take part in an international effort to provide the refugees with financial compensation that would also compensate Jews, who it maintained were expelled from the Arab countries (Lustick 2005: 121–122, Masalha 2003: 236, Klein 2006: 99, Tovy 2003).

Assad Abdul Rahman, former head of the refugee department in charge of the refugee file in the final status negotiations, quotes the official Palestinian position as formulated by Abu Mazen in his speech to the Palestinian Central Council on 9 September 2000 as follows:

> The Palestinians want Israel to take moral and legal responsibility for the refugees crisis. UNGAR 194 must be accepted so that all refugees are guaranteed the right of return, and by return we mean to Israel. Refugees who choose to return and those who do not must be compensated. Host countries must also be compensated. We refuse to mix the issue of Palestinian refugees with Jewish immigrants.
>
> (Abdul Rahman 2003: 15)

Yossi Beilin sums up what took place during the summit in the following statement:

> At Camp David there were no real negotiations on the subject. The Israeli view was that Israel was not responsible for the problem, doesn't have to pay for it and the number of refugees who will be admitted will be some hundreds every year and that's it. The Palestinians felt that Israel was not ready to even address the problem.
>
> (Eldar and Tamari 2002)

In fact, reasons for failure to reach an agreement at Camp David range from insufficient preparations and groundwork to faulty negotiating tactics and domestic party-coalition constraints on the Israeli side. In this regard, for example, the argument went that the composition of Barak's coalition government, based on moderate-to-extreme right-wing parties, meant the prime minister was unable to yield far-reaching concessions on a thorny issue such as that of refugees (Abdul Rahman 2003: 13–15, Beilin 2004: 156–158). Barak's strategy was for a comprehensive package deal, an all-or-nothing approach, even if that meant giving what he called 'far-reaching concessions' to the Palestinians (Abdul Rahman 2003: 10).

Although Palestinians had received the first significant indication of Israel's eagerness to strike a deal – and its willingness to retreat from long-established positions – in secret discussions held between representatives of Israel and the PA in Stockholm in the spring of 2000, in the subsequent Camp David summit there was no agreement with respect to the origins of the refugee problem nor about compensation or the number of refugees who would be absorbed by Israel (Tovy 2003). Contrasting this outcome with his previous understanding with Abu Mazen, Beilin states that on the subject of refugees, the 1995 document stipulates that the Israeli side recognises the material and mental suffering caused to the Palestinian refugees, and that both sides seek to establish an international organisation led by the government of Sweden to deal with the subject of compensation. Israel will participate in financing the international fund that will compensate the refugees and will continue to absorb refugees in the framework of family reunification and in special humanitarian cases (Beilin 2004: 168–169).

In an effort to break the negotiations deadlock, President Clinton unveiled some proposals to the parties in December 2000. In a subsequent speech to the Israel Policy Forum in January 2001, Clinton outlined the many elements of this proposal regarding borders, security, settlements, Jerusalem and refugees (Clinton 2001). The Clinton parameters noted that all refugees should receive compensation from the international community for their losses and assistance in building new lives. In this regard, they differed little from the Camp David formula. A new international mechanism would be set up to look after the rehabilitation of the refugees to which Israel would contribute as part of its compensation to the refugees. Thought to be inclined towards embracing the official Israeli position vis-à-vis the refugees specifically calling for reunification of families as sufficient fulfilment on its part of 194, the Palestinians announced their rejection of those proposals (Masalha 2003: 239, Tovy 2003, Abdul Rahamn 2003: 13). Nevertheless, six months after their failure to reach an agreement at Camp David in July 2000 and the subsequent outbreak of the second intifada in September of the same year, both parties continued their negotiations in Taba in an effort to secure an overall permanent status agreement before early Israeli prime ministerial elections in February 2001.

The Taba negotiations

Ultimately, the Taba negotiations failed to produce a comprehensive agreement on the refugee issue despite substantial discussion of the matter. Against the backdrop of escalating violence, negotiations were very difficult. Neither Palestinian nor Israeli public opinion was inclined to compromise. With Sharon's accession to the position of prime minister, the prospects for meaningful permanent status negotiations quickly faded.

Tackling the refugee file with much more detail than negotiations at Camp David, the talks between the delegations at Taba focused the most on rehabilitation of refugees and compensation modalities. Also worth mentioning is the fact that, unlike Camp David – where the Palestinians merely responded to the Israeli offers presented to them – at Taba the Palestinian delegation also presented its own proposals. In fact, the refugee dossier at Taba was the only one on which drafts had been exchanged (Beilin 2004: 246–247).

The EU non-paper – otherwise known as the Moratinos Document – is the accepted source on the contents of the Taba talks.[15] The document was authored by the EU Special Representative to the Middle East Process, Ambassador Moratinos, and his team after consultations with the Israeli and Palestinian sides present at Taba in January 2001. Article 3 of the Moratinos Document, concerned with the refugee file, states that the parties exchanged non-papers according to which both sides suggested, as a basis, that the parties should agree that a just settlement of the refugee problem in accordance with Security Council Resolution 242 must lead to the implementation of GA Resolution 194. Article 3.7 in particular states that '. . . it was suggested that the implementation of the agreement shall constitute a complete and final implementation of UNGAR 194 and therefore end all claims'.

Chief Israeli negotiator for the refugee file at Taba, Yossi Beilin, outlined the Israeli perspective in his non-paper, where he accepted responsibility for being a partner in its solution. The Israeli paper did not contain an explicit acceptance of 194. Israel was in fact not accepting responsibility in its legal sense. Instead, it offered a joint historical narrative in collaboration with the Palestinian side. In their non-paper at Taba, Palestinians had demanded that Israel recognise its moral and legal responsibility for the forced displacement and dispossession of the Palestinian civilian population during the 1948 war, and for preventing the right of return of the refugees to their homes in compliance with 194 (Palestinian Refugees 2001). This matter is subject to further discussion in Chapter 5.

Moving to technical details of the compensation package and the question of what is compensation to cover, Article 3.6 of the Moratinos Document states that the Palestinian delegation demanded restitution of refugee property, which the Israelis rejected. In his non-paper, Beilin had initially rejected the idea of restitution, favouring instead compensation programmes addressing financial and in-kind compensation for displacement and material loss. Such programmes, in the Israeli view, would also emphasise the economic growth of the relevant communities. Therefore, 'individual historic justice' and 'communal economic development' are the objectives that should guide the elaboration of these programmes from the Israeli perspective.

Delving further into details concerning the mechanism and modalities of compensation payment, Article 3.3 of the Moratinos Document states that both sides agreed to the establishment of an international commission and an international fund as a mechanism for dealing with compensation in all its aspects.[16] Both sides agreed that 'small-sum' compensation shall be paid to the refugees in the 'fast-track' procedure. Moreover, claims for compensation for property losses below a certain amount shall be subject to 'fast-track' procedures. There was also progress on Israeli compensation for material losses, land and assets expropriated, including agreement on a payment from an Israeli lump sum, or proper amount to be agreed upon, that would feed into the International Fund.

According to the Israeli side, the calculation of this payment would be based on a macro-economic survey to evaluate the assets to reach a fair value. The Palestinian side, however, said that this sum would be calculated on the records of the UNCCP, the Custodian for Absentee Property and other relevant data with a multiplier to reach a fair value. Such a structure was thought to insulate Israel from direct responsibility to the refugees themselves for the resolution of their status and claims. Israel opposed Palestinian demands that the state of Palestine supervise the distribution of funds, which Israel insisted remain under the control of a commission on which it and the Palestinian state were represented. Israel's own contributions were recognised to be substantial, but its share of the $20 billion amount under discussion at Taba was not specified. A significant part of Israel's contribution would be in real property, including settlements and their infrastructure transferred to Palestinian sovereignty in the West Bank, Gaza Strip and East Jerusalem.

As for the issue of compensation to host countries, Article 41 of the Palestinian paper demanded that 'the refugees' host countries (i.e., Lebanon, Syria, Jordan, Egypt, Iraq and the Palestinian Authority) shall receive compensation for the significant costs they bore in hosting the refugees'. On the other hand, Article 11 of the Israeli private response stated that 'the refugees' host countries shall receive compensation for the significant costs they bore in hosting the refugees. Future rehabilitation costs and investments shall be addressed according to the details of this agreement, via bilateral arrangements between the host countries and the International Commission.'

And finally, regarding compensation to Jews from Arab states, Article 3.5 of the Moratinos Document states that: 'The Israeli side requested that the issue of compensation to former Jewish refugees from Arab countries be recognized, while accepting that it was not a Palestinian responsibility or a bilateral issue. The Palestinian side maintained that this is not a subject for a bilateral Palestinian–Israeli agreement.'

Yossi Beilin, reflecting on the Taba talks, describes the compensation issue as complex, 'but it can be resolved' through the refugee rehabilitation channel facilitated by funds to be collected from various entities worldwide. The fund will be used for universal compensation to every refugee family, personal compensation for property presently in the possession of Israel, as well as compensation to be given to countries such as Jordan, which has absorbed refugees over the past few decades (Beilin 2004: 238–239). The pending issues, according to the Israeli politician, were to address 'what the Palestinians call Right of Return' and the question of the responsibility for creation of the refugee problem.

Beilin states that the agreement would include a concise history of events in the eyes of each party, recognition of the suffering and distress of the refugees and separate interpretations of 194, while agreeing that 194 would be implemented in line with the Clinton plan (Beilin 2004: 230).

The major contribution of Taba, in fact, was the detailed discussion of the technical aspects of the potential compensation agreement, hitherto unprecedented. Some observe the Israeli strategy as forsaking the refugees' historical and legal rights by seeking instead clear, detailed, practical and mutually acceptable arrangements between Israel and the PA that would end all claims related to the refugee file. By the same token, resettlement options and financial compensation were considered tools that Israel intended to use to achieve certain outcomes, namely that of ensuring the disappearance of the refugee camps and the removal of UNRWA, to build in disincentives for those choosing to return to Israel and to assure the political and economic stability for refugees in host countries (Masalha 2003: 240–244).

Taba was the last round of official negotiations between Israelis and Palestinians. Since then, the subsequent Road Map is the official document presented by the international community as a peace blueprint.

The Road Map

Presented by the Quartet – the US, the EU, Russia and the UN – in 2003, the Road Map represents the latest international attempt to offer a vision of a peace agreement for the Israeli–Palestinian conflict.[17] Unlike Taba, it did not provide many details on the refugee issue, particularly reparations. Rather, it seemed to be more concerned with the two-state form and border issues.[18] Regarding refugees – a topic to be discussed as a final status issue after the establishment of a Palestinian state – the Road Map concisely calls for an 'agreed, just, fair, and realistic solution to the refugee issue'. Brynen believes the inclusion of 'realistic' may be seen as suggesting that the Quartet does not foresee the likelihood of maximalist solutions to form part of an eventual peace agreement (Brynen 2003). Another important observation to be drawn from the Road Map is that it bases itself on 242, which, with regard to refugees, simply called for a 'just settlement of the refugee problem'. The Road Map also establishes as one of its foundations the Beirut Arab summit declaration of March 2002, also known as the Arab Initiative.[19] The summit's declaration section on refugees called for 'achievement of a just solution to the Palestinian refugee problem to be agreed upon in accordance with 194'.

This is seen as echoing the stance adopted by Palestinian and Israeli negotiators in the last round of negotiations at Taba in January 2001 (Brynen 2003). Apart from that, the Road Map is silent on all aspects of how the refugee issue might be resolved.

The Geneva Initiative

With strong public and media resonance when announced a few months after Taba and the Road Map, the Geneva Initiative is nevertheless not to be considered an official accord, nor a formal negotiations round between Israelis and Palestinians. Its major interest to this study is by virtue of its inclusion of detailed discussions of the refugee question heavily drawn on the progress achieved during the Taba talks.

The Geneva accord stipulated that implementation of the agreement constitutes the end of both refugee status (Article 7.6) and refugee claims (Article 7.7). Brynen notes that one important aspect of the accord contained in Article 17 calls for a Security Council (SC) or GA resolution endorsing any peace agreement. While a GA resolution would have little practical effect, an SC resolution would have considerable force of international law, superseding 194 and reinforcing the agreement's claim to represent an end to the conflict (Brynen 2004). On the other hand, the Geneva accord adopts no statement of moral regret or responsibility but rather includes proposals (in the context of Article 7 on refugees) for a series of 'reconciliation programmes' between the two sides.[20] In Klein's opinion, the Geneva understandings leave this task to the two civil societies, under the leadership of their respective governments. This strategy is based on the presumption that a diplomatic accord cannot suddenly change deeply rooted memories, nor modify national and historical myths overnight. Reconciliation and openness towards the narrative of one's fellow human beings are the result of long-term processes that take place within civil society. Diplomatic mechanisms in such a context can promote reconciliation processes but not dictate them (Klein 2006). Calling for compensation for refugeehood and for loss of property (Article 7.3.i), Article 7.12 specifically outlines the establishment of an international fund to which both Israel and the international community would contribute.[21] Moreover, Geneva outlines three ways in which refugees would receive compensation (Article 7.1.v.ii.1) (Article 7.10). As Brynen points out, the first and second elements of this are virtually identical in phrasing to that agreed at Taba. What has been omitted, however, is the Taba paper's proposal for a per capita payment to all refugees for suffering due to displacement. Instead, this has been replaced by the proposed collective compensation through the 'refugeehood fund'.

Collective compensation to a refugeehood fund supporting general community development programmes may not seem to be very real compensation to most refugees. The Taba proposals, by proposing some level of individual (per capita) payment to all refugees regardless of their property-ownership status would have more obviously and readily provided tangible benefits associated with peace (Brynen 2004). Worth noting is that there was little indication within the Geneva accord regarding compensation to host countries but for a general, undetailed 'there shall be remuneration' (Article 7.1 l.vi). Also worth noting is the absence of the issue of compensation to Jews from Arab states.

Pondering the developments on the diplomatic front, we notice that the scholarly interest in the Palestinian refugee issue regained vigour in the aftermath of the diplomatic revival associated with the Madrid Framework. The key themes that had preoccupied scholars in the early phases of the conflict were mainly the identification and evaluation of Palestinian losses in 1948. Decades later, the main scholarly focus was on more rigorous research concerning the origins of the refugee displacement and the extent of Israel's responsibility in causing this displacement.

Recently, various initiatives of Track Two efforts have been devoted to the Palestinian refugee problem. Such initiatives have particularly revived research interest in the practical aspects of compensation and sought to explore the refugee issue from a legal perspective.[22] Representative of the Track Two diplomacy is the Ottawa Process, held under the auspices of the Canadian International Development Research Centre (IDRC).[23] The first event within the Ottawa Process was a stocktaking, comprehensive Palestinian refugee conference held in Ottawa in 1997. A first attempt to link academic study of the refugee issue with policy-making and relevance to negotiators, the Ottawa 1997 compensation workshop relied heavily on the previous identification and evaluations scholarship, which was recently revived with the research undertaken by Michael Fischbach on the efforts of the UNCCP in evaluating Palestinian property and had thus shed more light on that whole body of scholarship. Also gaining ground were studies examining the various compensation models applied to other cases and thoughts offered as to how they could be linked to the Palestinian case. This interest in compensation mechanisms is also illustrated by a recent comparative study on compensation mechanisms and property restitution conducted by the International Organization for Migration (2008). Such is the current picture of the scholarship's interest in reparations-related issues to Palestinian refugees.

Conclusion

Throughout this chapter we have followed the various early and recent efforts related to reparations to Palestinian refugees. The establishment of the UNCCP by virtue of Resolution 194 represented the first international response to the refugee problem. The creation of a specific UN body to deal with the issue on a legal basis, however, was not in light of the problem being one of refugee displacement in the first instance but by virtue of it being a part of the overall Arab–Israeli conflict. The refugee issue was thus viewed as a channel conducive to an overarching peace. This was the very reason why the UNCCP efforts – crippled by the larger political constraints it faced – were relegated to a narrower scope of technical efforts regarding compensation. Those technical efforts, though, have neither tackled non-property-related losses, sources of funding, modalities of payment or, implementation mechanisms, nor was there a settlement of the moral element or the link between responsibility of Israel and provision of compensation. Nonetheless, those property identification and evaluation efforts are some of the most comprehensive to date and are likely to form the backbone of a future compensation agreement in relation to Palestinian refugees.

The beginning of the 1990s and the convening of the Madrid peace process was another international attempt to revive dormant efforts of peace between Palestinians and Israelis. Forty years after the third party effort of the UN, the peace process was conceived beyond the direct auspices of the international organisation and was based on Resolution 242 rather than 194, the former being open to broader interpretation than the latter. The refugee issue was discussed in this venue on a multilateral track although, by virtue of the nature of the peace initiative after years of dormant negotiations, the refugee question was only treated in terms of humanitarian considerations and no discussion of the reparations question took place. Soon after, Oslo shifted the focus of the peace efforts to a bilateral track and deferred discussion of the refugee issue to final status negotiations that eventually never took place.

The Camp David Summit convened by the US in 2000 was an attempt to bring together the two parties' leaders for an overall agreement. With the weight of the discussion more tilted towards the issues of Jerusalem and borders, the summit in fact lacked in-depth discussion of the refugee question in general, and reparations in particular, and fell short of reaching an agreement. Interestingly, a few months later, the Taba negotiations, confined to the Israeli and Palestinian delegations, produced what most analysts deemed to be the most comprehensive discussions of the refugee file, especially in terms of compensation, although concretely no agreement was reached. The focus is presently on another internationally designed peace blueprint drafted by the Quartet. The Road Map, concerned with establishing a Palestinian state in the first instance, hasn't put forward any vision for the refugee issue, which leaves the door open as to what may come next in relation to the refugee dossier. The Road Map in fact follows the same trend that emerged from the inception of the conflict in treating the refugee file as part of an overall conflict and the trade-offs involved concerning other thorny components of that conflict.

Throughout the diplomatic trajectory of the Arab–Israeli conflict, the issue of moral and legal responsibility of Israel for creation of the Palestinian refugee problem has been a regular feature without being bridged, even within those rounds of negotiations where the deepest discussion of the refugee reparations issue has taken place. This question of responsibility, closely linked with the interpretation of 194, has caused the hazy and constant shift in focus on basing the claims on 194 or not. During the two decades following the events of 1948, 194 remained the foundation for most international efforts to achieve a peace settlement. As the reader may have noticed, though, the relevance of 194 as a basis for a solution became rather murky even though it was never rescinded by the UN and is reaffirmed yearly by the GA. Whether it has in effect legally and politically superseded 242 is open to interpretation. This issue in fact illustrates how the views of both parties are strikingly disparate at all the rounds of talks even if negotiations seemed to gain grounds on the level of technical aspects of reparations. Israel's refusal to accept 194 as a basis for a solution denies the refugee problem from being treated as a legal one implying legal responsibility. This leads the Israeli side to present its arguments in terms of practical solutions and advocating the humanitarian dimension of the refugee problem. The Palestinian side, on the other hand, waving the international law card, views the refugee problem primarily as a legal one, a wrongful act requiring a remedy, and thus steadily demanding its claims to be based on 194 and advocating the rights of refugees.

It is worth pausing here to reflect on the development of the two parties' (Israelis and Palestinians) position vis-à-vis the refugee issue. In spite of the more detailed discussions at Taba, have the parties' positions changed over the decades of peace-related efforts? The Israeli preconditions, as presented at the mediation conferences of the UNCCP, were principally that it accepted no moral or political responsibility for the creation of the refugee problem, that compensation should be part of a general peace settlement and that there would be no restitution of property (Lynk 2003, Peretz 2001: 88, Caplan 1993).[24] In addition to these principles was the Israeli insistence that compensation be poured into a collective fund, which would be utilised for the resettlement of the refugees elsewhere, reflecting its optimal solution to the refugee problem. The essence in the Israeli position since the first peace efforts in 1949 has remained unchanged throughout.

The Arab position, on the other hand, at the UNCCP mediation conference was that Israel bore the principal responsibility for paying compensation. In the event that Israel would be unable to pay the full amount, the Arab position considered the UN also responsible because of its role in the 1948 partition. The Arabs further insisted that Palestinian refugees had to be given free choice about returning to their homes, and only then could compensation be determined as between those returning and those resettling elsewhere. They have also demanded that compensation be paid to individual claimants, should reflect the true value of the property and that the refugees must be represented at the different stages of the negotiations. At present, the Palestinian position is anchored on demanding implementation of 194, demands acknowledgement of responsibility and is willing to discuss compensation on a rights-based approach.

Pondering the direction taken by the academic scholarship regarding Palestinian refugees throughout the past decades, we notice that much of it is dedicated to issues surrounding the right of return, humanitarian conditions, situation in host states and historical and legal responsibility for the refugee exodus. Much less has been devoted to the issue of reparations, particularly regarding its political dimensions. Moreover, while there has been considerable progress on the technical elements of the reparations question; political considerations on the two parties' sides, the nature of the trade-offs with other components of the conflict and the disparate views of the nature of the conflict have not changed. The contentions regarding responsibility and the linked manoeuvres of the centrality of 194 as a legal basis for a solution reflect a certain controversy. Such a controversy is caused by the conflicting views of reparations to Palestinian refugees as a historical injustice requiring redress, a legal problem in need of a legal solution, a political pawn between parties of a political conflict or merely a humanitarian problem in need of a humanitarian, forward-looking solution.

Whereas this chapter has shed light on the history of the search for reparations in the Palestinian refugee case, an understanding of what reparations are follows in the analysis. What is the difference between the terms 'reparations', 'redress', 'compensation', 'indemnification' and 'restitution'? Is it a matter of money payment? an acknowledgement of a wrongful act? a fulfilment of legal principles? And what is the guiding perception? The following chapter looks at how the term is perceived in the various disciplines and how it will be employed in the present study.

2 Reparations: in search of a definition

> . . . [o]nly when present pain rooted in past harms was addressed and, to the extent appropriate, redressed could there be justice. And only when there was justice could there be reconciliation and a foundation for genuine hope and cooperation.
>
> (Professor Eric Yamamoto, quoted in Minow 1998: 102)

Professor Yamamoto's quote encompasses the many ingredients found in the general notion of redress: the search for an adequate address to a past injustice in pursuit of justice as a route to reconciliation. In its broader context, the idea of redressing past injustices evolved throughout history and has significantly developed throughout the course of the past century. Clustered under various definitions of redress, reparations, compensation and restitution – to name but a few – the literature abounds with interlinked terms used interchangeably. Efforts have thus been exerted in an attempt to understand why nations apologise, the meaning of human injustice, structuring a theory of redress and the various forms of the latter.

Chapter 1 concludes with questions surrounding the general notion of amending displacement and dispossession as pertinent manifestations of violations to human rights. The overview of the diplomatic endeavours in this regard, in the context of Palestinian refugees, suggests efforts on various tracks. The latter involves the admission of responsibility towards the plight of the Palestinians, the legal implications of implementing UN resolutions as a basis for a potential solution to the problem, issues surrounding restitution of property and compensation for material and non-material damages.

Building on that, this chapter is concerned with grappling with the definition of reparations. Scattered between disciplines as diversified as law, philosophy, politics and history, various approaches to the notion of reparations surface in the literature. The following pages thus proceed towards presenting an overview of the different approaches to reparations with the purpose of underlying how this study approaches reparations. The first section is dedicated to discussing reparations within the scope of international law as a distinct discipline, offering contributions on how reparations are conceived and practised. Equally important in devoting analysis to the legal notions of reparations is the fact that the latter will ultimately be expressed in the form of a legal agreement. While subject to the prevailing balance of power and systemic considerations, such an agreement will nevertheless encompass principles of law and standards of law instruments ascertaining a matrix of rights and forms of redress. Moreover, one party to the conflict, Palestinians, base their demands for reparations on a rights-based approach and thus advocate legal arguments in this regard.

The second section in this chapter is dedicated to overviewing reparations in practice and the various ideas put forward regarding redress in several disciplines such as politics, philosophy and history. By no means mutually exclusive, the notion of redress combines interdisciplinary approaches and adopts analytical tools transcending across the borders of one particular discipline. Combined, the two sections represent an attempt to put together the common elements of reparations and, by consequence, pave the way for the third and final section of the chapter explaining how reparations are perceived in this book and applied to the analysis of the case studies.

Reparations in international law

This section aims to shed light on some of the legal aspects of reparations, notably the definition of related terms in international law. In doing so, it particularly focuses on the notion of reparations in relation to state responsibility, in addition to the debate over the relevance of 194 as a basis for reparations to Palestinian refugees. It is worth noting that such issues in particular are often advocated by Palestinian refugees in their legal demands for reparations.

Reparations, as an international law concept, is the remedy for violations of international law. Historically, the 1928 Permanent Court of International Justice Chorzow Factory – a landmark case in the development of the concept of reparations – ruled that 'reparation must, so far as possible, wipe out all the consequences of the illegal act and re-establish the situation that would, in all probability, have existed if that act had not been committed' (quoted in Shelton 2005: 32).

Modern legal definitions regarding determination of a wrongful act are based on the International Law Commission (ILC) articles on State Responsibility and the Draft Basic Principles and Guidelines on the Right to a Remedy and Reparation for Victims of Violations of International Human Rights and Humanitarian Law (Draft Principles on Reparation), which were prepared under the auspices of the UN Special Rapporteur on the Right to Restitution[1] (see Crawford 2002 and Office of the UNHCHR 2008).

Reparations in this context are thus due according to Article 31(1) of the ILC Draft articles stipulating that '[T]he responsible State is under an obligation to make full reparation for the injury caused by the internationally wrongful act.' Section 2 of the article asserts that injury includes both material and moral damage caused by the internationally wrongful act of a state. According to Article 34 of the ILC Draft articles, 'reparation shall take the form of restitution, compensation and satisfaction, either singly or in combination'. Accordingly, legally speaking, reparation encompasses three main types of remedy: restitution, compensation and satisfaction. According to Article 35 of the ILC Draft articles, restitution means:

> to re-establish the situation which existed before the wrongful act was committed, provided and to the extent that restitution: (a) is not materially impossible; (b) does not involve a burden out of all proportion to the benefit deriving from restitution instead of compensation.

As stated above, restitution in kind does not exclude any of the other forms of reparation referred to in Article 34 of the ILC Draft articles. If it is impossible to restore the conditions that existed prior to the human rights violations, remedies are often achieved through compensation, which involves monetary payment for material and moral injury. Satisfaction addresses non-material injuries. According to Article 37(2) of the ILC Draft articles, '[S]atisfaction may consist in an acknowledgment of the breach, an expression of regret, a formal apology or another appropriate modality.' Satisfaction for the injury is also available 'insofar as it cannot be made good by restitution or compensation' (see Crawford 2002). The above-mentioned principles and definitions necessitate further discussion of state responsibility and 194 as a basis for reparations to Palestinian refugees.

State responsibility

Legally speaking, state responsibility establishes an obligation to make good any violation of international law producing injury. The idea originally arises out of the legal maxim stated by Grotius in 1646 that 'every fault creates the obligation to make good the loss' (Lee 1986: 537). As mentioned above, legal scholars base modern arguments regarding the legal source for state responsibility on the ILC Articles on State Responsibility (Crawford 2002, Shelton 2005: 50–103). Donna Arzt, for example, argues in favour of state responsibility as the pre-requisite for compensation on the premise that claims for relief under international law always begin with the law of state responsibility (Arzt 1999).

It is noteworthy to mention at this point that, traditionally, as states were the conventional subjects of international law, state responsibility applied only on the state-to-state level in principle (see Crawford 2002). Duties owed to individuals were thus left out. The ILC Articles on State Responsibility affirm this traditional state-centric definition of state responsibility and set out reparation, restitution, compensation and satisfaction as the basic legal tools states have to remedy injuries. A further development is the fact that many states have now taken on new legal obligations that are unilateral or vertical in the sense that they concern duties owed by states to individuals. It is thought that these developments reflect the relatively recent but fundamental shift in international law towards recognition of the rights and duties of individuals (see Shelton 2005: 104–173 and Office of the UNHCHR 2008). This development led to the incorporation of human rights into international instruments. Subsequently, there currently is general agreement that an 'international wrongful act', for which a state is held internationally responsible, includes specifically action in violation of human rights (Lee 1999).

In fact, the Basic Guidelines base themselves on breaches of human rights. In his report mentioned above, UN Special Rapporteur on the right to restitution, Theo van Boven, concluded that:[2]

> such gross violations of human rights and fundamental freedoms as genocide, torture or other cruel, inhuman or degrading treatment or punishments, systematic racial discrimination, and a consistent pattern of gross violations, entail the obligation to provide for compensation as a means to repair a wrongful act or a wrongful situation. Such obligation exists under a well-established principle of International Law.

The principle that refugees in particular are entitled to restitution for their lost property is increasingly gaining recognition in international law. Drawing on the general rule of state responsibility, Susan Akram argues that the state responsible for the illegal expropriation must reverse the effect of that violation through full property restitution. She points out the case of Bosnia, where more than 50 per cent of all property claims have resulted in the restitution of the homes and lands to their owners after the conflict ended. According to her, restitution in the Bosnian case has been the goal of the reconstruction process (Akram et al. 2005).

Another related principle now applies not only to aliens' property but also to citizens fleeing from their own state. Principle 4 of the International Law Association's 1992 Cairo Declaration of Principles of International Law on Compensation to Refugees, stipulates that '[a] State is obligated to compensate its own nationals forced to leave their homes to the same extent as it is obligated by International Law to compensate an alien'.

While international law establishes criteria for determination of wrongful acts as well as obligation to repair for injuries caused by the breach of legal norms through various forms of reparations, the fact remains that states can often evade their duties with regard to individual victims of violations of human rights law because of the lack of robust enforcement mechanisms (see Bradley 2005: 4). By the same token, Lee believes that as long as the principle of reparations remains valid, it matters little whether reparations are settled through courts, international organisations, ex gratia payments or diplomatic negotiations (Lee 1999). Furthermore, a relevant question put forward by Arzt is whether international law requires that a state be found at fault in order to make redress for injuries. In other words, is all wrongful international conduct blameworthy? She cites leading jurist Ian Brownlie, stating that international tribunals usually follow the theory of objective responsibility: provided that agency and causal connection (attribution) can be established, a breach of international law occurs through the result alone. Even where a state's agents have acted beyond their authority (*ultra vires*) or, for that matter, in the absence of intention to harm (*dolus malus*) or the presence of good faith, it will bear responsibility for all its acts which fail to conform to international legal standards. This approach, according to Arzt, may be applicable in convincing Israel that it can provide reparations without having to admit fault (Arzt 1999).

Equally important in the legal discussion of reparations in relation to

Palestinian displacement and dispossession is the relevance of 194 as a basis for legal remedy.

United Nations General Assembly (UNGA) Resolution 194

The first UN resolution that refers to refugees displaced within Palestine during the 1948 war is Resolution 194 (iii) of 11 December 1948 adopted by the General Assembly. Paragraph 11 states that the GA:

> . . . resolves that the refugees wishing to return to their homes and live at peace with their neighbors should be permitted to do so at the earliest practicable date, and that compensation should be paid for the property of those choosing not to return and for loss of or damage to property which, under principles of international law or in equity, should be made good by the governments or authorities responsible . . .

194 is often cited in the Palestinian refugee context as the legal principle calling for the right of refugees to return and for compensation.[3] Noteworthy, as pinpointed by Lynk, 194 establishing the availability of return, compensation and restitution for Palestinian refugees was the international community's first affirmation of these principles of compensation in international law in the context of a displaced population (Lynk 2003).[4] 194 is commonly cited by refugee law scholars as a primary international law source for the right of refugees and displaced persons anywhere in the world to compensation and restitution (Lynk 2003). Departing from the history of drafting the resolution, Fischbach maintains a different argument. According to the resolution, the only possibility under which returning refugees could be compensated was if their property had been damaged or destroyed wantonly without military necessity. In other words, the resolution did not call for compensating repatriated refugees for confiscated property. Israel was under no obligation to pay repatriated refugees for land and movable property that it had confiscated. The decision to exclude this possibility was deliberate (Fischbach 2005: 76–77). Furthermore, the final version of the resolution spoke only of compensation and contained nothing about restitution of property specifically, either for returning or non-returning refugees, other than the implicit call for restitution contained in the call for refugees wishing to live at peace to be allowed to 'return to their homes'.[5]

The debate over the validity of 194 is rife and has engaged many scholars. The following is not an exhaustive exposure of conflicting opinions but rather offers an idea of the main arguments contended. One such argument affirms that 194 explicitly states that the repatriation, compensation and restitution of the refugees should be made according to principles of international law or in equity. Luke Lee argues that by deliberately choosing this particular drafting, the GA clearly signalled that it was restating pre-existing law on the principle of compensating wrongs in international law rather than simply establishing a new legal obligation (Lee 1999). As such, this resolution acquires further strength (Lynk 2003). Moreover, Lynk holds the opinion that 194 gains strength and significance by the virtue of having been repeatedly affirmed by the GA at least 140 times (Lynk 2003). Also, it is thought that 194 provides an appropriate standard of law to be used in regard to repatriation and compensation of the displaced Palestinians because it reflects customary international law and because in Resolution 242, the Security Council in effect incorporated Resolution 194 by calling for a 'just settlement of the refugee question' (Quigley 1999).

On the other hand, refuting 194 as a legal basis for the settlement of the Palestinian refugee problem, Don Peretz thinks that in international law, the right to compensation does not apply to persons displaced by war, as only individuals directly persecuted are classified as refugees and entitled to payment. Compensation, therefore, is an obligation that rests 'upon countries that directly or indirectly force their own citizens to flee and/or remain abroad as refugees'. According to Peretz's logic, the great majority of Palestinians fleeing Israel and Jews leaving Arab countries, departed en masse as a result of war conditions, not individualised persecution according to their countries of origin. Consequently, there is no effective remedy in international law for a citizen in his own state if his property has been expropriated. Thus, in the Arab–Israeli conflict, the right to compensation is derived largely from UN General Assembly resolutions on the refugees. Settlement of the compensation issue will ultimately depend on agreements voluntarily entered into by Israel and Arab parties to a peace settlement (Peretz 1995: 1).

Another opinion advocated by Eyal Benvenisti considers that 194 is equivocal in relation to compensation ('compensation *should* be paid . . . for loss . . . which, under principles of international law or in equity, *should* be *made good*'). According to Benvenisti, the Report of the United Nations Mediator Count Bernadotte – which served as the basis for this resolution – mentioned the 'payment of *adequate* compensation'.[6] Moreover, 194 refers to 'loss of or damage to property' instead of simply 'property' in the Bernadotte report. These discrepancies in the scholar's view, between the resolution and the report that follow similar discrepancies in the attitude towards the demand for physical return, indicate that the drafters of this resolution wanted to avoid the clear standard of 'full compensation' and to limit the potential heads of damages for property.[7] According to Benvenisti, this interpretation of 194 is fully in line with general principles of international law. Lapidoth also sides with the opinion refuting the binding nature of 194. The argument she advocates claims that under the UN charter, the GA is not authorised to adopt binding resolutions except in budgetary matters and with regard to its own internal rules and regulations. Lapidoth also believes the provision concerning the refugees is but one element of the resolution that foresaw a final settlement of all questions outstanding between the parties (Lapidoth 2002).

This section, focusing on reparations within international law, has presented various aspects of reparations as an umbrella term for the concept of redress to an injury caused by a breach of international law norms. The modern development of the legal notion of reparations began in an absolutist form, as evident from the Chorzow Factory ruling in its attempt to repair the harm by reverting it. International law jurists thus visualised remedy through the reversal of the injury. Further developments in the legal realm occurred through the evolution in the standards of what constitutes a wrongful act as well as the various forms of remedy addressing the wrongful act, namely: restitution, compensation and satisfaction. Those recent standards reflect a more malleable understanding of the core of the reparations act in the spirit of the law. In that context, state responsibility and the relevance of UNGA Resolution 194 have been discussed as a basis for legal demands for reparations to Palestinian refugees.

Another main observation drawn from the legal approach to reparations is the centrality of the element of obligation as a characteristic of the establishment of a reparations agreement in international law. Although many analysts do contend that the manifested lack of an enforcement mechanism to impose on states carrying out their obligations under international law does weaken the obligation factor, the latter principle – at least in theory – is a main characteristic of international law reparations agreements.

The previous legal overview has also brought into the limelight the impact of the inclusion of human rights violations in demands for reparations. International law evolution progressing from being state-centric towards incorporating individual human rights established the norm that an international wrongful act for which a state is held responsible includes violations of human rights. In more concrete terms, this has accordingly put forward an increase in importance of the entitlement of refugees in particular – as victims of human rights violations – for compensation for their displacement and lost property.

Adding to the contributions of international law principles to the notion of redressing violations of human rights, 194 enters the scene as a pertinent legally relevant international law resolution to the Palestinian refugees question in particular. Notwithstanding the debate over its basis for a reparations claim, it is worth noting that the GA resolution triggered the debate over mutual exclusivity, as well as the hierarchy of preference of the three options of restitution of property, compensation and return as appropriate solutions to the Palestinian refugees case. A far less observed factor, although no less important in its significance, is the fact that 194 neither mentioned satisfaction, admission of liability nor apology as components of a solution to the Palestinian refugees problem.

In broad terms, the general idea detected throughout the previous pages reveals that the international law understanding of justice is the address of the commitment of a wrongful act through various legal forms already previously determined. However, international law obligations devoid of the power of enforcement are constantly subject to the friction between the legal and the political. A settlement of a conflict in the international system does not thus necessarily imply full implementation of relevant international law principles.

If such is the nature of the legal approach to reparations, other disciplines have generally discussed violations of human rights as a wrongful act necessitating redress, the former not necessarily being a breach of law and the latter not aiming to ascertain a right. The other approaches to reparations – as shall be apparent from the next section of this chapter – view reparations as a path to remedy injury caused by a wrongful act.

Reparations in international practice

Departing from the premise that justice cannot be absolute and that the past is not reversible, ideas have been put forward towards an understanding of reparations. Aside from the legal arguments, definitions and principles surrounding the concept of redress and amending an injury determined by a breach of legal codes, other disciplines have harboured thoughts regarding redress in a broader and different perspective than the realm of international law. In his introduction to Minow's study,

Between Vengeance and Forgiveness, prominent South African judge and war crimes prosecutor, Richard Goldstone, states that:

> In a perfect society victims are entitled to full justice, namely trial of perpetrators and if found guilty adequate punishment. That ideal not being possible some societies find other solutions. A national amnesia is bound to fail. Managing the past has to be implemented but there is no standard formula. In most cases the choices will be limited by political, military and economic conditions. And whatever solutions, the results will be mixed.
>
> (Richard Goldstone, quoted in Minow 1998: x)

Goldstone's quote emphasises what the following pages seek to probe, namely that the various approaches to reparations are in fact an array of interpretations of justice and attempts to operationalise it. The search for justice and the route best taken in its pursuit is the subject matter of thoughts offered in regard to reparations as a general notion of redress. As is the case with other philosophical terms, there is no consensus either on the meaning or on the applicability of justice in the international realm. From a realist standpoint, the recognition of a decentralised international state-centric system, characterised by an absence of a single legitimate authority, means that justice takes a back seat to considerations of order. For idealists, on the other hand, justice is a pre-requisite of a stable and lasting order. Realists argue that the issue of justice is secondary and derivative, while non-realists maintain that it is primary. They consider that the idea of context is irrelevant, for 'right' conduct is universal and therefore what is considered good or evil in one context is *ipso facto* good or evil in another. The issue has been a contentious one throughout the history of international thought. At one extreme, political realism argues that international politics is centrally amoral. Self-interest is the key and states create their own morality. A toned-down version of this view is the argument that moral obligations do impinge on world politics. Between the two basic realist/idealist positions there are variations on the meaning and significance of international justice and most opinions adopt a stance on a compromise or synthesis between the two extremes. That is, that transnational obligations and rights are important and certain obligations of common humanity undoubtedly exist, but their realisation is circumscribed by the characteristics of the international political system. In this context, international justice is a term usually referring to a set of moral standards over and above those prescribed by law (Penguin 1998b).

Rights, the obligation to amend an injustice and remedies is the language spoken by international law in pursuit of justice through reparations. Other disciplines draw on a different vocabulary and points of reference in their search for justice, moving away from punishment and the obligation element heavily evident in the legal approach. Absent may the obligation be, the responsibility, if not legal – rather moral or out of self-interest – is there.

In its entry on 'reparations', the *Penguin Dictionary of International Relations* defines the term as:

> . . . compensation claims made of an effected upon vanquished by the victors following the cessation of hostilities. Reparations may involve financial payments and/or physical requisition of goods. By exercising reparations the victor(s) may be seeking to indemnify itself/themselves for losses incurred during the war. Additionally, reparations may be seen as an instrument that will reduce the ability of the vanquished to wage war or otherwise pose a security threat in the future.
>
> (Penguin 1998c)

Unpacking this definition sheds light on several issues of relevance to the broad notion of reparations in addition to its historical unfolding. When put in comparison with the modern literature on reparations presented throughout the chapter, this definition indicates that from a historical standpoint, the act of reparations initially involved an act of war in its traditional sense, in addition to a clear structure of victor and vanquished as the parties to a reparations claim. Moreover, it was the standard practice that victors *imposed* reparations on the vanquished. From another perspective, the forms of redress as outlined by the definition were confined to financial payments in addition to restitution proper. The incorporation of other forms of reparations, such as apologies for instance, is a novel phenomenon in the sphere of reparations practice. The following pages illustrate how the modern literature on reparations has developed in comparison with the traditional definition presented above.

Consequently, this section is divided into two parts. The first covers a spectrum of redress theories and perspectives within the modern literature on reparations. The second part focuses on other ideas concerned with redressing displacement and dispossession specifically.

Perspectives of redress

Scholarly and practical interest in reparations and their role in post-conflict situations has significantly expanded over the past years. I wish to shed light here on a number of perspectives pondering various aspects of reparations with the objective of grappling with the issues that are of interest within the politics of reparations. I will particularly look at the contribution of Roy Brooks, Elazar Barkan and Martha Minow for the variety of dimensions brought out in their respective analyses.[8]

Roy Brooks discusses the various conditions that he deems necessary for successful redress of human injustices and presents them as the elements of his theory of redress.[9] To him, the key to redress is through legislating rights and remedies to injustices (Brooks 1999b: 6). The second condition necessary for a successful redress is the political leverage exercised in favour of the claim. Public and private pressure is necessary for the success of redress rather than mere demands of logic, justice and culture. This element in Brooks' opinion clearly illustrates that not all meritorious claims succeed. Strong internal support is the third element of successful redress in the sense that the victimised group itself must exhibit unquestionable support for the claims being pressed (Brooks 1999b: 6). This internal cohesiveness in support of the redress claims explains – according to Brooks – why the African-American slavery redress movement for example falls behind the successful Japanese-American redress efforts. Nevertheless, while Brooks acknowledges that the politics of redress claims overshadow their merits, such claims must still be meritorious, this being the fourth and final element of Brooks' theory of redress (Brooks 1999b: 7).

The four elements of the redress theory thus presented, Brooks proceeds to elaborate on what precisely constitutes a meritorious claim. According to him, the latter would be one that satisfies certain criteria. Identifying a human injustice that must be well-documented is one factor. Another one is the distinctiveness of the victims as a group whose current members must continue to suffer harm causally connected to a past injustice (Brooks 1999b: 7). Of particular significance is the fact that the definition of a human injustice according to Brooks is derived from the concept of human rights as a subsidiary of international law. This implies that a human injustice is the violation or suppression of human rights or fundamental freedom recognised by international law (Brooks 1999b: 7). Brooks also affirms the fact that the harm connected to a past human injustice raises the complex question of privity and how a claimant is to establish such privity between himself or his group and the perpetrator when the latter belongs to a different era (Brooks 1999b: 8). This concept of privity is for instance used to decline African-Americans' claims for redress for slavery.[10]

Having outlined the elements of a redress theory and established the criteria of what constitutes a meritorious claim, the following question of importance to Brooks becomes that concerning the adequate form of redress (Brooks 1999b: 8). Here, Brooks is preoccupied with questions such as: Is there one adequate form of redress? Should governments issue apologies? Should apologies be made in conjunction with payments to victims? Could redress consist of money paid to victims without issuing an apology? Does money have to reach victims themselves or could it be in the form of investments, services or both in the victim's community in lieu of compensating victims individually? (Brooks 1999b: 8). Brooks' discussion and attempts to categorise forms of redress are in fact an answer to a question predominantly posed in the literature on reparations: is there a hierarchy of forms of redress and a most-adequate model?

Addressing the issue, Brooks begins by distinguishing between redress responses that are remorseful and others that are not (Brooks 1999b: 8). According to him, reparations are those redress responses that seek atonement for the commission of an injustice. By the same token, responses in which the government does not express atonement are dubbed as settlements, a compromise formula that gives the victim a monetary award on the one hand while giving the perpetrator a chance to end the dispute without a finding of liability (Brooks 1999b: 9). The author emphasises that reparation is easily distinguishable from a settlement by the presence or absence of an accompanying statement of apology in the sense that an apology expresses an admission of liability.

Reparations and settlements according to Brooks' definitions can be subdivided into monetary and non-monetary responses.[11] Monetary or non-monetary reparations and settlements, in turn, can be directed towards the victims individually or collectively. A reparation or settlement directed towards the individual is intended to be compensatory. In other words, to return the victim to the *status quo ante*. One directed towards the group is designed to be rehabilitative of the community (Brooks 1999b: 9). Accordingly, South Africa for example, has opted for reparations rather than settlement. The Government's Truth and Reconciliation Committee (TRC), which in 1998 ended two and a half years of investigations into apartheid-related injustices, has provided reparations in the form of individual compensation and community rehabilitation.[12]

To Brooks, then, redress is the umbrella term subject to division into several types. Generally speaking, his elaboration of a theory of redress adds the power ingredient that lacks in the legal approach, the role pressure plays in the push for a reparations claim and categorises redress in light of that. Moreover, his understanding of the action of seeking redress could be described as future-looking, for the author is preoccupied with the idea that apologies are essential to the non-repetition of 'shameful acts' (Brooks 1999b: 4). This view is contrary to redress, primarily seeking to repair an injustice to amend the past. In the Palestinian rhetoric, for example, reparation is generally viewed as a redress to an inflicted injustice rather than a broader preoccupation with fear of the same injustice reoccurring. In his insistence that apology is the differentiating factor between reparations and settlements, Brooks neglects the fact that an official admission of liability in the guise of an apology is likely to trigger legal responsibilities, whereas settlements, according to the author's definition, may avoid this thorny issue for the perpetrators. This in fact follows the same line of thought echoed by Arzt – mentioned in the previous section – regarding her evocation of Brownlie's theory of objective responsibility. Another worthy observation concerns Brooks' definition of settlement as being exclusive of any legal element in its basis. If his theory of redress is based on a meritorious claim, which he states as being a violation of human rights, it becomes unclear how an apology can be the differentiating factor between reparations and settlements. In other words, how in Brooks' theory can settlement be a redress act if not based on dealing with the claim as one with legal merits?

Another significant contribution to the literature on reparations is the conceptualisation put forward by Elazar Barkan. Unlike Brooks and most other reparations scholars, Barkan employs restitution as his umbrella term for the concept of reparations. Barkan attempts to overview many redress cases and extract certain principles that form the essence of his understanding of what restitution is. Accordingly, he sees in those restitution cases a pattern of what he calls a potential international morality. This notion is formed alongside his observation of a common willingness on behalf of perpetrators of an injustice to acknowledge a wrongful act and opt to compensate for it (Barkan 2000: ix). In Barkan's view, the observable fact of nations acting morally and acknowledging their own gross historical injustices is a novel phenomenon in the international arena. Barkan perceives the international system prevailing in the aftermath of the Second World War as a political environment where morality and justice are replacing realpolitik as the drive for politics, and thus increased attention is paid to moral responsibility (Barkan 2000: xi). As such, the need for restitution to past victims has become a major part of national politics and international diplomacy (Barkan 2003: 91). Barkan even pushes it to the point whereby 'the moral dispute [over historical injustices] has come to be about interpretations, means, and timing, more than about principle' (Barkan 2000: xii). Subsequently, restitution represents the moral channel that bridges historical animosity between enemies (Barkan 2000: xii). This understanding of restitution contrasts the enforced retribution or punishment and the old custom of imposed war reparations epitomised by the Versailles Treaty of 1919, whereby traditionally, the winner imposed various payments on the loser. As Barkan proceeds to explain, the trend was reversed in 1945 when the Allies did not impose reparations on Germany. Instead, the US accepted the burden of rebuilding Europe and Japan and initiated the Marshall Plan. This, in the historian's view, introduced a novel factor in international relations: rather than holding to a moral right to exploit enemy resources, as had been done previously, the victor underscored future reconciliation and assisted its defeated enemies in re-establishing themselves (Barkan 2003: 95).[13] While Barkan rightly points out that this was a turning point for the concept of restitution shifting from its vindictiveness element, his overlooking of the fact that the threat of the communist spread in Europe was a major incentive for the American aid to Western Europe is not be to dismissed.

In that same context, Barkan points out that Germany, mainly acting on its unique need to re-establish political and moral legitimacy, sought to repent from its sins under Nazism by reaching an agreement with its victims (Barkan 2003: 95). Regarding this case, Barkan argues that the Germans paid compensation not to the winners but to those they victimised the most. The perpetrator compensated the victims of its own volition in order to facilitate self-rehabilitation. This admission of guilt had to be done in concord with the victims; the idea of compensation, the rhetoric of guilt and limited recognition and forgiveness were translated through the legal medium of restitution. While Barkan's view on the German–Jewish reparations case is valid, it remains nevertheless incomplete. One question is, why weren't all those victimised by the Nazis compensated for? Moreover, where would the pressure exerted by the Jewish groups in search for reparations from the post-war German Government be placed in his equation?

History in Barkan's view thus acts as a formative political force drawn upon to facilitate reconciliation (Barkan 2000: x). In other words, painful historical injustices are subject to victims' attempts of redress through negotiating a political settlement with the perpetrators. In other words, a reconsideration of historical narratives acts as the vehicle through which politicians can re-examine particular beliefs that inform animosities and thus can facilitate a new approach to the conflict (Barkan 2005a: 230). This view illustrates Barkan's understanding of an injustice as not being confined to a legal violation of human rights. This concept of redress is therefore rather closer to Brooks' definition of settlement whereby a conclusion of the conflict is reached by a compromise solution rather than a rights-based one. Unlike Brooks, though, Barkan does not attempt to categorise the forms of redress. To Barkan, the modern discourse on restitution takes the form of political negotiation between perpetrator and victim. Therefore, the historian argues that instead of categorising all cases according to a certain blueprint, the discourse depends on the specific interactions in each case (Barkan 2003: 92–93). In that context, the case of the American Government compensating Japanese-Americans interned in camps during the war is a successful redress case because it quantified a historical injustice and translated it into a specific sum acceptable to both the victims and perpetrators as compensation (Barkan 2003: 95–96, Brooks 1999a). Apology in this context does not mean the dispute is resolved but is in most cases a first step, part of the process of negotiation (Barkan 2003: 98). Contrary to Brooks' views, apology to Barkan does not necessarily entail responsibility nor does he discuss responsibility in its legal implications (Barkan 2003: 99).

In Barkan's own words, a strong case for restitution would underscore a moral economy that would calculate and quantify evil and would place a price on amending injustices. Such a theory of justice, the historian reminds us, would inevitably suffer from all the shortcomings of utilitarianism. Yet, the moral high ground, maintaining that nothing can compensate for atrocities, would not amend an injustice either. In this context, one virtue of moral economy of restitution is that it does not propose a universal solution but strives to evaluate conflicts in light of a vague standard to be pragmatically mediated by the protagonists (Barkan 2003: 101). This understanding of redress totally sets aside a rights-based approach to reparations claims.

In a more recent publication devoted to the Palestinian predicament, Barkan contends that the dynamics of realpolitik and morality are central to the Palestinian demand for the right of return as a form of restitution to their demands of redress to the historical injustice inflicted on them (Barkan 2005b: 86). In his opinion, the conflicting views between the protagonists of the conflict of what the right of return means provides much heated public rhetoric, thus hindering a solution plan and inflating maximalist positions (Barkan 2005b: 86). From the Palestinian perspective, 'the claim of right might have become an ideological credo turned into a political stumbling block' (Barkan 2005b: 87–88). Accordingly, Barkan embarks on analysing the clashing views on the right of return between Israelis and Palestinians and firmly presents the argument that searching for a solution based on the notion of right is the road to no solution at all. Therefore, the guiding principle for redress to the injustice of displacement and dispossession, in addition to accepting historical responsibility, is not by implementing the right of return but rather lies in a symbolic gesture and an in-kind reparation (Barkan 2005b: 100).

In summary, by evoking the shift in the focus of reparations from the Versailles spirit of vindictiveness to that of the post-Second World War environment, Barkan's approach to reparations is also future-looking. Barkan offers no definition of injustice, no categorisation of redress and his philosophy relies on perpetrators' willingness to redress, overseeing the role of pressure exerted by the victimised group to seek reparations.

Martha Minow, on the other hand, focuses on the various forms of redress – as formal responses to atrocity – discussing their positive and negative repercussions. In that context, reparation is viewed as one alternative among several other transitional justice measures seeking to address mass violence (Minow 1998: 2).[14] The writer endeavours to explore what each alternative can and cannot accomplish, acknowledging that the limitations to each response are influenced by the fact that context (system) matters and that a response can never be adequate (Minow 1998: 4–5). By consequence, legal responses are inevitably frail and insufficient. However, inaction by legal institutions means that the perpetrators prevailed in paralysing the instruments of justice (Minow 1998: 5).

This understanding of reparations as a form of restorative justice, in Minow's analysis, moves away from the idea of prosecution as a response to a historical injustice. Unlike punishment, which imposes a penalty or injury for a violation, restorative justice seeks to 'repair the injustice', 'to make up' for it (Minow 1998: 91). Hence, restorative justice in its various forms takes precedence over punishment or law enforcement (Minow 1998: 92). In that context, South Africa's TRC emphasises truth-telling, public acknowledgement and actual reparations as crucial elements for restoration of justice (Minow 1998: 92). In Minow's analysis, reparations are unable to undo the violence that was done. Yet even inadequate monetary payments or an apology can pave the way for a sense of recognition and renewal for survivors, observers and offenders (Minow 1998: 93).

Minow puts forward several reasons why she prefers symbolic reparations and negotiated settlements rather than restitution of pre-existing entitlements (Minow 1998: 112). In reference to restitution in its technical definition of re-instating property, Minow underscores that one of the problems of restitution is when innocent individuals obtain and build their lives around lands that were wrongly stolen from the original inhabitants. In such a situation, restoring the actual property after it has passed through a chain of ownership means committing a current injustice to rectify a past one (Minow 1998: 108).[15] Moreover, another problem engendered by restitution, according to Minow, lies in the fact that even if it works to redress misappropriations of long ago and even if it is designed to spread the burden among all intervening owners, it still carries a dilemma. Such a dilemma can clearly be seen in South Africa and Eastern Europe, where massive patterns of poverty and inequality present immediate and urgent issues of injustice.[16] In these contexts, historically oriented restitution efforts are both too partial and too inadequate to the survival tasks of rebuilding national economies and civil societies (Minow 1998: 109–110).[17]

Regarding the weight of apology within reparations, Minow says that the explicit aim and the actual effects of the reparations law in the case of the Japanese-Americans illustrate the symbolic significance of official acknowledgement of wrongdoing, paying respect to a community of survivors (Minow 1998: 100). A relevant question that may be raised at this junction relates to differentiating between the weight of apology for a community, such as the Japanese-Americans enjoying full citizenship and adequate welfare, as opposed to a displaced, dispossessed and largely stateless community such as Palestinian refugees. In this regard, Minow's input is that these public acknowledgements of wrongdoing and statements of contrition reflect a growing international interest in restorative steps towards justice (Minow 1998: 114). However, Minow considers apologies to be superficial, insincere or meaningless unless accompanied by direct and immediate actions, such as payment of compensation, that manifest responsibility for the violations (Minow 1998: 116). She says 'they [apologies] may . . . be the most inexpensive and least difficult actions available . . .' This, however, contradicts her statement one page further when she says 'full acceptance of responsibility by the wrongdoer is the hallmark of an apology'. Although a legal scholar, Minow seems not to dedicate sufficient analysis to the weight of an official apology and link it with legal responsibilities engendered by a state's formal acknowledgement of liability. Moreover, in the case of Palestinians, for example, the issue of a wrongdoer is in itself contested with Israel's denial of involvement in the creation of the Palestinian displacement. On the other hand, the case of Korean comfort women against the Japanese Government also illustrates the victims' struggle in providing evidence of who the wrongdoer was. Minow contends that it falls to grassroots and international groups of advocates and writers to create a demand and an appreciation for the ideal of legal responses to mass atrocity. And it is this ideal, according to Minow, not the actual practices, that must be conveyed if the movement for international justice is to build (Minow 1998: 126).

Forms of redress

The discussion above denotes how scholarship and practice alike have resorted to various forms of redress as reparatory measures. I wish to further discuss this matter in the following pages.

The most notable forms of reparations debated by the various disciplines are restitution of property, financial compensation and apologies. While international law heavily draws on tackling restitution of property, as well as financial compensation, as remedies for a violation of rights, the increasingly important element of apology featuring more prominently in other disciplines is less discussed by legal codes.

However, the modern history of reparations indicates an increasing attention to the apology element as an integral component of addressing a past injustice. The ideas discussed earlier in the chapter demonstrate awareness among the authors of the apology angle within reparations. The latter is particularly evident in a number of cases in the modern history of reparations. Combined, these cases highlight the prominence of an official apology within a reparations claim as well as the dual relationship between apology and financial compensation, among other issues.[18] The recent Australian official apology to its Aborigines is a good example. After years of struggle for recognition of the injustices committed against them, the Australian Prime Minister delivered an apology on behalf of Parliament while at the same time declining to offer financial compensation, proposing instead rehabilitation programmes.[19] The US reparations for Japanese-American survivors of the evacuation and internment is another case in point. President Reagan signed into law the bill that expressed apology as well as authorised financial compensation. Reagan said 'no payment can make up for those lost years. What is most important in this bill has less to do with property than with honor.

For here we admit wrong' (Minow 1998: 112–113, Yamamoto and Ebesgugawa 2006). This redress case is often mentioned in the literature on reparations to highlight the atonement aspect of the US Government and its desire to seek contrition. Yet, many commentators neglect the fact that such an apology wouldn't have occurred without the campaign pushing for it, nor the legal implications of such a public official statement.

The case of the Korean comfort women is also of importance to the argument. Although the existence of the comfort women operation (*jugun ianfu*) was first exposed in 1948 when Batavia (now Jakarta) hosted public trials concerning the sexual internment of Dutch women, it was not until 1990 that a Japanese official in the person of Prime Minister Miyazawa Kichi offered an unofficial apology for the acts perpetrated by the military against the comfort women.[20] More recently, the Japanese Diet, although refusing to issue an apology, has allocated money to administer a fund for Asian women. The form and source of such redress, however, raised important questions (Brooks 1999a: 87). More controversial than Japan's refusal to apologise was its approach to monetary redress. Japan established the Asian Women's Fund to aid comfort women in need and support projects addressing contemporary women's issues. The fund purports to represent the Japanese people's 'feelings of apology and remorse' by allowing them to contribute directly. The fund is financed by private donations and the Government only pays administrative fees (Brooks 1999a: 89). Japan's response is an example of redress in the form of community rehabilitations. Rather than paying compensation to individual victims, redress money is used to improve conditions (Brooks 1999a: 89). This attempt of redress was met by criticism. Comfort women and advocacy organisations argue that this is not redress in the form of reparations, for atonement can only be achieved through money paid by the Government in the form of personal compensation along with a formal apology from the Diet. They maintain that the Asian Women's Fund is a welfare system because individual payments are based on socio-economic needs rather than moral restitution. Such payments add to the overall sense that Japan is failing to take responsibility for its actions (Brooks 1999a: 89, Hicks 1999: 113–125). It took changing attitudes towards women's rights, as well as campaigns by women, to turn the comfort women issue into a larger one over women's rights (Hicks 1999: 114). At some point in 1990, Emperor Akihito expressed 'intense sorrow' at the wrongs inflicted on Korea. Korean activists, however, did not regard this as atonement for the lack of adequate apology (Hicks 1999: 116). Meanwhile, in June 1990, the Japanese foreign ministry denied any government responsibility for the sexual slavery of Korean women. No public apology, disclosure, memorial or compensation was forthcoming (Hicks 1999: 117). Many women refused the payments, seeing them as an attempt by Japan to evade its responsibility. Only about 260 former sex slaves received money – 2 million yen (£10,110) each. The fund was discontinued in 2007 and no plans have been announced for a replacement (McCurry 2005). To this day, the Diet has not issued an official apology.

The 2007 bicentenary of the abolition of the slave trade is another example of demands for apology. Two hundred years on, the Queen is asked to say sorry for Britain's role in the slave trade. But an apology alone is not considered to be enough by those soliciting it. Nor are financial reparations for that matter. How the country should face its past role and the current issues of importance to black Britons today are among the issues tackled by the campaigners. The latter understand reparations as a set of acts granting Africans a new sense of identity. In other words, making an 'apology of substance' accompanied by educational and other reforms and consider it *insulting* to try and put a monetary figure on the millions of lives lost in the genocide (Smith 2004). Another most recent case in metropolitan France sheds more light on the centrality of the apology factor. In the early 1960s, the Creuse department suffered youth exodus whereas La Réunion was home to high birth rates. The latter's MP therefore devised a plan whereby 1,641 children were shipped to the Creuse between 1963 and 1980. Decades later, 19 of them are suing the state for violating French and international laws and conventions on children's rights. The contenders are not demanding money – a symbolic euro in damages – as reparations but rather an admission of a wrongful act (Henley 2005).

It is worthy to notice in this respect that the Palestinian Refugee ResearchNet (PRRN), for example, as one of the most comprehensive research entities on Palestinian refugees, refers to 'refugee compensation' as the issue of both compensation (monies paid for lost property) and reparations (monies paid in recognition of the historical injustice which created the refugee issue). There is no mention of apology as a form of reparations (Palestinian Refugee ResearchNet 2008b).

The discussion of the various forms of reparations is directly linked to what the parties aim at from seeking reparations. For example, Waldron believes that reparations, whether in the form of payment of money or the restitution of lands and artefacts, plays a role in the embodiment of communal remembrance. Aside from offsetting losses, reparations thus symbolise a society's undertaking not to forget or deny that a particular injustice took place and to respect and help sustain a dignified sense of identity in memory for the people affected (Waldron 1992: 6). This idea was behind the Japanese-American redress movement.

Lynk, on the other hand, thinks that the route to the future begins with ascertaining the legal rights violated. The legal scholar states that if compensation and restitution are to play a forward-looking role towards healing the transparent wounds of the decades-long conflict, and building the foundation for a prosperous and secure future in the region, then the available rules found in international law are both the principled and the most instructive road to follow (Lynk 2003). The benefits of legally based reparations with an eye on the future include the deterrent factor in committing acts generating 'refugeedom'. Moreover, compensation and restitution serve to repair some of the individual/group dignity lost by the refugee through their violation of human rights by mass displacement, which reduces the financial burdens of refugees. The compensation principle may also assist with the reconciliation of the parties or groups to the conflict that sparked the mass population displacement, as part of a broader range of restorative remedies such as a frank apology, the revelation of the truth, substantial reforms to political and social institutions, public educational campaigns, etc . . .

From another perspective, the idea of backwards-/forwards-looking is particularly apparent in the questions related to the persecution angle of reparations. In that sense, Minow poses the question whether all societies should pursue prosecution in order to comply with international human rights standards. She argues in this regard that alternative legal responses have recently been invented, such as East Germany's extension of public access to previously secret police files and Canada's grants of lands as restitution to First Nations groups, for example, as means to establish a break from the past (Minow 1998: 2–3). Moreover, the South African TRC illustrates an innovative and promising effort to combine an investigation into what happened, a forum for victim testimony, a process for developing reparations and a mechanism for granting amnesty for perpetrators who tell of their role in politically motivated violence.

Backwards-looking then is more concerned with the nature of the harm, the type of violation and ascertaining a right. Future-oriented targets reconciliation. This means that future-oriented or past-oriented is another way of expressing the 'just' and 'adequate' or the 'right' vs. the 'practical' debate discussed earlier. Reparations solely based on international law overlooks the issue of finding power to enforce the law to attain justice.

Before moving to how this study perceives reparations, it is worthwhile discussing how reparations have been invoked in relation to redressing cases of displacement and dispossession in particular.

Redressing displacement and dispossession

A number of approaches, particularly 'full restitution' and 'adequate compensation', have been put forward to suggest redress to displacement and dispossession. The full restitution approach (*restitutio in integrum*) acknowledges that to repair the bond between the refugee and the state of origin, the restitution process must address both material and moral damages. While property restitution and compensation may be used to repair material harms and promote physical security and well-being, moral damages are better addressed through apologies, trials and truth commissions designed to uphold state accountability (see Bradley 2005: 14–15).

The Durban Declaration from the World Conference Against Racism embraces this development-based vision of restitution. Although the debate in Durban mostly pertained to reparations for slavery, the conference concluded that restitution should be used not only to *redress* historical injustices, but also to *address* the legacies of injustice. That is, where harms such as exile have spanned generations, compensation should be used as 'a vehicle for rectifying the social and economic problems that underpin today's victims' continuing marginalization' (Bradley 2005: 15). Bradley argues that although remedies for refugees have typically been limited to the return of real property, the state is obliged to provide 'full restitution', which addresses property issues but also speaks to non-material human rights violations through mechanisms such as apologies, reconciliation commissions and criminal tribunals. Her argument is based on the idea of compensation being part of a best possible satisfaction of a just return.

'Adequate compensation', on the other hand, is a notion argued for by legal scholar Eyal Benvenisti in relation to redressing displacement and dispossession problems. Adequate compensation was discussed by the GA in 1981. The notion was subsequently elaborated upon by Benvenisti and the UN Group of Governmental Experts on International Cooperation to Avert New Flows of Refugees. The concept was developed with a view to resolving the issue of property restitution for Palestinian refugees but is considered to have significant implications for other restitution and return processes (Bradley 2005: 13).

It is worth mentioning that this concept has developed as opposed to 'full compensation' and the set of difficulties it raises. Benvenisti cites, in support of his theory, the example of the German Federal Constitutional Court, which stated in its 'Land Reform' decision of 1991 that the standard of compensation for property expropriated between 1945 and 1949 in the former German Democratic Republic (GDR) need not be at full market value, and a lesser amount would be permissible under the German Basic Law. A similarly nuanced formula – Benvenisti reminds us – is found in the Dayton Accords of 1995 concerning Bosnia, whose Annex 7 (Agreement on Refugees and Displaced Persons) mentions 'just compensation in lieu of return'. This adequate compensation framework thus rejects the Chorzow Factory philosophy that restitution must fully eliminate the consequences of a harmful act on the grounds that it is not pragmatic when dealing with large refugee communities. It rather calls for an ad hoc appraisal of the various interests and constraints involved. At times, this principle could mean more than the historic value (plus interest) but less than the full current market value. At other times, when rehabilitation of refugees requires more funds than the value of their abandoned property, 'adequate' or 'just' compensation might mean more than the full value of the property. In that sense, Benvenisti considers these principles as forward-looking, for he believes that a compensation scheme that is inspired by consequential considerations and distributive justice may be preferable to a rights-based scheme aimed at effecting corrective justice. Such a prospective outlook carries the promise of the rehabilitation of emerging economies during a relatively short period. This policy proved very successful in West Germany after the Second World War. In addition to reviving the German economy and infrastructure, it helped to absorb and rehabilitate millions of German refugees from the East, to whom no compensation for lost property was provided (Benvenisti 1999).

Moreover, according to Benvenisti, compensation in lieu of repossession of property is viewed as an alternative in the international efforts to resolve the refugees problem in both Cyprus and Bosnia. The UN initiatives to resolve the Cypriot refugees' claims and counterclaims, for example, emphasise compensation as the preferred alternative and offer a procedure for processing claims. Similarly, the 1995 Dayton Accords provide a general framework for compensating refugees who would prefer it to repossession (Benvenisti 1999).

Adequate compensation in that sense is considered to be taking into account both parties' interests and constraints. As it relates to the Palestinian–Israeli issue, calculations of adequate compensation take into account Israel's financial limitations, the time elapsed since the Palestinians were displaced, refugees' ability to prove property ownership and the massive and growing number of Palestinian claimants (Bradley 2005: 13).

Atif Kubursi tackles the notion of what an adequate compensation would be from an economic point of view.[21] The logic of his thoughts in this regard is that human beings, when unimpeded, would seek to attain the highest level of utility given their economic endowments and prices (Kubursi 1988: 189). Given the chance, individuals will take advantage of any exchange opportunity to move to their highest level of satisfaction where their willingness to trade is matched exactly by their ability to do so. Circumstances outside the objective conditions of the market that prevent the economic agents from reaching their preferred status result in loss of satisfaction and welfare. The size of these losses is generally identified as the difference between the maximum level of satisfaction possible and that which is realised under the forced circumstances. Alternatively, it is equal to that monetary compensation that would permit the higher level of utility to be utilised (Kubursi 1996: 2). This concept of economic loss also suggests that social losses are the sum total of individual losses. Moreover, according to Kubursi, compensation is synonymous with indemnification in the legal sense of undoing damage done and losses suffered. Total indemnification means in essence a return to a situation that existed before the loss was incurred. If it is done by way of restitution, the old situation is restored *in specie*. If, on the other hand, it is done wholly or partially by way of compensation, the consequences of the damage are liquidated, although the old situation is not restored in the true sense of the word. To Kubursi, such a return to the old situation is possible only by way of total restitution or total indemnification, and only when changes in the general financial, economic, social and demographic situations are taken into account (Kubursi 1996: 4). Consequently, compensation is a mechanism to reinstate the individual in the situation he or she had chosen before other circumstances intervened (Kubursi 1996: 1). Therefore, he describes compensating Palestinian refugees as follows:

> Our expression of these losses in financial terms does not mean that the figure we reached would compensate the Palestinians for the loss of Palestine. It is simply a historical and monetary valuation of the injustices perpetrated by the Zionists, no more and no less.
>
> (Kubursi 1988: 189)

Goodwin-Gill also has an input on the debate of full vs. adequate compensation. In his opinion, recent arbitral practice reveals increasing acceptance of the principle that 'full compensation' is indeed often required, although in state practice, especially where lump-sum settlements are agreed, only part of the value may be paid. The disadvantage of the latter – only a portion of the value is paid – may be offset by the fact that if everything went to arbitration, many claims might fall for lack of proof, while considerable resources would need to be expended in the processes of adjudication. In such circumstances, the notions of what is 'appropriate' or 'adequate' compensation may be calculated not only by reference to past losses, but also in the light of an assessment of present and future needs (Goodwin-Gill 2000: 49).

Bradley, in turn, bases herself on the notion of justice to form an opinion on approaches such as that of adequate compensation. In her view, albeit practical and adaptable, the adequate compensation framework fails to model the type of redress process that could enable just conditions of return or even resettlement for refugees. Employing the term restitution – as did Barkan – as an umbrella term for redress, Bradley believes that if restitution is to promote justice for refugees, it must involve not only compensation for lost property, but also the return of property and accountability for the human rights violations that led to and exacerbated displacement (Bradley 2005: 14). She also brings out the point that there is concern that compensation may be seen as a means of legitimising human rights violations, particularly ethnic cleansing, as it may mistakenly imply that money can substitute for the protection of human rights. Quoting Benvenisti, Bradley also brings out a further problem with adequate compensation, that of releasing the state from any further obligations towards refugees, usually without admitting responsibility for any wrongdoing (Bradley 2005: 14).

Transforming abstract notions of state responsibility and just return into a reconciliation and repatriation process that reflects the specific needs of each refugee situation is a complex challenge to be navigated through restitution (Bradley 2005: 6–7). Klein follows the same line of thought and believes that in the case of the Palestinian refugee problem, the issue at stake is a displacement problem requiring return of the displaced and that restitution becomes an element of satisfying an optimal state of return. Thus, ensuring a 'just return', according to this argument, implies a futuristic look in the form of a stable political future. Reparations here is a tool for a 'better', more stable, peaceful future (Klein 2006).

Throughout this chapter we have seen how the evolution of the concept of reparations moved on from being linked to an act of war to a more associated connection with a historical injustice, thus distancing from the concept of victor/vanquished. The development of the concept also progressed towards a wider inclusion of forms of redress. By considering that reparations also indicate a willingness of non-repetition of the injustice, the process has in fact broadened, taking a future-looking perspective concerned with reconciliation between the parties. Those issues reflect the importance of establishing a more concrete understanding of how this study approaches reparations, the elements it comprises and the aim it seeks. In other words, deciding on what the core of the redress is. The remainder of the chapter elaborates on those issues.

Reparations in the scope of this study

From the ideas presented and discussed throughout this chapter, issues at stake when addressing the idea of redress from different perspectives suggest they revolve around the following: identifying a past harm/injustice/wrongful act, the form of reparation, in addition to the final aim of reparations.

The legal, moral, historical or political standpoints of the protagonists influence the basis of the reparations claim and thus the identification of the nature of an injustice. Reparations then may be a right in itself, conducive to the end of a conflict or a means of restoring a previous condition. Once this question is addressed, another one arises about whether the determination of a wrongful act implies a model reparations form. Stated differently, if reparations take several forms, does the nature of the injustice necessarily lead to adopting a certain form of remedy as most adequate? This set of questions is also linked to the final objective of reparations as being backwards-looking or future-oriented. Forming the main pillars of the notion of reparations, those three elements are invariably interlinked and cannot be separated.

In light of the discussion presented above, this book employs the term reparations as the general umbrella term for redress. Reparations in this sense will focus on three forms: restitution, in its narrow definition of returning property; compensation, as financial payments; and apologies, as a formal act of contrition from the perpetrator of an injustice to the victim (as a group). With this understanding, reparations could be seen as composed of four main elements: the establishment of an injustice, the establishment of a responsibility (moral/legal), the form of remedy and, finally, the final aim of the reparations process. In other words, reparations is the answer to the set of corresponding questions consisting of: what is the wrong done? Who is responsible? What is the form of redress? And what is the aim? Added to these elements, and influencing the path to reparations, is the extent to which reparations for a specific injustice (displacement, dispossession) are linked to other components of a conflict and the inevitable trade-offs between them.

The following chapters aim to illustrate how this understanding of reparations features in each of the comparative case studies addressed in this book. Analysing the interaction between the position of each party to the conflict as well as the external involvement in how they affect reparations in both its form and basis are to illustrate the reparations process in each case. Some of the pertinent questions to be covered by the comparison are centred around the following: to what extent can the gap be bridged to reach a balance point conducive to a favourable environment to the signing of a reparations agreement? What is the consensus that could be reached about what constitutes a plausible solution? How can a balance be struck between the legal and the political? Should the rights be forsaken for the solution or should a solution come only through the implementation of rights? Is a third party involvement necessary for facilitating a favourable environment? What would be the nature of this external involvement?

3 The German–Jewish Reparations Agreement of 1952

The signing of the Restitution Agreement between Israel and Germany remains an unforgettable experience. It was, incidentally, the first time that I had met Chancellor Dr. Adenauer personally. It was an important political event of far-reaching international significance; in fact, it was quite without precedent and has become a chapter of major importance in Israel and German history. It was a political act which redounded to the credit of the democratic, post-war Germany and which has become a source of important constructive aid to Israel. The moral credit it bestowed on the Federal Republic is due first and foremost to Dr. Adenauer who initiated the agreement and led it to its successful conclusion.

(Moshe Sharett, then Foreign Minister of Israel, quoted in Vogel 1968/69)

The German–Jewish Reparations Agreement (hereinafter the Reparations Agreement) – also known as the Luxembourg Agreement – of 1952, signed between the Federal Republic of Germany, the state of Israel and the Conference on Jewish Material Claims Against Germany (hereinafter Claims Conference (CC)) is the first case study we will look at.[1] The main points of the agreement were payment of DM3 billion (about $715 million) and payment of DM450 million (about $107 million) to the state of Israel on behalf of the Claims Conference.[2] Under the terms of the agreement, payments were to be made in 12 annual instalments.[3] In addition, in one of the two protocols signed together with the Claims Conference, Germany undertook to pass an indemnification law covering compensation payable to individual victims of the Nazi persecutions who had suffered imprisonment, mutilation and loss of profession or property, and a law restoring property seized by the former Third Reich and other bodies.[4]

To unravel the particularities of this case of reparations, an overview of the early attempts of redress prior to the Luxembourg Agreement is presented. This historical outline is followed by details of the negotiations between the parties. As shown in Figure 3.1, understanding the reparations process will particularly focus on the interaction between the parties to the agreement, in addition to the role of external involvement. It is worthy to note at this instance that the Jewish party is divided into two: the state of Israel and the Claims Conference. An elaboration of this matter is provided throughout the course of the chapter.

Historical background

Throughout the Nazi military progress in Europe during the Second World War, several thousand European Jews fled for their lives, abandoning their homes in territories falling under German rule, thus leaving behind nearly all their possessions. During this process, the Nazi Government confiscated abandoned Jewish property (Sagi 1980: 2). In reaction, ideas were burgeoning within Jewish circles worldwide over claims to be presented to Germany after the war for compensation for expropriated Jewish property. Accordingly, individuals and groups in England, Palestine and the US formulated various plans and proposals. Compensation to individuals and to the Jewish people as a whole for the material losses suffered was demanded at conferences in Baltimore in 1941 and Atlantic City in 1944, enjoying the support of Jewish organisations throughout the world (Sagi 1980: 2, Roth 1982).

Efforts in this context became more concrete in 1945 when Chaim Weizmann, on behalf of the Jewish Agency (JA), submitted to the

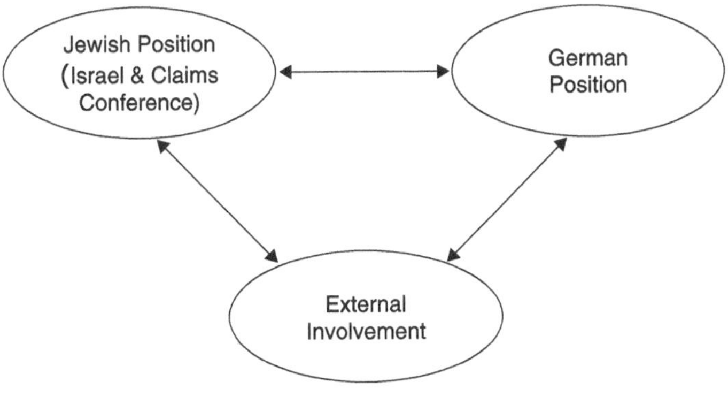

Figure 3.1 Reparations as an interplay of the interaction between the parties to the agreement.

governments of the US, the USSR, Britain and France a memorandum demanding the restitution of existing property to the owners – individuals or institutions.[5] The memorandum, spelling out the foundations of the subsequent comprehensive Luxembourg reparations treaty, also requested heirless Jewish property to be restored to the representatives of the Jewish people and that the latter should be allotted a proper percentage of German reparations to be entrusted to the JA in Palestine (Encyclopaedia Judaica 1971, New Encyclopedia of Zionism and Israel 1994). Weizmann further appealed to the Allied Powers to include this claim in their negotiations for reparations with Germany in view of the 'mass murder, the human suffering, the annihilation of spiritual, intellectual and creative forces which are without parallel in the history of mankind' (quoted in Encyclopaedia Judaica 1971).

The issue of Jewish reparations claims against Germany was later picked up by the newly born state of Israel two years after its establishment. On 24 October 1950, the governments of the US, the UK and France addressed a note to Israel (as well as to 54 other countries) announcing their intention to take legal measures to put an end to the state of war against Germany and they suggested that the Israeli Government should, if it thought fit, adopt similar measures (P.G. 1954). Israel's initial response was negative. On 16 January 1951 it replied in a note to the four powers occupying Germany declaring it could not envisage taking similar action, but asked that the four powers in their future agreements with Germany should reserve for Israel the right to put forward a claim on behalf of the Jews persecuted under Hitler. Israel went on, stating that as a country with a large Jewish immigration, it was particularly qualified to speak in the names of the victims of Nazism (P.G. 1954: 260).

Due to the deadlock and later interruption of the Allies' negotiations for reparations, no further development took place until 12 March 1951 when the Israeli Foreign Minister, Moshe Sharett, submitted another note to the four allies demanding reparations from Germany, thus reversing his government's policy towards the matter (P.G. 1954). A series of exchanges between Israel and the three Western powers followed, while the Soviet Union remained silent and never acknowledged Israel's demands. The answers received by Israel made it clear, by implication, that a reparations settlement could only be achieved through direct negotiations between Israel and Germany (New Encyclopedia of Zionism and Israel 1994). This indicated one of the main characteristics of the German–Jewish reparations agreement, which went through a negotiation process solely involving the concerned protagonists negotiating parameters of a settlement themselves. The following sections discuss the position of the parties in relation to reparations in both its basis and form, and illustrate the process through which the reparations claim went through until the signature of the agreement in Luxembourg in 1952.

Party 1: the Jewish position

As pointed out in the introduction to this chapter, the German–Jewish Reparations Agreement was in fact signed between three parties rather than two: the state of Israel, the Claims Conference and Germany. While Israel and the CC both represent the claimants, their attitudes towards spelling out the reparations claim, their concerns and their motivations were not always matching and the form of reparations included in the final agreement was different. Therefore this section, concerned with the overall Jewish position, is subdivided into two parts. The first one is devoted to the state of Israel's position towards the reparations claim, while the second sheds light on the Claims Conference's stance.

Position of the state of Israel

The Israeli decision to request reparations from Germany first came in the form of an indirect approach when the Israeli Government decided to send the above-mentioned 12 March 1951 note to the four powers demanding reparations from the Federal Republic and the GDR. Pressing for reparations from Germany was not a target of Israel's foreign policy when it was established in 1948. Several things influenced the newly born state so as to revert its policy orientation regarding the matter. As the following paragraphs illustrate, the challenge in the reparations journey was not in the negotiating process itself over details of the reparations agreement. Rather, the challenge lay in the preceding phase of articulating the decision to seek reparations on the one hand, and formulating the basis for the reparations demanded from Germany on the other hand.

The set of prevailing circumstances on the international scene, as well as domestically, caused Israel to consider the question of reparations and to adopt an indirect approach to the matter at first instance. In that context, when the three Western Allied Powers decided to end the state of war and ask Germany to pay war reparations, they subsequently sent on 24 October 1950 a communiqué to Israel expressing their wish that Israel do the same. This request 'stunned' the Israeli Government, which had hitherto believed that post-Nazi Germany could not be readmitted to the international community until it had restored its relations with the

Jews. In effect, Israel considered that the Allies' decision recognised Germany's rehabilitation without any atonement for its crimes against the Jewish people, and without agreement from either the Jewish people or the Israeli Government. In this context, the rebuff of the boycott policy pursued thus far by the Israeli state, which was meant to intensify pressure on Germany and increase the cost of Israel's 'seal of approval', seemed irrelevant in the wake of these fast-moving developments (Auerbach 1991: 277). Germany's astounding recovery and rapid reintegration into post-war political dynamics became the most important development in the international arena in 1950–51. As the Cold War intensified, Germany became more important to both superpowers (Auerbach 1991: 276).

On the domestic scene, analysts go as far as describing Israel at that stage as 'dominated by a catastrophic deterioration in the country's economic situation'. The first item on Ben-Gurion's agenda was immigration and the enormous expenses it entailed, stretching the nascent state's meagre resources. Additionally, security issues related to strengthening the fragile armistice between Israel and its neighbours called for equally high budget allocations. It could thus be understood why a pressing need to attract foreign currency to cover the Government's mounting deficit was a factor altering foreign policy decisions. The perspectives of reparations were therefore perceived by the Israeli leaders as a life-saving flow of capital that would aid the economy without increasing the debt burden (Auerbach 1991: 276). This in fact meant that Ben-Gurion swiftly grasped the economic significance of the idea of reparations and was even more aware of its political ramifications, which became increasingly important in light of international developments.[6]

This perception of what reparations meant to the Israeli leadership was soon manifest in state policy when, in January 1951, the Government met and adopted a resolution for Israeli representatives 'to apply to the central governments of the occupying powers concerning Germany's promise of reparations and restitution of Jewish property'. Thus, the strategy of pursuing reparations from Germany was officially spelled out (Auerbach 1991: 277).

The significance of the note Israel subsequently addressed to the Allies – mentioned above – resides in the fact that it reflected Israel's perception of reparations. Stating as its purpose facilitating the re-settling of Jewish refugees from Europe in Israel, the latter pointed out the financial responsibility of the Bonn Government, which had recognised itself to be the successor of the Third Reich. It also demonstrated how the German people were continuing to enjoy the fruits of Nazi massacres, described the action taken by Israel for the resettlement of displaced persons and maintained that the German people should contribute to the re-establishment of the survivors (Giniewski 1959: 171). In other words, Israel's position was to advocate German financial responsibility in covering costs of resettling the displaced whose displacement it was responsible for. Israel was clear in making this point despite the government now in power in Germany not being the one having caused the displacement. The note in fact indicates that at this stage, Israel's position meant that its perception of the act of reparations was linked to Germany's responsibility towards the resettlement of the refugees by paying financial compensation to the state representing them. It was neither presented as an act of contrition nor as a demand for remedying breached rights. Further developments in the reparations track – discussed later in this chapter – indicate that while emphasis on German responsibility shifted from financial to moral, the absence of legal rhetoric in the search for reparations remained as a main characteristic of the German–Jewish reparations case.

In such an approach to the issue of reparations from Germany at this initial phase, Israel was following some advisory proposals that indicate that the form of reparations was not originally defined but rather left to the negotiations themselves. Dr Hendrick van Dam, General Secretary of the *Zentralrat der Juden in Deutschland*, had prepared a memorandum (1 July 1950) for the Israeli Government that outlined concrete proposals for negotiations between Israel and its German counterpart. Clause 6 proposed:

> . . . that the [Israeli] government send a 'Reparation and Indemnification Mission' with power to negotiate with the German government agreements on compensation for Jews living in Israel, the transfer and export of goods, etc., to prepare the general claims for reparations. The mandate of the mission's agreement, irrespective of our wishes, must accord with the facts the mission is likely to find. In negotiations with the German government, proper credentials should be formally submitted if in the light of prevailing conditions this would appear advisable.
>
> (Vogel 1968/69: 7–8)

A question that may be asked at this junction is: why did Israel opt for resorting to the Allies to make their demands for reparations rather than directly addressing the German Government? This policy attitude was in fact adopted in light of the strong objection to the idea of reparations in

Jewish public opinion circles. Overcoming such an obstacle to pave the way for reparations was perceived to be possible through indirect approach, as a gradual step to the actual reparations negotiations. Israeli and Jewish public opinion were strongly concerned about relations with post-Nazi Germany and reactions were potent regarding contact with Germany (P.G. 1954: 266, Auerbach 1991: 278). The principle of material reparation was repugnant to large segments of the Israeli population, who felt that it was morally wrong to accept 'blood money' from the Germans. To them, it recalled the Teutonic *Wehrgeld*, the blood-price whereby, in past times, the most abominable crimes could be atoned for (P.G. 1954: 267). As Auerbach points out, Ben-Gurion had two arguments to publicly justify accepting reparations from Germany. The first was based on recovering as much Jewish property as possible, thereby extricating the 'Jewish legacy from the murderers' hands . . . so that the murderers do not become the heirs as well . . .'. The second argument was based on illustrating how reparations monies would be used to finance the absorption and rehabilitation of the Holocaust survivors in Israel (Auerbach 1991: 284). Israel's need for foreign aid was also advocated. It was pointed out that American aid was becoming increasingly dependent on political considerations in addition to the philanthropic support of world Jewry showing signs of tapering off.

Hence, German reparations were distanced from any insinuations of *Wehrgeld* allegories. Instead, reparations were marketed as a contribution to the establishment of 500,000 displaced persons in Israel. As to the moral objection of meeting the assassin of yesterday at the conference table, it was emphasised that it would be 'even immoral to allow the culprits or their heirs to enjoy the fruits of the crime' (P.G. 1954: 267). What the Jewish leader succeeded in doing was to present the issue of reparations as an act of historic justice: the return of stolen goods by the murderers in order to rehabilitate the survivors (Auerbach 1991: 287).

In a subsequent public declaration, the Israeli Government made a first step towards its shift to directly address reparations claims to Germany. In his capacity as the Israeli delegate to the UN, Abba Eban stated:

> The discussions have shown that the Western Powers are not prepared to represent Israel concerning her claims against Germany. Consequently Israel must decide whether the plundered property is to remain in the hands of the murderers, or whether she must embark on direct negotiations with the German authorities.
>
> (quoted in P.G. 1954: 266)

In a powerful article advocating direct negotiations, Nahum Goldmann (joint chairman of the JA, acting president of the World Jewish Congress at the time and future president of the Claims Conference) addressed the Jewish world, attempting to assuage its opposition to the idea. He skilfully distanced the reparations issue from conciliation aims and limited the matter to seeking restoration of looted property: '. . . To take the position that we don't want our own property returned to us by the Germans, would be, in my opinion, absolutely immoral' (Goldmann 1952).

Nevertheless, when the issue of direct negotiations with the Bonn Government came before the Knesset on 7 January 1952, it reportedly provoked a heated discussion in the press and public opinion.[7] The opposition centred in a wide assortment of parties. The Knesset debate took place against a background of a violent demonstration in proximity of the building. Begin's speech in the Knesset illustrates the fierce opposition to the idea of reparations from Germany. During the Knesset debate, Begin said:

> We will fight to the end . . . There are things in life that are dearer than life itself; there are things in life that are more dreadful than death. And this is one of those things for which we will give our lives, for which we are prepared to die. We shall leave our families, bid farewell to our children – and negotiations with Germany will not take place.
>
> (quoted in Rubinstein 1962: 29–30)

On 8 January, the Knesset approved the government request for authorisation to begin direct negotiations with Germany by a vote of 61 to 50 with 5 abstentions (New Encyclopedia of Zionism and Israel 1994). Yet, since the Israeli public was not yet receptive to an attitude as flagrantly realistic as this, a moral 'coating' was required. It was thus considered that an official statement by the German Government, including recognition of its responsibility for crimes against the Jewish people and willingness to make redress, would serve as proof of Germany's sincere desire to rid itself of its Nazi past. The main difficulty facing the Israelis at this point centred on extracting such a declaration without meeting the Germans directly.[8]

In other words, internal opposition to the idea of seeking reparations from Germany contributed towards the development of another main feature of the German–Jewish reparations claim. The Government of Israel deemed it necessary to obtain a formal acknowledgement of

Germany's moral guilt before proceeding with issues of financial compensation. The act of contrition thus acted as a *sine qua non* in the politics of reparations preceding the agreement and formed a part of the path leading to the conclusion of the treaty.

Against this background, the first meeting between Israeli and German officials to deliberate the reparations claim was shrouded in a thick mantle of secrecy. According to Auerbach, the main purpose of the meeting was to make it clear to Chancellor Adenauer that, before any negotiations began, the Government of Germany would have to issue a public declaration including the following points: expression of shock and regret concerning the crimes committed against the Jewish people during the period of Nazi rule; recognition of the German people's obligation to ensure that no German government repeat similar crimes against humanity; acknowledgement that although the crime could be neither forgiven nor expunged, Germany had an elementary obligation to correct the damage it wrought; and finally that Germany must promise to do everything it could to expedite the claims for restitution, indemnification for damage to life and property, and collective reparations to the Jewish people (Auerbach 1991: 279–280).

It was still necessary for Germany to invite Israel to negotiate its claim. On 6 December, at Goldmann's request and with Ben-Gurion's agreement, a meeting was arranged between Goldmann and Adenauer. At the end of the meeting, Goldmann allegedly dictated to Adenauer's secretary a letter that was addressed to Goldmann and signed by Adenauer. This letter contained an explicit invitation to the Israeli Government to enter into dialogue with representatives of the German Government concerning reparations, based on Israel's letters of 12 March 1951. As such, it initiated the birth of the formal process towards a reparations agreement (Auerbach 1991: 287). This marked the shift of the struggle between Israel, Diaspora Jews and the Germans on the idea of reparation itself towards one concerning the extent, form and conditions of payment of reparations.

Position of the Claims Conference

The idea that there would be two separate negotiations tracks between Germany and Israel on the one hand, and Germany and the Jewish Diaspora on the other hand, emanated from both the Jewish and German sides. This section explains why there has been a division in the Jewish camp and how this division led to the birth of an umbrella organisation representing Jewish Diaspora negotiating with Germany a separate claim; an entity whose name reflected the perception of its founders of the purpose and nature of reparations.

The birth of the Claims Conference, as an umbrella organisation representing Jewish Diaspora in its negotiation for reparations from Germany, was a culmination of efforts to unite a worldwide Jewish endorsement to Israel in its endeavours to earn reparations. In anticipation of its imminent negotiations with Germany, the Israeli Government took the initiative of bringing together Jewish organisations of the Diaspora so as to complement its mandate as representative of world Jewry, hence the Israeli request to Nahum Goldmann to use his offices at the World Zionist Organization to convene a preliminary meeting of the various Diaspora Jewish organisations to discuss the matter (Zweig 2001: 26, Goldmann 1969: 254–255).[9]

From the perspective of the most prominent Jewish organisations, Israel's reparations claims and those of world Jewry would have to be presented separately if they were to have any success in the negotiations (Zweig 2001: 26). By the same token, to be fully able to endorse the Israeli Government's endeavours, world Jewry had to gather under the banner of one single umbrella organisation in view of Adenauer's specific statement that the German Government wished to negotiate both with the Israeli Government and 'representatives of Jewry'. Therefore, the general meeting that gathered representatives of the Jewish organisations was originally planned as a public demonstration of support by the Jewish world for the principle of negotiations with the Germans. The meeting also endorsed the leadership of the Israeli Government in such negotiations and discussed the strategy to follow with the Germans (Zweig 2001: 27).

Each of the 22 invited organisations attending the meeting in New York had been selected to represent a broad range of Jewish communities, whether geographically or ideologically. Putting pressure on Western powers to gain their support for the reparations demands was also a matter taken into consideration by the Jewish leaders. Therefore, effort was exerted to ensure the attendance of the major organisations operating in the Western world. As Goldmann subsequently stated:

> At first we invited the important organizations in the countries of the Western powers in order to exert pressure on these powers. We could not invite the Jews of the East [Bloc], because they are unable to come and attend the Conference. The idea was that these bodies in the Western countries should exert influence on their states and thus

> put pressure on Germany. We invited all the larger organizations in Europe, England, Canada and America.
>
> (quoted in Zweig 2001: 27)

In addition, representative bodies of the Jewish communities of South Africa, Australia and Argentina were also invited.

The question of pushing for reparations against Germany was debated among the 22 organisations present at the New York meeting. The main outcome was full agreement on backing Israel's global claim against Germany, yet disagreement on their own path of negotiation as a separate entity presenting a separate claim.[10] Achieving such widespread support from the Jewish organisations for reparations negotiations presented the Jewish leaders with the mandate they wanted both to endorse Israel's demands and to begin contacts with Germany on behalf of the Diaspora organisations. This was no meagre achievement in the history of the Jewish reparations from Germany. Goldmann had played an important role as a link between the Israeli Government and the Diaspora Jewish organisations. He had succeeded in the impressive task of unifying the Jewish organisations after they were each working with different aims and strategies. The Jewish leader was able to shift the aim of the organisations from the mere tasks of relief aid and local restitution efforts to embarking on a common idea of reparation, thus paving the way for the strategy of the organisation-to-be in the forthcoming negotiations.

The significance of this full agreement on backing Israel in its journey towards seeking reparations from Germany is that it demonstrated that reparations was a goal that overcame general apprehensions on behalf of the organisations and the dynamics of their inter-relationships. Moreover, it proved to be directed by the futuristic perspectives of allocating reparations monies. The leading Jewish organisations were apprehensive about the common public Jewish endorsement to the state of Israel, which would leave the task of negotiating to the Israelis while accepting a purely symbolic role for the Jewish organisations. In their opinion, this would not only upset the balance of inter-organisational relations that had evolved on the question of reparations since the end of the war, but would also undermine their position in any subsequent allocation of reparations achieved (Zweig 2001: 28). It is worth noting that this was a time when the major Jewish organisations were in the process of accommodating to the transformation of the Jewish world caused by the creation of the state of Israel three years earlier. Since the 1930s, the interests of the Jewish communities living in various countries were catered for by the World Jewish Congress as well as the American Jewish Community (AJC). Each of the two organisations had developed its own strategy and methods of operation. Israel's creation as a state of all Jews introduced an additional and more influential protector of Jewish interests, which ultimately made both the Congress and the AJC reconsider their international activities. Moreover, the division of Jewish philanthropy between the needs of Israel, those of disadvantaged Diaspora communities and the requirements of the local communities where the funds were raised was another area of potential discord and worry among the Jewish organisations (Zweig 2001: 29).

Once the decision to create the common negotiating organisation was made, the full name it chose for itself – the Conference on Jewish Material Claims Against Germany – expressed a fundamental position of the various Jewish organisations towards the aim of reparations and the form it would eventually take. To the founding members of the Claims Conference, negotiations with Germany were limited to pragmatic material matters and did not imply any degree of reconciliation. Negotiations in that sense would not undermine Germany's moral debt and only the material claims would be discussed within them. This view was expressed in a public statement released after the New York meeting in which representatives of the organisation agreed on establishing the Claims Conference to represent them in negotiations with Germany (Zweig 2001: 30–31, Sagi 1980: 77):

> Crimes of the nature and magnitude perpetrated by Nazi Germany against the Jews cannot be expiated by any measure of material reparations . . . [but] every elementary principle of justice and human decency requires that the German people shall, at least, restore the plundered Jewish property, indemnifying the victims of persecution, their heirs and successors, and pay for the rehabilitation of the survivors.

The principle of negotiations now endorsed, the newly born Conference's next task was organisational: establishing a framework for continuing the consultations between its constituent organisations and formulating the details of the Jewish claim in anticipation of the forthcoming contacts with Germany. Details of the claim are discussed later in this chapter. The following section outlines the German position towards reparations to the Jewish world.

Party 2: the German position

The first manifestation of the German position regarding reparations to dispossessed Jews came in the guise of a statement that Chancellor Konrad Adenauer made during an interview with the *Allgemeine Wochenzeitung* a few weeks after the establishment of the Federal Republic:

> The Federal Republic is particularly concerned that Jewish citizens should be recompensed for the economic losses they sustained. In this respect existing legislation needs to be amended and improved. The State of Israel has come to represent Jewry as a whole. The Federal Government, as an earnest of its intention to make amends for the wrong which Germans have inflicted on Jews from all over the world, will put development aid to the value of 10m. DM at Israel's disposal.
>
> (quoted in Vogel 1968/69)

This statement contained the German perception of reparations to Jews. It acknowledged Jewish losses, acknowledged amendment of laws as a remedy to the wrongful act, acknowledged Israel as the representative of the harmed and acknowledged the intention to pay a sum that it spelled out as development aid rather than a compensation for a wrongful act in the strict sense of the term. This initial position was subject to alterations, as apparent from the subsequent formal German declaration to the Bundestag regarding its decision to enter negotiations with the Jewish world.

In February 1951, the Bundestag debated the problem of reparation.[11] On 27 September 1951, the Federal Chancellor stated in a Bundestag declaration that he had not only decided to pass a comprehensive restitution law, but also to inform the state of Israel of the Federal Republic's willingness to negotiate a reparation agreement:

> In view of Nazidom's ruthless destruction of all Jewish property, any reparation agreement has to face the grave problem of Germany's limited ability to pay, brought about by the bitter need to provide for her own countless war victims and expellees. The Federal Government is, however, prepared to solve in co-operation with representatives of Jewish organizations and the state of Israel, which has offered sanctuary to so many of the Jewish refugees, the problem of material reparations in order to make some contribution towards healing the deeper wounds inflicted by the enormity of suffering. The

> Government is profoundly aware of the need to revive the spirit of humanism and make it flourish, and regards it as the German people's foremost duty to serve this spirit.
>
> (quoted in Vogel 1968/69: 8)

An overwhelming majority of Bundestag deputies shared the Chancellor's attitude and cleared the way for the negotiations leading up to the Luxembourg Agreement. The German position regarding reparations had thus slightly shifted from its initial statement, as apparent from above. Recipients of reparations were specified as being all world Jewry instead of considering the state of Israel as the only representative of the victims. Moreover, from the German perspective, redress for the historical injustice was to be reached through indemnification laws and material compensation.[12] In the aftermath of this statement began several steps of rapprochements between Germans and Israelis initiated by some meetings between delegates of the two sides. The general argument during those meetings was that Germany, in order to come to terms with herself, would regard the acceptance of reparations by Israel as a favour and gesture of goodwill. There was no question of trying to minimise German guilt. But financial attempts to make at least material amends were considered to 'help to ease the German conscience' (Vogel 1968/69: 6).

In fact, Germany was willing to embark on the negotiating track as a ticket to the new post-World War II international system. To achieve that goal, it had to find a way to distance itself from the Nazi regime. Repairing the wrongs perpetrated against the Jews was perceived as reaching this objective and, by consequence, the necessity from its point of view to sign an agreement with representatives of all Jews and not just the state of Israel (Rubinstein 1962: 31, Auerbach 1991: 275). This was part of the general policy framework on the political scene of post-war Germany. Political circles were preoccupied with the idea that the new Germany could only inspire confidence and trust and re-establish its reputation in the world if the Federal Government was to dissociate itself from the past by a genuine and tangible effort to compensate and rehabilitate those who had lost so much. Such an effort would also serve to remind the German people of the recent past and the need for a new beginning.

That 'overcoming' of the legacy of the past apparently took two main forms in official German policy-making: legal and moral. Therefore, this period was related to the need for short-term stabilisation of a society that, following years of occupation, had to take increasing responsibility for its own well-being. On the other hand, it was related to the need to produce more sustained political, judicial and intellectual standards for confronting that same past. The Adenauer era's 'policy for the past' therefore dissolved into a shared engagement for a post-national future (Frei 2002: xi–xiii). One of the main components of this policy characterising the first years of the German state, and enjoying a high degree of consensus, was completing a normative separation from Nazism, manifesting itself in various aspects of legislative and executive action (Frei 2002: 303). The Bonn Government made no secret of the advantages it expected to accrue to it from paying reparations to Israel. Adenauer himself, the day after the agreement was ratified in the Bundestag, said:

> The government is extraordinarily pleased about the ratification of the agreement, since it will be of great significance for future relations between Germany and the rest of the world. The prestige of the German people, which suffered from the Nazi chief's crimes against the Jews, will gain much in the eyes of the free world from this agreement.
>
> (quoted in Rubinstein 1962: 31)

An editorial comment in the *Herald Tribune* at the time said that West Germany:

> by acknowledging her moral debt and by trying to pay it off through financial outlays, has taken an important stride towards regaining her pre-Hitler status as a respected and responsible nation.
>
> (quoted in Rubinstein 1962: 31)

In adopting such a policy, Adenauer did not seem to face any serious domestic opposition regarding the issue of reparations to the Jewish people apart from a small minority drawn from the various branches of neo-Nazism.[13] The Germans thus decided to sound out Israeli authorities and representatives of Jewish organisations as to whether they would be interested in such an attempt of reparations. As Germany and the Jewish world embarked on negotiating details of working out the form of reparations, Adenauer wrote in a letter to his Minister of Finance, Fritz Shaeffer, on 29 February 1952:

> that the negotiations should be prepared and conducted in a spirit which paying due regard to the moral and political uniqueness of our obligations, would abstain from raising objections which under different circumstances would certainly be understandable.
>
> (quoted in Vogel 1968/69: 8)

Therefore, that the German policy of pursuing reparations to the Jews was based on moral contrition, as it was announced, is difficult to believe. Nor could it be attributed to a combination of moral and political considerations that led Adenauer to make his statement in the Bundestag and sign the reparations agreement a year later as Rubinstein wrote (1962: 31). Rather, reparations to the Jewish world were perceived by the German Government as a policy consolidating its presence in the post-World War II political scene, and were thus an act of political pragmatism.

External involvement

The case of the German–Jewish reparations agreement is one characterised by a path to reparations involving the two parties concerned with no external intervention putting forward solutions. The interaction of the concerned parties has thus been the sole influencing factor on the nature of the reparations agreement, both in its form and basis. Therefore, discussion of external involvement in this section is limited to considerations taken into account by the parties themselves and some degree of influence exercised by some international players, but can by no means be characterised as direct significant intervention. The following paragraphs present a general idea of considerations the main players may have taken into account throughout their path to reparations. Also highlighted are early attempts to link the German–Jewish path to compensation to Palestinian refugees in the early years of the conflict, as an Israeli attempt to gain pressure from the American Government, which was interested in finding a solution to the Israeli–Palestinian conflict.

Since the very inception of the reparations efforts on behalf of the Jewish and Israeli side, the Allied Powers manifested no special interest to enforce Israel's claims. While the Soviet Union did not reply at all to Israel's note of 12 March 1952, the Western powers responded by citing legal and other reasons for their refusal to force Germany to make reparations payments to the state of Israel, and recommended that Israel enter into direct and free negotiations with the Government of Germany on this matter (Auerbach 1991: 278, Rubinstein 1962: 30).

The international atmosphere towards the end of the 1940s suggested a lack of urgency for the Western powers to intervene in full strength for a reparations agreement between the Jews and the Germans. Despite the growing realisation of the impact of the Holocaust, the attitude of the powers, and particularly of the United States, were more concerned with considerations of the Cold War, the Marshall Plan and the growing threat of communism. Germany's geographical location and potential strength could not be ignored. Thus the Allies' plans for punishing Germany soon gave way to plans for its rehabilitation and re-integration. Germany was to be brought closer to Western Europe and fitted into the economic, political and military organisations being set up there (Sagi 1980: 60). Hence, the United States was not about to alienate Germany, an important potential ally, by pressing her to pay a large sum in reparation to another state. Economic considerations further reinforced this tendency. Germany was still being assisted and supported by the Marshall Plan, and in the United States its ability to carry the burden of reparation was seriously doubted. It was feared that, in consequence, the bill would ultimately be paid by American taxpayers (Sagi 1980: 60). Therefore, to secure acceptance of the Jewish claim without having themselves to coerce Germany into paying, the Americans were ready to recommend direct negotiations between Germany and Israel. They were prepared to exert their influence over Germany in the course of the negotiations, but not to claim the money from Germany for Israel (Sagi 1980: 61).

The Israeli Government, in its part, was keen on having the American support for its negotiations with Germany and, therefore, tried to attract American interest by linking the matter to compensating Palestinian refugees. It is reported that Israeli Foreign Minister Sharett told US Undersecretary of State George McGhee in March 1951 that the reparations were a possible source of funding for compensation to Palestinian refugees. Around the same time, Ben-Gurion noted: 'certainly we wish to give reparations to the Arabs but we cannot until we have been paid for all we lost in Germany, Hungary, Poland or Austria' (Fischbach 2003a: 189, Pappe 2001: 268).

The reaction of the Arab states towards the reparation talks was of some importance at this junction. The Arab states reacted to the reparation talks even before an agreement was signed. In March 1952, Syria, Lebanon and Iraq approached the US, the UK and France and stated that the Palestinian refugees should benefit from any future German reparations to Israel. Jordan wrote a similar note to the UK and France, while in April 1952 the Yemeni Government gave its verbal assent to the idea. In June, the Arab Higher Committee wrote directly to the West German Government asking it to sequester the reparations for use by the refugees. The Germans reportedly ignored the letter, arguing that the Arabs were not a party to their talks with Israel. Some Arab governments approached the Germans as well. Privately, however, the German Government conceded that the Arabs had a point and stated that some of the money should in fact benefit the refugees. Arab states then threatened to boycott Germany, something the US was keen to avoid. They consequently told the Syrians that 'they would be killing their own case for compensation' by such a course of action. Therefore, when it signed the reparation agreement, the German Government risked alienating its Arab trade partners. Nevertheless, the Germans deemed the agreement with Israel more important (Fischbach 2003a: 188–189, Rubinstein 1962: 41, Talhami 2003: 45–48).

The United States continued to examine linkage between the two issues. The State Department drafted a memorandum in January 1953 entitled 'Arab Refugee Compensation and the Israeli–German Reparations Agreement'. Among the ideas contained in the document was the belief that *theoretically* the two issues were separate but that *politically* it would be helpful to connect the two issues to forestall an Arab boycott of West Germany. The document suggested that the Americans use Israel's great anxiety about securing German parliamentary approval of the deal as a 'sanction' to get it to move forward on the compensation issue. The United States could reasonably ask Israel to link the two issues, however, only if it increased its aid to Israel. The maximum amount necessary for this was $20 million a year. This would require the United States to give up its hope of ending Israeli grants-in-aid sometime around fiscal year 1951. Later, on 4 March 1950, the American ambassador to Israel suggested to Sharett that Israel issue a public statement renewing its willingness to pay compensation in order to forestall the threatened Arab boycott of West Germany. Sharett replied that he already had passed on an indirect message to Egypt that Israel's offer still stood 'for the time being'. He added, however, that Israel's domestic political scene made it difficult for him to issue such a statement at that time. In the end, no German reparations payments were diverted to the Palestinian refugees (Fischbach 2003a: 191).

The path towards reparations thus resumed with no further external pressure. The following section discusses how the positions of the parties to the agreement influenced the nature of the reparations claim, both in its basis and form.

The nature of the reparations claim

This section is intended to address the nature of the reparations claim, aiming at understanding how the positions of the parties, outlined in the previous sections, interacted to influence the basis of the claim (legal, moral, political) in addition to the form it finally took.

Formulation of the Israeli claim

The reader may recall from the introduction to this chapter that earlier informal reparations calls originally demanded for restitution and compensation for Jewish possessions expropriated by the Nazi regime. This sub-section highlights the reasons behind the request on behalf of the state of Israel of a global claim from Germany, and the basis of the demand for this global claim.

Prior to the birth of the Israeli state, addressing individual claims was tackled by restitution laws instituted by the Allies in the zones of occupation (Sagi 1980: 38–48, Pease 1976). The restitution laws enacted in the American, British and French zones, respectively, each referred to successor organisations to be created to take custody of ownerless and heirless property. Accordingly, the first successor organisation, the Jewish Restitution Successor Organization (JRSO), was set up in Germany by the American administration in June 1948. The JRSO presented tens of thousands of claims to heirless property. The monies received were primarily utilised for welfare, for aid to the JA, and for the cultural and religious needs of communities re-established in Germany (Sagi 1980: 41). The JRSO also presented claims for the restitution of the property of communities, organisations and institutions.

As the question of restitution and compensation to individuals was being dealt with, the demand for global reparations by Germany to the Jewish people as a whole was also put forward. In its Note of 16 January 1951, the Israeli Government stated that it reserved the right to devote a special Note to a problem not covered by the existing laws in Germany concerned with restitution and indemnification – the problem of the reparation owed by Germany to the Jewish people in its entirety. The argument went on to specify that the Jewish masses throughout Europe were murdered and there was no one to present individual claims for the restitution of their property or payment of compensation (Sagi 1980: 55). Therefore, Israel asked that measures should be taken to permit persons dispossessed of their property, who had left Germany, to claim restitution, in addition to giving the persons having the right to restitution and compensation the legal possibility to transfer money and goods abroad (P.G. 1954: 260).

The major significance of this Note was that the Israeli resolution to enter into direct negotiations with Germany led to the formulation and presentation in writing of two types of claims to the four powers: the first relied on precedents and existing laws concerning the restoration of stolen property to individuals. The second claim was presented in the letter of 12 March: the two Germanys were asked to pay the Jewish people $1.5 billion in reparations. This demand was later raised in the Israeli note of 16 March 1951 to the four powers. Here, for the first time, the global claim against Germany was presented in full detail and with all the supporting arguments. Nine months later, it was accepted by Konrad Adenauer as the basis for negotiations between Germany and Israel and the Jewish organisations, and it served as the basis for the agreement reached at the close of the negotiations in Wassenaar (Sagi 1980: 55). The Note stated the following:

> The amount to be claimed must be related, on the one hand, to the losses suffered by the Jewish people at the hands of the Germans, and on the other, to the financial cost involved in the rehabilitation in Israel of those who escaped or survived the Nazi regime . . . Israel can base its claim only on the expenditure in connection with the resettlement of the Jewish immigrants from the countries formerly under Nazi control. Their number is estimated at about 500,000 which would involve an overall expenditure of 1.5 billion dollars.
>
> (New Encyclopedia of Zionism and Israel 1994).

Several observations can be drawn from this Note: on the one hand, the claim presented by the state of Israel to act as the legal recipient of German reparation funds was based largely on the fact that of the nearly 200,000 Jewish displaced persons who had been located within the German borders at the end of the Second World War, 130,000 had emigrated to Palestine/Israel. This claim was based on the financial cost involved in the rehabilitation in Israel of those who had escaped or survived the Nazi regime. The financial expense incurred by Israel in the absorption of 500,000 Nazi victims would be covered at $3,000 per capita. Israel was keen on stating that its claim bore no relation to the real value of the Jewish property looted (which would represent a much higher figure), but was based on the expenditure actually incurred in resettling the immigrants. Neither could there be any question of regarding the payment as moral reparation (P.G. 1954: 261). On the other hand, the sum to be demanded had to bear a relation to the injury suffered by the Jewish people at the hands of the Nazis and, at the same time, to the financial cost involved in rehabilitating the survivors in Israel. The Israeli Government was not in a position to secure and submit detailed data on seized Jewish property, estimated at $6 billion (Sagi 1980: 57).

Accordingly, it only remained for Israel to base its claim on the sums needed for the absorption and rehabilitation of the 500,000 survivors of Nazism. Moreover, in his speech to the Knesset (which was devoted entirely to the subject of the Note), Sharett pointed out that payment of the reparations demanded by Israel would not release the German Government from its responsibility for payment of individual compensation. It was merely to serve as a contribution towards closing the account between the German people and the Jewish people (Sagi 1980: 57).

As indicated earlier, the Israelis, on the cautious acceptance of Adenauer's declaration, were faced with two steps: first, to emphasise it was a material matter only and would not atone for the crime; the second challenge was the task of unifying the Jewish front.

Discussions on this matter took place in Israel between members of the Government and Goldmann. The Government's intention was to emphasise world Jewry's support for its demands. A proposal for coordinating the activities of the Israeli Government and the Jewish organisations was prepared. This proposal was opposed by Goldmann, who contended that too much stress was put on the right of the state of Israel to represent the Jewish people and had not given the Jewish organisations their due (Sagi 1980: 75). The government representatives argued that if the Jewish organisations brought forward an additional claim to heirless property, in accordance with the Atlantic City resolution, it would not complement the Israel claim but would compete with it even though its basis was not the same. It was feared that it was impossible to present Germany with two parallel global claims since it was prepared for a settlement of one global reparation for the Jewish people (Sagi 1980: 75). A compromise was finally reached: a conference of important Jewish organisations would be called to express support for Israel's claims and also for the demand for individual indemnification for Nazi victims throughout the world, but this conference would not draw up an additional global claim (Sagi 1980: 75), hence the New York meeting of the 22 Diaspora organisations mentioned earlier in the chapter.

However, the global claims of Israel and the Claims Conference differed – not only in kind but also in the grounds on which they were based. While Israel's global claim related to the cost of absorbing and rehabilitating the victims of Nazism, the Claims Conference's claim was based on heirless and unclaimed Jewish assets, other than those that would be reclaimed by individuals or successor organisations. This matter is further discussed below.

Formulation of the Claims Conference claim

Earlier in this chapter, the reasons behind the birth of the Claims Conference as an umbrella organisation demanding reparations from Germany were discussed. This subsection outlines the Conference's endeavours in formulating the nature of its reparations claim.

The final agreement signed between the Claims Conference and Germany consisted of two protocols.[14] The first protocol covered individual indemnification, whereas the second one awarded the Conference DM450 million on the global claim. On the same day, an agreement was signed in New York between the Conference and the Government of Israel, setting out that a sum of DM517 million was to be made available to the Conference for expenditure outside of Israel.

This form of the claim did not start off as it finally appeared in the signed document. At the opening of the negotiations, the Claims Conference submitted its claims, which consisted of restitution laws, the need for implementation of restitution, federal government responsibility for acts of the Reich, extension of indemnification laws, extension of categories of claimants, responsibility for seizure of property by party and Reich institutions outside Germany, in addition to the global claim of $500 million (Sagi 1980: 115). The shift along the negotiating process reflects the considerations held by the Claims Conference in their demands for reparations. The futuristic perception the Jewish organisations had for the post-agreement role of the Claims Conference not only influenced the final form of the reparations demanded from Germany, but was also reflected in the clash with the Israeli Government over the issue of the global claim and how it was solved.

Although the principle of presenting two separate claims both by the Claims Conference and Israel had been set earlier on, the idea that the Conference would present a global claim of its own was new and triggered an internal debate within its members, as well as with Israel (Zweig 2001: 33).

Goldmann's role was again crucial at this stage. In his personal address to the New York meeting, he emphasised several issues that marked the trajectory subsequently adopted by the Claims Conference. The future president of the organisation stressed the necessity of Jewish unity so that the German side would not attempt to set Jewish groups against each other during the negotiations, and also so that the entire Jewish world would share the responsibility for dealing with the Germans. Moreover, Goldmann advocated presenting a global claim rather than an itemised one laden with complex legal specifications. This opinion was new to Jewish experience, hitherto grounded in the individualised legal restitution effort undertaken by the JRSO, which had so far been in charge of restituting heirless Jewish property in West Germany.[15] The Jewish leader further pointed out to the meeting that time was working against the Jewish world. As Germany's economy recovered, and as its strategic importance for the West grew due to the Cold War, Germany's need to come to terms with the Jews would decline. He felt that if the organisations waited much longer, they risked endangering reparations as a whole. Detailed, legalistic negotiations would only give the German Government an opportunity for delaying a real settlement (Zweig 2001: 29).

Therefore, during the winter of 1951–52, and up to the start of the negotiations in Wassenaar in the Netherlands in March 1952, two opposing points of view on the form of the reparations claim surfaced: should the claim presented by the Conference to the German Government be a detailed, individualised one, or a global general claim? (see Zweig 2001: 33, P.G. 1954: 256). The organisations based in Europe and most actively engaged in the practical tasks of restitution and relief argued for as large and as detailed a claim as possible. On the other side of the spectrum, the Committee of Experts in New York wanted a restricted, defined and realisable claim. The Conference also considered that the best way of representing the interests of the individual victims of Nazism would be to press for improvements in the existing German legislation relating to restitution and compensation. A detailed list of the necessary improvements was thus prepared. On the other hand, the Conference was of the opinion that neither an expanded claim for the individual victims nor the continuing work of the successor organisations in reclaiming heirless property identifiable in the Western zones of Germany or in West Berlin nor even the large Israeli global claim (for $1.5 billion) would ever restore all the plundered Jewish assets. Moreover, none of these claims would provide enough funds to meet the continuing needs of the organisations outside of Israel that were active in relief work.

Those circumstances foreseen by the Conference convinced it that only a global claim additional to that which Israel was preparing to present when the negotiations opened would give the Claims Conference the means to aid those refugees who did not want to settle in Israel. Thus, shortly after the New York meeting, the Conference experts suggested that the Claims Conference would have to present a global claim of its own based on the heirless assets that could not be reclaimed by any other means.

The decision to present a global claim posed a problem, though, for it was likely to clash with Israel's own global claim and limit its chances of success. The Germans proposed that if agreement was reached with Israel, the Claims Conference should receive only half its claim. Germany argued that the Israeli claim was based not only on the costs of rehabilitation but also on the contention that Germany had no right to profit from heirless property. Accordingly, the remaining half of the Claims Conference claim would be included in the payment to Israel (Sagi 1980: 115–116).

It is important to note here that the Claims Conference members and the Israeli delegation discussed the matter. It was argued that as long as Israel too based its claim on the value of heirless property, the Germans would stick to their position. This would harm the Claims Conference claim while not increasing the size of the Israeli claim. Thus, the Israeli claim should not be based only on the cost of rehabilitation as this would make German reparations an *ex gratia* payment. Israel had to put its claim due on a moral footing and not on charity (Sagi 1980: 116).

Accordingly, in December 1951, Israel suggested a compromise formula, which Goldmann presented to the Executive Committee of the Conference. Israel agreed that if there was to be only one global claim, then one-third of all funds obtained would be allocated to the various Diaspora organisations.[16] The matter was finally settled by the Conference's decision to carry on its initiative regarding its global claim while conceding to give priority to Israel's own claim and the individual restitution claims of the heirless Jews it represented. By adopting this stance, the Jewish organisations proved to have a futuristic view, for they were thus ensuring a life for the Claims Conference after the negotiations were completed. It retained the opportunity of playing a major role in the reconstruction of the Jewish world with the reparations money it was to receive from Germany (Zweig 2001: 34, Sagi 1980: 140).

In sum, the global claim of $500 million presented by the Conference during the negotiations with Germany at Wassenaar was based primarily on heirless assets, although it represented only a small proportion of them. In sustaining its global claim, the Conference also referred to the moral element of reparation. At this stage, the issue of pressing need was a motivating factor in the action of the Claims Conference, which was aware that its global claim would have to cover relief, rehabilitation and resettlement expenditures not for one or two years but until the displacement problem had been resolved. Given these facts, the $500 million global claim of the Conference was seen as an achievement for the optimists within the new organisation, while at the same time being considerably less than the Conference's real needs (Zweig 2001: 35).

By mid-August 1952, the size and purposes of the global payment to the Claims Conference had been agreed with the Germans. As the latter had made clear that any payments would have to be in the form of goods to Israel, the Conference was obliged to reach an agreement with Israel on the conversion of the German goods into the foreign currencies, which the Conference could use outside Israel.

During the very complex negotiations with the Germans, who held a strong negotiating stance according to their interests on how they wanted the reparation to be channelled and the implications triggered by Israeli interests, which ultimately led to diminishing the total amount of the claim, the Claims Conference had nevertheless succeeded in achieving its two principle objectives: securing a German obligation to make major improvements in the rights of individual victims of Nazism to restitution and indemnification, as well as a commitment towards a global payment.

In fact, the attitude of the Claims Conference towards the nature of its claim was ultimately more complex and different than that of the state of Israel. As the representative of world Jewry, the CC claimed the payment of a compensatory lump sum of $500 million in respect of heirless Jewish property and, above all, it asked for the implementation of Adenauer's promise to introduce overall legislation, applicable throughout the federal territory, on restitution, compensation and indemnification for all forms of persecution and spoliation, and for the extension of this legislation to those categories of persons whose property has been plundered but who were not yet beneficiaries under the differing laws of the various German zones.

The German view

From the German perspective regarding the nature of reparations, Adenauer accepted the claims that had been presented in the Israel note of 12 March 1951 as a basis for the negotiations. In compliance with Goldmann's requests, Adenauer stated in his letter that the German Government considered the question of reparations a moral obligation and saw the German people as honour-bound to do everything possible to atone for the wrong that had been done to the Jewish people (Sagi 1980: 80–81). Therefore, the issue at stake for the Germans was neither the moral contrition basis of reparations nor was it the nature of the harm. The issue at stake was not compensation as the adequate form of reparations as much as it was on the amount offered as compensation to Israel. As shall be apparent in the following paragraphs, the issue vis-à-vis the Claims Conference took a different twist.

The opening statement of the Germans during the negotiations in Wassenaar on 12 March 1952 recalled the commitment undertaken by Adenauer in his speech but immediately went on presenting arguments contending that Germany could not meet the claim. German negotiators argued that Germany's ability to transfer money and commodities abroad was limited by regulations laid down by the Allies and by considerations connected with the London debt conference. In addition, it argued that its capacity to pay was also limited by other current obligations relating to the intake of refugees and their rehabilitation.[17] However, once the contact had been established, this relationship between the reparations talks and the London negotiations was the main bone of contention between the two delegations. Moreover, arguing from their country's economic and financial situation, the German delegation made no recommendation as to the date and methods of payment of the debt. In fact, this proposal in no way represented a formal offer from the German Government, but was merely a suggestion from the delegation (P.G. 1954: 262, Rubinstein 1962: 33).

At the same time, Israeli representatives, through British and American intermediaries, were exerting pressure on Adenauer to resist his domestic political and financial circles that opposed the Israeli claims and argued for a differentiation between the talks in Wassenaar and in London. They also rejected the distinction made by the Germans between what they owed and what they could afford (Auerbach 1991: 285–286). On 8 April, the talks ground to a halt and the deadlock was resolved only months later. The Chancellor could not but realise that the moral prestige that he hoped to acquire from the treaty could be obtained only by a serious undertaking which excluded any possibility of evasion. Therefore, at the beginning of June, he made a concrete offer, this time independent of the problem of commercial debts (P.G. 1954: 263). This offer was considered acceptable by Israel and negotiations were resumed in The Hague on 24 June.

The global as well as individual restitution and compensation claims the Conference presented during the first phase of the negotiations in Wassenaar proved to be of considerable interest to the German side. In 1950, the International Refugee Organization had transferred to the German Government responsibility for the care of the 125,000 'hard core' displaced persons (DPs) still in German territory.[18] Some 46,000 to 50,000 were still in DP camps. Of those, the remaining population of

Jewish DPs presented particularly difficult social welfare problems. Two years after the West German Government had been charged with responsibility for these people, the Claims Conference's global claim offered a prospect that the Jewish world itself would help resolve at least part of the problem of those 'hard core' refugees (Zweig 2001: 35).

When presented with the Conference's claim, the German delegation asked for details both of the justification of the Conference's global claim (the plundered heirless assets that could not be restituted through the relevant legislation) and of the current needs of the Jewish organisations in the fields of relief, rehabilitation and resettlement of the victims of Nazism. When presented with the required documents from the Conference, the German reply was an offer of DM450 million (payable in goods to Israel) to be allocated by the Claims Conference. A further DM50 million was set aside for allocation by the German Government specifically for Christian converts of Jewish origins who were victims of Nazism. The Germans made clear in their reply that they did not accept the legal basis of the Conference's global claim (the unidentifiable heirless assets). They also added that they considered the fund to be a 'hardship fund' to be used solely for the relief and rehabilitation of victims of Nazism in the narrowest sense, not for the repayment to any Jewish organisation of funds expended on these items in the past, or of cultural programmes (Zweig 2001: 37–38). Furthermore, the Germans linked the fund to a final agreement on the programme of legislation designed to facilitate the payment of individual indemnification. They let it be known that the DM450 million offer had very nearly not been approved by the German cabinet, and that the Conference was close to having been turned down. It is thought that by defining the DM450 million as a 'hardship fund' the German delegation made it clear that the intention was to provide the means for the Claims Conference to aid those who were unable to seek redress through the German courts. Thus the Conference would in fact relieve the German Government of the burden of dealing with part of the 'hard core' problem passed over to it by the International Refugee Organization (Zweig 2001: 38–39).

This view of the purpose of the payment was very different from the view of the Claims Conference. The Conference's intention of providing relief, rehabilitation and resettlement possibilities for the victims of Nazism went far beyond the German understanding of a hardship fund for individual claimants who had not received any compensation, or those who might feel that they had been insufficiently compensated by Germany. The matter was pursued throughout the second phase of the negotiations when the Conference fought for the principle of need as the principle guiding allocations of funds derived from their global claim. The argument was resolved when both sides agreed that the Claims Conference would allocate the funds to victims of Nazism according to the urgency of their needs and according to priorities determined by the Conference itself. The Jewish organisations had thus won the right to determine policies and priorities, while the German Government only reserved the right to receive a full annual accounting of the Conference's use of the funds.

Conclusion

The German–Jewish Reparations Agreement of 1952 is the first reparations case considered within the comparative framework of this book. Over the preceding pages, this chapter has presented an attempt to answer the broad question posed by the study: how did the formulation of the reparations claim in its form and basis take place? Accordingly, the chapter has proceeded so as to highlight the position of each party towards the idea of reparations, the factors influencing their perception of the injustice and thus the basis and form of reparations. In this present case, one of the claimants was the state of Israel, in the name of the Jewish victims who had fled Nazism. Also claiming reparations was The Conference on Jewish Material Claims Against Germany, in the name of both the victims of Nazi persecution who had reached countries other than Israel, and of the Jewish people as a whole entitled to global reparation for Jewish property that had been left heirless.

In its final version, the agreement stipulated payment of a global claim in the form of goods to the state of Israel, as well as another specified sum earmarked to the Claims Conference. In addition, in a separate protocol signed with the Claims Conference, Germany undertook to pass an indemnification law covering compensation payable to individual victims of the Nazi persecutions who had suffered imprisonment, mutilation and loss of profession or property, as well as a law restituting Jewish property seized by the former Third Reich.

Apart from the global compensation claim, the indemnification and restitution laws, reparations to the Jewish world as represented by the state of Israel and the Claims Conference also took the form of an acknowledgement on behalf of the German Government of the historical injustices its predecessor inflicted on the Jews. This, in fact, illustrates two main characteristics of this reparations case. First, agreement by both parties on responsibility for the wrongful act and, second, that reparations were based on an act of contrition. The German–Jewish Reparations Agreement was not a reparations case rooted in a language of lost rights on behalf of the victims. It rather represented a claim based upon the victim party demanding for a moral contrition in relation to the injury inflicted upon it. Moral contrition, though, in spite of smothering the reparations process and constituting the solid articulated basis of the claim, was not the motivator for the search for reparations on behalf of the claimants. Instead, the unfolding of the reparations story in the German–Jewish case suggests that it was the aim of reparations that dictated the moral mantle engulfing the claim.

Neither were reparations in this case initially perceived by the parties as a reconciliatory step. While various opinions retrospectively discuss the role of the Luxembourg Agreement as a conciliatory chapter in the history of German–Israeli relations, this chapter has demonstrated how the aim of the reparations agreement on both sides was rather short-sighted when the decision to pursue negotiations was made. It is therefore difficult to agree with opinions (Auerbach 1991: 287, Wolffsohn 1993, Deutschkron 1970) that consider reparations as the kick-off step in a deliberate policy conducted by Ben-Gurion aimed at achieving a coveted normalisation with Germany.

The analysis of the Israeli position revealed how the Government perceived a reparations treaty as a means of obtaining a capital boost to its nascent suffering economy. The chapter has also demonstrated how the obstacles facing the Israeli side in carrying on with its decision to pursue reparations were the factors influencing the Government's approach towards the form of reparations. The wrongful act was thus put in the service of the overall aim of reparations. Once the aim of reparations was decided as a means to gain financial compensation, the obstacle of antagonistic public opinion was the reason behind the moral guilt basis of the claim. By the same token, the issue of property restitution was also utilised to assuage angry public opinion. On the other hand, the division of the claimant part into two, as well as the birth of an umbrella organisation negotiating for reparations, stemmed from the need to assist Israel in its claim and also to unify the Jewish front in dealing with Germany. The clash, however, between the newly established organisation and Israel reflected the experience of restitution the Jewish world was subject to, in addition to bearing in mind the final use of reparations. Moral contrition was again a means rather than an aim. As for Germany, reparations to Jewish victims of Nazism were considered as a policy strategy leading to its admission into the post-war international community. In that sense, reconciliation with the Jewish world from the

German perspective was not perceived as a goal as much as it was seen as a means.

The success of the German–Jewish Reparations Agreement was thus first and foremost a factor of the concept of 'opportunity', which both sides saw the Reparations Agreement fulfilling. At a common temporal point, each party in its own way perceived reparations as an act conducive to a desired objective. This concept of opportunity, which overshadows the politics of this reparations case, is a factor that will be equally present – although differently – in the analysis of the reparations story in the case of Cyprus, as the following chapter unveils.

The German–Jewish reparations case is also characterised by an absence of external involvement, both in terms of offering direct pressure on the parties or in proposing a set of solutions to reparations. Nor was there a link between reparations and other components to a conflict. The two parties were confined to discussing one particular problem without having to negotiate trade-offs of a larger conflict in need to be addressed.

Additionally, this reparations case was devoid of legal rhetoric. Legal connotations were rather derived from the signing of the treaty, which set a precedent in terms of property restitution in international legal and diplomatic history. As noted in the analysis, legal tools were not advocated by the claimants. Instead, legitimacy of the claim was derived from the moral contrition the victim employed against the perpetrator of the wrongful act. This absence of the language of rights and calls for legal responsibility on behalf of the claimant party may partly be attributed to the Versailles spirit (discussed in the previous chapter), the absence of international practice as well as the lack of legal precedence in this sphere.

Another important theme discerned from this case study is the precedence of a non-state actor negotiating and signing a reparations agreement with the state responsible for the inflicted harm. The victims of the historical injustice of displacement and dispossession had succeeded in shifting scattered individual institutions devoted to tasks of relief and restitution to a global entity seeking to negotiate for overall reparations.

In the following chapter, the study moves on to analyse reparations within the case of Cyprus in an attempt to unravel the characteristics revealed by the interaction between the protagonist positions and the external involvement in the formulation of reparations claims.

4 Cyprus

> As I came near the Cyprus conflict, I became immersed in a tangled and anguished dilemma: was justice to be found South or North of the provisional line of division of the island? I could not answer this question, but encountered an irrefutable premise: the absence of a common objective makes disintegration unavoidable.
>
> (Hugo Gobbi, former Secretary-General Special Representative to Cyprus (Gobbi (no date): 45)

This chapter is devoted to the second case study covered by this book, the one concerning reparations in relation to settlement of the displacement and dispossession dossier of the Cypriot conflict. Accordingly, the chapter examines how the positions of the parties and external involvement interact in their search for reparations to the displacement and dispossession caused by the conflict in Cyprus. And by consequence, how has this interaction affected the nature of reparations in both its basis and form?

Prior to delving into the details of this chapter, it is of importance to draw attention to a number of issues. First, the Cypriot conflict is an intractable and comprehensive one in the sense that a search for a settlement has been an overall endeavour encompassing all the conflict elements. Hence, displacement and dispossession are but one sub-theme and have not been treated separately from the overall conflict. However, the purpose of this chapter is not to analyse the entire Cypriot conflict, but rather to present the latter as a necessary background to the displacement/dispossession angle and how it has been tackled in the search for a solution. Second, it is also important to mention that whereas, arguably, the conflict roughly began in the 1960s with the independence of the island, this study solely focuses on the events of 1974 onwards when the

Turkish military intervention on the island and the resulting displacement and dispossession took place. These events have formed the basis of numerous UN attempts to propose solutions to the Cypriot conflict and shall be examined throughout the chapter. Third, reparations in the Cypriot context, as far as this study is concerned, relate to that part of the proposed solutions aiming at redressing displacement and/or dispossession. Finally, I wish to note that the present book recognises the controversy created by the use of certain politically sensitive terms. Terminology such as 'intervention' or 'occupation', for example, generally denote a certain perception of the conflict. This study does not adopt any such position and only attempts to analyse certain aspects of the conflict with respect to all points of view.

The chapter begins with a historical background illustrating the overall evolution of the conflict and the core issues of importance to a settlement. This is followed by two sections each depicting the two protagonists' – the Greek Cypriot and the Turkish Cypriot – positions regarding the displacement/dispossession issue. The nature of the external involvement in the conflict is subsequently analysed. Finally, the last section, focusing on discussing the nature of the reparations claim, will look at the basis and form of reparations within the United Nations settlement proposals relating to the Cypriot conflict. The reader will notice that the sections devoted to the positions of the parties are rather short in comparison with the German–Jewish case. In parallel, the section covering external involvement is much longer than its predecessor. Rather than suggesting inconsistency, such a difference brings out some of the major characteristics of these two reparations cases. As apparent from the previous chapter, the German–Jewish case is one where the protagonists' positions played a major role in the mutual formulation of the reparations claim. Cyprus, by contrast, is a case where the United Nations has played a major role as a mediator and has proposed several peace plans in its attempt to settle the conflict. Such characteristics are inevitably reflected in the section lengths of each chapter.

Historical background

The purpose of this section is to shed light on the Cyprus conflict both in terms of its historical evolution as well as the main elements deemed to be of particular concern to a settlement.[1] An understanding of those main elements and the priority given to each by the protagonists sheds light on the nature of the trade-offs within a settlement, and by consequence, the impact on the issue of displacement/dispossession.

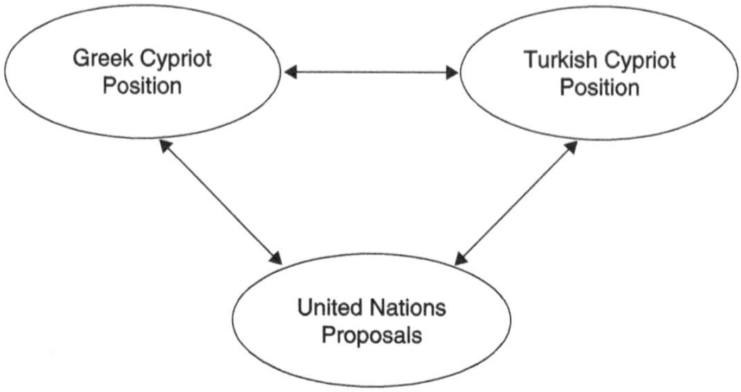

Figure 4.1 Reparations as an interplay of the interaction between the parties to the agreement.

In 1960, the Zurich–London agreements granted Cyprus independence from Britain.[2] The constitution of the new Republic of Cyprus was designed to reflect the island's two ethnic communities' – Greek Cypriots and Turkish Cypriots – attempt to co-exist under one united state.[3] Greece, Turkey and Britain were designated guarantors under the Treaty of Guarantee. This Treaty forbade secession or the union of Cyprus with any other state. It also gave to the three guarantor powers the duty to consult together to preserve the territory and the constitutional order of the newly established state of Cyprus and, if such consultation did not lead to agreement on the steps that needed to be taken, it permitted each of the guarantor powers to intervene unilaterally with a view to restoring the *status quo ante*.

The newborn state faced precarious conditions as relations between the two communities quickly deteriorated. The Turkish Cypriots accused the Greek Cypriots of treading on their constitutional rights and the latter, in turn, accused the Turkish Cypriots of abusing their veto powers to hamper legislation.[4] In fact, analysts believe that the tension between the two Cypriot communities since the establishment of the republic was due to the disparity between the two parties' perceptions of the nature of the state. While Greek Cypriots viewed the bond between the communities as one of majority–minority, the Turkish Cypriot side had considered it as being between two politically equal communities.[5] This rift has grown to mar all attempts of settlement in the history of the conflict.

Inter-communal violence broke out and continued throughout the 1960s, with human rights abuses on both sides, and many Turkish Cypriots reclining into enclaves throughout the island.[6] The conflicting views over Cyprus between Greece and Turkey further fuelled hostilities between the Cypriot communities. Greece believes that, historically, Cyprus is part of the Hellenic world, as do Greek Cypriots, and thus favoured uniting the island with the mainland (*enosis*). Turkey, on the other hand, valued the strategic importance of Cyprus and advocated partition (*taksim*).[7]

In 1974, the military government in power in Greece instigated a coup, overthrowing Archbishop Makarios, president of Cyprus, and attempted to unite the island with Greece. Fighting and violence erupted. Invoking the Treaty of Guarantee as the basis for its action, Turkey launched a military assault on the island on 20 July 1974. After two successive waves, Turkish forces successfully occupied a large segment of land in the north of Cyprus, amounting to 38 per cent of the entire island.[8] The ensuing events led to the Greek Cypriot civilians fleeing south and the Turkish Cypriots north. An estimated one-third of the population of Cyprus, amounting to around 180,000 people, were displaced during and immediately after the fighting. The buffer zone between the two cease-fire lines, demarcated in an attempt to stop the fighting and occupied by United Nations Peacekeeping Forces in Cyprus (UNFICYP), marked the new status quo of the island characterised by an almost total segregation of the Greek and Turkish ethnic communities of Cyprus. The events of 1974 had in fact divided the island into two separate entities, the internationally recognised Cypriot Government in the south and a Turkish Cypriot community in the north.[9] Although Greek Cypriots and Turkish Cypriots have been governed under separate administrations since 1963, this de facto practice has been legally acknowledged by Greece and the UK with the conclusion of the 30 July 1974 Geneva declarations, which recognises (para 5) 'the existence in practice in the republic of Cyprus of two autonomous administrations, that of the Greek Cypriot community and that of the Turkish Cypriot community'.

A formal exchange of populations took place in 1975 following an agreement between Glafcos Clerides, President of the Republic of Cyprus in the south, and Rauf Denktash, leader of the Turkish Cypriot community. Consequently, only but a few Greek Cypriots continued to live in the north, mostly in the Karpas Peninsula (the panhandle), and an even smaller number of Turkish Cypriots remained in the south. On the other hand, Turkish soldiers who had fought in Cyprus were allowed to settle with their families and given homes. In addition, a significant number of immigrants from Turkey had been allowed to settle in the north. Both the displaced Turkish Cypriots from the south and the settlers from Turkey were granted homes and property abandoned by

Greek Cypriots in their flight from the north, thus further complicating the issue of property restitution in all future negotiation rounds and conflict settlement attempts (Hannay 2005: 6).

The Turkish Cypriots' perspective of the conflict was that the events of 1963 indicated that the Greek Cypriots had trespassed the constitution and the latter was therefore no longer valid. And since the Greek Cypriot takeover of the Government since 1963 was unconstitutional in Turkish Cypriot eyes, there was resentment towards the UN and the other international organisations' treatment of the government in the south as the sole legitimate government in Cyprus. Denktash argued that until that recognition was reversed, either by recognising the Turkish Cypriots on an equal but separate basis or by derecognising the Greek Cypriots, there could be no forthcoming solution to the Cyprus problem. However, the refusal of the UN to abide by the Turkish Cypriot demands led to a feeling of suspicion towards the UN Secretary-General's (SG) offices. In addition, the Turkish Cypriots acquired a conviction that UN peacekeepers could not protect them from Greek Cypriot harassment (Hannay 2005: 5)[10]. The Greek Cypriots, on the other hand, highly regarded their recognition as the sole government of Cyprus by the international community and exploited their legitimate presence in the various international forums to undermine the Turkish Cypriots' position, claims and attempts to secede. They were of the conviction that the Turks had always wanted to annex Cyprus for its strategic value and that the Turkish Cypriots' complaints about their plight was merely special pleading to provide cover for this policy (Hannay 2005: 5).[11]

UN involvement in Cyprus began with the deployment of its peacekeepers in 1964. As stated above, the SC continued, following the breakdown of the 1960 constitution, to treat what was now effectively a Greek Cypriot administration as the constitutional government of the Republic of Cyprus (Hannay 2005: 5, Richmond 1998: xv–xvi). From 1974 onwards, successive low- and high-level meetings, inter-communal talks and special representatives of the UN SG working with the two sides led to a series of attempts to propose solutions to the conflict encompassing the elements of a comprehensive settlement. The last such attempt, known as Annan Plan 5, failed and the situation on the island has been at a stalemate since then. On 24 April 2004, the Greek Cypriot and Turkish Cypriot communities voted in simultaneous and parallel referenda on whether to approve the UN-brokered Annan Plan, which would have ended the 30-year division of the island by establishing a new 'United Cyprus Republic'. A majority of Greek Cypriots voted 'no' whereas Turkish Cypriots voted in favour. A few days after this political shock, on 1 May 2004, Cyprus entered the European Union still divided, with the EU's body of legislation and standards (*acquis communautaire*) suspended in the north.

Several core issues will need to be resolved if there is to be a comprehensive settlement of the Cyprus problem. These issues pertinently featured in each round of negotiations and settlement proposals, including the Annan Plan.[12] The remainder of this section provides an overview of the substance of these core issues, highlighting the parties' traditional positions towards each of them. While the most important core issues are covered here, the displacement/dispossession file is discussed separately in later sections.

Governance and sovereignty, with what they entail regarding constitution and power-sharing, are the prime core issues of concern to the parties in their search for a solution to the conflict on the island. It is generally agreed, in the framework of a search for a solution, that a new constitution is to define the make-up of the unified state. Greek Cypriots support a settlement based on a bi-communal, bi-zonal federation that allows for a central federal government with certain clearly defined competences to allow Cyprus to operate as a single state and two component entities. With regard to legislative power, Greek Cypriots favour 'effective equality' rather than equality based on numerical representation. The Turkish Cypriots' main priority is the desire to gain political equality. Their starting point is that the basis for a solution should stem from the new realities of the island. In other words, they back a new partnership state of two component states as opposed to the continuation of the existing state of Cyprus. Stated differently, Turkish Cypriots want two sovereign states, or a bi-zonal, bi-communal confederation of two sovereign states (see for example Hannay 2005: 28–31). Related to that, and as Lord Hannay – special British representative – states:

> no issue was raised more frequently by Denktash than that of status, and he never made any secret of the fact that he regarded getting satisfaction on this matter a precondition for negotiating on the other core issues.
>
> (Hannay 2005: 39)

The question of guarantorship also incited disagreement. Greek Cypriots want no guarantorship or would alternatively consider an EU or UN guarantorship. Turkish Cypriots, on the other hand, want the 1960 Treaty of Guarantees to remain without any change (which allows for a unilateral right of intervention from Turkey). Security in fact is of primary importance to both sides. Turkish rhetoric frequently described Cyprus as a 'floating aircraft carrier' or a 'dagger pointing at Turkey's heart'. While it is thought that the Turks could contemplate a considerable reduction in their troops on the island in the context of a settlement agreement, they remained disinclined to a complete military withdrawal. Moreover, it had always been emphasised by Greek Cypriots that if they were to make major concessions to the Turks and Turkish Cypriots on this issue of security (as the Turks and Turkish Cypriots would have to do over territory and property), it was essential that there should be a robust international military presence on the island (Hannay 2005: 21–34). Additionally, Greek Cypriots demand absolute freedom of movement, settlement and property (the Three Freedoms) while Turkish Cypriots demand restrictions for maintenance of bi-zonality. And finally regarding settlers/immigrants, Greek Cypriots demand that all Turkish settlers should go back to mainland Turkey, whereas Turkish Cypriots demand that all Turkish immigrants should stay in Cyprus (Hannay 2005: 43–44).

Party 1: the Greek Cypriot position

Lord Hannay describes the displacement and dispossession component of the Cypriot conflict as follows:

> None of the . . . core issues was more complex and none was more sensitive than the question of property – what was to be done about the property rights and claims of Greek Cypriots displaced from the north of the island and of Turkish Cypriots from the south.
>
> (Hannay 2005: 37)

A 2004 estimation of the number of displaced Cypriots on both sides puts the total figure at 265,000 (CIA 2009). The displacement dossier within the Cypriot conflict carries certain characteristics that are important to outline as a prelude to the specific position of each party, as will be discussed in the following pages. In this particular case, the displacement and dispossession problem consists of several pertinent issues, such as return of the displaced to their former homes, in addition to property restitution and/or compensation for lost property. Also, since the inception of the problem and because of the nature of the events of 1974, what took place then and the geographical division of the island between two ethnic communities, the issue of displacement was linked with the territorial adjustments and the Three Freedoms. These links have had a direct impact on the negotiations of the issue and have affected the Greek Cypriot position in the search for a solution. After the cessation of hostilities in 1974, the proportion of territory under Turkish Cypriot control was slightly over 36 per cent of the territory of the 1960 Republic of Cyprus, while the territory under Greek Cypriot control was around 63 per cent. These figures contrasted with population figures of broadly 80 per cent Greek Cypriots against 18 per cent Turkish Cypriots. In light of these facts, it was accepted by all concerned, including the Turkish Cypriots, that any settlement would have to include a territorial adjustment to the benefit of the Greek Cypriots (Hannay 2005: 35–37). Therefore, the Greek Cypriot position was to push for a substantial territorial adjustment in their favour while seeking to link the three related issues of territory, property and the right to settle in the north (Hannay 2005: 35–36, Tocci 2004: 23–27). To them, the key to any territorial settlement was the proportion of the displaced Greek Cypriots expelled from the north who could be returned to the adjusted territory.

On the dispossession resulting from the displacement, the traditional Greek Cypriot position is that every single Greek Cypriot with a valid claim to property in the north should have the right to return to it (Hannay 2005: 37–39). The Greek Cypriots did, however, recognise that the idea of all displaced Greek Cypriots returning to the north was unrealistic and, given the large number of Greek Cypriots who had lived in the north prior to 1974, not compatible with a bi-zonal solution. They believed that, in any case, relatively few Greek Cypriots from the north, many of whom had completely rebuilt their lives over the past 30 years and who were reasonably prosperous and well established in their new homes, would choose to live in what would be a Turkish Cypriot-administered component state. They were also prepared to contemplate a range of tight quantitative and transitional arrangements, including a moratorium on returns in the early years after a settlement, which would limit the number of Greek Cypriots who would be permitted to return to their properties in the north. Such an approach had begun to be discussed in the 1992 negotiations when it had been known as the 'fishing net' and they were prepared to resume this discussion. What they would not accept was an approach that extinguished any right of return from the outset and offered only one option: financial compensation.

From another perspective, it has been widely agreed between the concerned parties that there would be no room for individual claims and that the issue of property would be settled all together. However, the issue of the *Loizidou* case in the European Court of Human Rights (ECHR) posed a significant challenge to this consensus on the globality of the compensation claim. Titinia Loizidou, a displaced Greek Cypriot from the north, filed a case before the ECHR. Mrs Loizidou won her case in 1996 when the Court found that she had been wrongfully dispossessed of her property in the north by Turkey (not by the TRNC, which the ECHR did not recognise) and in 1998 awarded her a large sum in damages with interest. As soon as this case – in which Mrs Loizidou had the support of the Greek Cypriot Government – was won, a large number of similar cases were filed before the ECHR. The case had important implications to the settlement negotiations. It was in effect crucial that any property settlement negotiated should be accepted by the ECHR as invalidating the base for bringing individual legal proceedings before the Court. It was considered less likely that they would do this if the settlement simply extinguished any right of return and offered compensation rather than providing alternative remedies for those who had lost their property (Hannay 2005: 39).

Party 2: the Turkish Cypriot position

The Turkish Cypriot position towards the displacement and dispossession dossier asserts no recognition of the right of return of displaced Greek Cypriots and that all claims should be settled by global property exchange and/or financial compensation (Hannay 2005: 37–39, Tocci 2004: 27–30).[13] The Turkish Cypriots' preference is payment of compensation in the form of global exchange of titles. They argue that all Greek Cypriot-owned property in the north should notionally be exchanged for all Turkish Cypriot-owned property in the south. Each side should keep what it has and distribute property to its people in accordance with what they lost. Moreover, they argue that the financial value of the property lost on each side is the same because, even though the Greek Cypriots lost more land, its value is significantly less due to the poor state of the north's economy following years of economic embargoes (Garlick 2003: 4).

In conjunction with this line of thinking, Turkish Cypriots refused to contemplate even the most informal discussion of the territorial issue until the very last stage of the negotiations, and until their preconditions on recognition and sovereignty had been met. Denktash maintained the belief that he would gain substantially from the governance and security aspects of a settlement, both of which would be resolved on a basis which met most of the Turkish Cypriots' longstanding demands. On each of the other core issues, territory, property and the linked issue of the right of Greek Cypriots to reside in the Turkish Cypriot component state, he knew he would have to make concessions. These concessions would make it clear that the new Cyprus would not only be bi-zonal but also bi-communal, whereas his own ideal outcome was to pocket gains on governance and security while not conceding anything inconsistent with his preferred two-state solution. Hence, his approach was to de-couple the three issues and present unyielding positions on each (such as his proposal for settling all property claims by compensation and allowing no Greek Cypriot returns to the north). This was the exact opposite of the Greek Cypriot approach (Hannay 2005: 36). Tocci explains the matter further by highlighting that on questions of rights and freedoms, the Turkish Cypriot leadership agreed on the freedom of movement throughout the island, but objected to the full liberalisation of the freedoms of property and settlement. The displaced would not be allowed to return to their properties if these were occupied by homeless or displaced persons, if they had been altered or converted to public use, if they were occupied by war veterans or if they were located in potential hotspots (Tocci 2004: 30).

External involvement

In this section I analyse the external involvement in the Cypriot problem, especially in regard to the search for a solution to the displacement problem. The Cypriot case is characterised by an impressive number of influential players, their interests and policies heavily at stake. Therefore, a broad overview of the roles played by Greece, Turkey, the UK, the US and the USSR is presented below. However, this study particularly focuses on the role of the UN and does so by examining how attempts to address displacement and dispossession have featured in each settlement proposal, culminating in the last of those, the Annan Plan 5. This detailed analysis of UN draft solutions is followed by a summary of the EU dimension. The EU accession dynamics of the island have had a deep impact on the politics of the conflict and thus cannot be overlooked.

The involvement of Greece and Turkey in the internal affairs of Cyprus predates the establishment of the Republic of Cyprus in 1960. Throughout the period of British rule, from 1878 to 1960, Greece actively supported the Greek Cypriot action for *enosis*. During the same period, Turkey came in support of the Turkish Cypriots and their goal of partition as a counterweight to the Greek and the Greek Cypriot demands (Joseph 1985: 71–83). Joseph argues that the involvement of Greece in Cyprus has taken place exclusively on ethnic grounds. In his view, there are no other sources of Greek concern or interest in Cyprus as the island lies some 500 miles from the mainland and cannot be of any particular economic or military interest (Joseph 1985: 111).[14] Regarding Turkey's role in Cyprus, the conclusion can also be drawn – according to Joseph – that ethnic factors have been the primary cause and instrument for intervention. However, it could be added that strategic considerations have played an important role in shaping and implementing the Turkish policy. Hence, ethnic and strategic factors have been congruent and mutually reinforcing in causing Turkish involvement in the Cypriot conflict (Joseph 1985: 111–112).[15]

Since the fighting of 1974, the two Cypriot sides have attempted, with the help of their motherlands, to maximise their political rights over each other and minimise the involvement of the opposing side's motherland. These conflicting interests were however subservient, for much of the Cold War period, to the dominant Western interest of retaining influence on the island, in the region, and in preventing Greco–Turkish conflict from escalating, thus safeguarding the influence of the Western alliance. According to this line of thought, during the Cold War period the de facto partition of the island after 1974 was considered in the interest of the Western alliance (Richmond 1998: xv–xvi). In fact, Richmond argues that external involvement in Cyprus is characterised by all parties intervening not for the sake of a settlement but for the sake of some other goal. In his opinion, international interest has been directed at preventing the Cyprus problem from sparking off a wider conflict and it is to this that the interest of the two communities have become subservient, and towards which UN involvement has actually been directed. The focus has been on preventing war, not on promoting peace. Cyprus has been viewed by the international community as a potential spark of a damaging conflict between Greece and Turkey, which during the Cold War would have had serious implications for NATO and would have provided ammunition for the Soviet Union, which had shown interest in Cyprus (Richmond 1998: xvi).

The US and the USSR, preoccupied with considerations emanating from their global, military, economic and ideological objectives and responsibilities as superpowers, found themselves contesting for control and influence over Cyprus and the region. The US attitude reflected the containment doctrine that has been the driving force behind American foreign policy since the Second World War. As a Cold War protagonist, the US intervened to prevent expansion of Soviet influence and protect vital Western security interests in the region. The main American goals were to bring Cyprus under Western control and protect the unity of NATO by preventing a Greek–Turkish war. The Soviet Union, thinking and acting along similar lines, intervened to counteract American policy and goals and benefit from the conflict that involved American allies. The undermining of Western strategic interests through NATO disruption and the maintenance of a pro-Soviet independent Cyprus were Moscow's basic goals (Joseph 1985: 155–156).[16] O'Malley and Craig argue that, whereas history records that Cyprus was divided because of a Greek-inspired coup and a Turkish invasion, it was a conspiracy by America and Britain which stood by to divide the island. They argue that the Cyprus crisis was no failure of American diplomacy but a deliberate Cold War plot to divide the island and save the top secret spying and defence facilities from the twin threats of a communist takeover or British withdrawal (O'Malley and Craig 1999: ix, x).

By and large, it was the US and Britain, the two leading NATO countries having major interests in Cyprus and the region, which were disturbed by the developments in and around Cyprus. They tried to drag NATO into the conflict as an instrument of peacekeeping and mediation. Beyond the immediate task of peace restoration, NATO intervention was intended to pave the way for the establishment of a lasting Western control over Cyprus and the elimination of the sources of Greek–Turkish friction over the island. The Anglo–American initiative failed because it did not receive any support from within or outside NATO. Other NATO countries were reluctant to participate in a NATO operation in a non-aligned country prescribed by the US and Britain. Cyprus rejected intervention by a regional political military alliance with which it had no affiliation and opted for the UN (Joseph 1985: 191–192).[17] The British were disinclined from the outset to allow themselves to be dragged back into Cyprus. They thus reconciled to the UN being a preferable instrument for conflict prevention and resolution (Hannay 2005: 6).

The preceding section has outlined the traditional positions of the two parties in relation to displacement, which represents the maximalist demands when viewed from a negotiating perspective. As the UN has been playing the role of mediator and has interfered to propose a solution to the conflict, tracing the various UN attempts allows reflection on the following: what kind of proposal has the UN put forward in its attempt to deal with displacement and dispossession? Have those proposals changed from one settlement framework to the other? To what extent was there a compromise in those proposals compared with the maximalist positions? And how does the last of these proposals – the Annan Plan 5 – fit in the understanding of reparations in the scope of the present book? The remainder of the chapter probes these questions.

Early settlement attempts[18]

The GA unanimously adopted Resolution 3212 of 1974, which became the basis of the UN position towards the Cyprus conflict. In addition to calling for withdrawal of all foreign troops from the island and condemning the illegality of their presence, Article 5 of the resolution also acknowledged the displacement problem by stating that '. . . all the refugees should return to their homes in safety and calls upon the parties concerned to undertake urgent measures to that end'. Moreover, the resolution also calls for conducting negotiations under the framework of the UN.

In the immediate aftermath of the events of 1974, inter-communal talks took place and were limited to humanitarian issues such as the exchange of population between the two sides of the island. During the subsequent Vienna Talks in January 1975, both parties declared their support for the principle of an independent, non-aligned and demilitarised Cyprus. Beyond these broad concepts, however, there were serious differences over the form of government, the size of the area to be retained by Turkish Cypriots, the return of the displaced, the principle of compensation for property losses and the timing of the withdrawal of Turkish troops.[19]

After intensive efforts by UN SG Waldheim, the 12 February 1977 High-Level Agreement was reached between Makarios and Denktash. Far from being a detailed settlement, the 1977 Agreement – consisting of four points – emphasised the priority of the issue of a federal bi-communal state in the overall search for a settlement to the conflict. This emphasis was apparent as it overshadowed other provisions included in the basic document. Point 3 in particular states that:

> Questions of principles like freedom of movement, freedom of settlement, the right of property and other specific matters, are open for discussion, taking into consideration the fundamental basis of a bi-communal federal system and certain practical difficulties which may arise for the Turkish Cypriot community.[20]

By conceding federation, the Greek Cypriots effectively recognised that the bi-communal unitary state of 1960 had gone beyond recall and that in the future Cyprus would need to consist of two units (Hannay 2005: 8).

In 1979, a second high-level agreement was reached. The talks conducted in Cyprus under the chairmanship of the UN SG's Special Representative in Cyprus, Hugo Gobbi, continued without a major breakthrough.[21] However, the Ten-Point Agreement of 19 May 1979 reaffirmed building on the 1977 Agreement and UN resolutions relevant to the Cyprus question. It went on to add that there should be respect for human rights and fundamental freedoms of all citizens of the republic.

While the 10 points did not resolve any substantive issues, they nevertheless introduced a new element regarding the re-occupation of Varosha (an abandoned city in the north since the 1974 events). The principle of relocating the refugees displaced from Varosha back to their hometown, and linking it with the location of the territory in question, was to gain further importance in the negotiations between the parties over the displacement and territorial adjustments, particularly in the 1992 Set of Ideas, as shall be discussed further on.

The gaps between the parties remained unbridgeable when Denktash unilaterally proclaimed the north of the island to become an independent state in November 1983. SC Resolution 541 condemned this move and, to this day, only Turkey recognises the Turkish Republic of Northern Cyprus (TRNC). The 1983 declaration considerably complicated the search for a settlement but did not halt it. In fact, less than a year later, the two sides met UN SG Pérez de Cuéllar in Vienna in August 1984 and agreed on initiating proximity talks.[22] This paved the way for a direct summit between the leaders of the two communities. Subsequently, in a January 1985 summit meeting, UN officials presented a draft framework agreement for the establishment of a bi-zonal, bi-communal federal republic, thus formalising that the solution would be bi-zonal as well as bi-communal. The parties, according to many accounts, had been briefed on its contents but not directly involved in its drafting. UN efforts in the months that followed were unsuccessful in mending the rifts.

The situation prior to the 1992 Set of Ideas was thus as follows: SG de Cuéllar had assigned his two aides, Camillion and Feissel, to meet separately and jointly with the Cypriot parties to draft an outline that could be based on an 'ideas paper' that the UN circulated on a non-committal basis to the parties. This step was in fact considered close to Turkish Cypriot demands, as the concerned document referred to the separate status of the two communities and to bi-zonality as an enshrined principle in a prospective settlement. From the Greek Cypriot perspective, the increasing emphasis on rights and freedoms in settlement proposals since the 1977 agreement lent weight to the claims of the displaced Greek Cypriots and underlined the Greek Cypriots' growing insistence on the acceptance of the Three Freedoms of movement, residence and ownership of properties. This heralded the emergence in negotiations of serious differences between the two sides in their view of the nature of the Cyprus problem and the ways to solve it. For the Greek Cypriots, unity was the key word. The other key words were freedom and fundamental rights as accepted by UN international covenants and by Europe. This Greek Cypriot line of banking on international legitimacy to give a push to their claims and rhetoric acted differently on the Turkish Cypriot policy. The Turkish Cypriots were stressing the importance of each state's sovereignty and territory as the basis on which to build. Hence, the internationalisation of the dispute provided an opportunity to declare the TRNC as an act of ascertaining sovereignty based on the right of self-determination. Afraid of being regarded by the world as a mere minority in the Republic of Cyprus, the Turkish Cypriots stressed that the only way to establish a future federation was by agreement between two equal peoples (Dodd 1988: 36–38).

The Ghali Set of Ideas 1992

When aired in 1992, the overall contribution of the 'Set of Ideas' was that it went far beyond the 1977 and 1979 high-level agreements on which it was based, and brought together for the first time all elements of a comprehensive settlement covering all areas of contention between the two parties.[23] The 100 points document generally called for establishing a bi-zonal, bi-communal federation with extensive autonomy for the two component parts, a substantial territorial adjustment to the benefit of the Greek Cypriots with limited returns of displaced Greek Cypriots to the north, a continuation of the Treaty of Guarantee, a reduced Turkish and Greek military presence and an international peacekeeping force.[24]

Regarding displacement and dispossession, the UN document takes the link between territorial adjustment and displacement further than all previous proposals. Accompanied by two alternative maps, the document stipulates that the Turkish Cypriot side gives up 7–8 per cent of land it controls, reducing its territory to about 29 per cent of the island. The document does not give figures of how many displaced Greek Cypriots can return, though. Section IV, devoted to displaced persons, offers for the first time a proposal dealing with the dispossession element of the Cypriot displacement problem. By recognising property claims of both Greek and Turkish Cypriots, the 1992 Ghali Set of Ideas set the basis of its philosophy towards the dispossession component of the conflict. Based on the principle of recognising property rights of the displaced, the Set of Ideas acknowledged restitution of property as the adequate remedy for the dispossession. However, bearing in mind the need to take into consideration the issue of territorial adjustment, the

UN document set limitations on full restitution of property. What Point 77 of the Set of Ideas thus proposed was that with regard to property ownership in areas subject to territorial adjustment, properties could be reinstated to dispossessed owners. On the other hand, for dispossessed owners who are not subject to territorial adjustment, there would be alternatives available, including compensation and the setting-up of an independent property board that would administer claims for reinstatement, which would include non-Cypriot members. When the Annan process was launched, it based its philosophy on much of what Boutros-Ghali proposed, as shall be illustrated further on.

Endorsed by the SC in Resolution 750 soon after the negotiations had been suspended in 1992 as 'an appropriate basis for reaching an overall framework agreement', the Set of Ideas took on more the character of a set of firm proposals for a solution than a number of points for discussion (Dodd 1988: 45). Moreover, the fact that discussions began with territorial adjustments and Greek Cypriot displaced persons is viewed as a victory for the Greek Cypriot side since these were among their main concerns.

The Set of Ideas, on the other hand, also met some of the demands of the Turkish Cypriot side, such as in the guarantee and in not promoting the Three Freedoms to the forefront of discussions (Dodd 1988: 50). It was the Turkish side that produced a response to the Set of Ideas and was criticised for finding some of the proposals unacceptable while accepting 91 of the 100 points. By contrast, the Greek Cypriots did not commit themselves by merely indicating that the Set of Ideas could form the basis for discussion. To them, it was a success that the Turkish Cypriots were reacting strongly against a document that had the backing of the SC. Greek Cypriots were thus occupying the moral high ground (Dodd 1988: 50, Hannay 2005: 52).

Negotiations were suspended for the Greek Cypriot presidential elections in early 1993. The narrow victory of Clerides, who campaigned against the Set of Ideas, meant that the negotiations for a settlement faltered. In reaction, the UN tried throughout 1993 and 1994 to get agreement on a major package of confidence-building measures, the most significant of which would have led to the return of Varosha to the Greek Cypriots and to the reopening of Nicosia Airport. However, these negotiations also failed to come to fruition (Hannay 2005: 8–9). In parallel, Cyprus's application to join the EU was making steady progress. The EU dimension of the Cyprus problem was thus becoming more prominent than it had ever been in the past. And while it was possible to hope that it would act as a catalyst towards a comprehensive settlement, it was equally feared that it would lead towards the definitive partition of the island.

Annan Plans

Indirect negotiations resumed in 1999–2000, shifting to direct talks between the two communities in 2002. On 11 November 2002, Annan Plan 1 was created as the most extensive document ever submitted, proposing a constitution, settlement of property rights, territorial adjustment and security arrangements among other things. The objective was to get the leaders to sign an agreement of principles that would be binding on the parties by 12 December – the date of the European Council meeting where it would be decided that Cyprus, together with nine other states, would be admitted to the EU. Following the reactions of the parties, the UN submitted a revised version of the plan – Annan Plan 2 – on 10 December 2002. On 12 December the parties did not agree. The UN set its eyes on an agreement before 11 March 2003. Another revised plan – Annan Plan 3 – was submitted on 26 February 2003. On 11 March, the Greek Cypriot side set the conditions under which it would be willing to put the plan to a referendum. The Turkish Cypriot side declined. The process was not revived until February 2004. The aim this time was to get the two sides to sign an overall agreement before 1 May 2004 so that the accession of Cyprus to Europe on 1 May 2004 would be that of a united Cyprus republic. The parties agreed on a process that would inevitably result in a final document – produced in 2004 – that would be put to two separate simultaneous referendums on 24 April 2004.

The logic of the UN thinking during the period preceding the Annan process was to step in with some initiative of its own on the basis of the negotiating demands of each party. The broad lines the UN built upon were the following: political equality and non-domination for the Turkish Cypriots; and for the Greek Cypriots, indissolubility of the common state, an international force with a UN mandate, a property settlement based on an appropriate combination of restitution, exchange and compensation. Denktash was still tough on the issue of property, claiming that he would reject any solution based on any element of return to the north by Greek Cypriots and that all settlement of property claims was to be done by compensation. The UN, however, was of the conviction that a document that contemplated doing so would be both non-negotiable with the Greek Cypriots and indefensible because it would be a legitimisation of ethnic cleansing and would defy the jurisprudence emerging from the ECHR (Hannay 2005: 120–125).

Consequently, the renewed efforts of the UN – conducted by Alvaro de Soto, the newly appointed SG's Special Adviser on Cyprus – materialised in the 'Preliminary Thoughts' he presented to each party (Hannay 2005: 125–127). The relevance of de Soto's Preliminary Thoughts is that they built on some major points already made in previous settlement attempts and confirmed them as pillars of the future versions of the Annan Plan, thus signalling a continuation in the trend for the solution framework. A common thread along previous and future settlement attempts was the inclusiveness of a coveted solution, which would be a comprehensive one covering all areas of contention, to be agreed upon simultaneously. Moreover, the principle of conclusiveness was also set in the sense that the settlement eventually agreed upon would be final. In addition, the Preliminary Thoughts picked on the Set of Ideas' principle in remedying dispossession with a mixture of restitution, compensation and exchange linked to the extent and nature of territorial adjustment included in the settlement plan.

The SG's subsequent personal involvement not only confirmed the principles set by de Soto's ideas, but also ushered in a shift in the nature of the UN intervention from talks to negotiations. This also meant that it would do so without seeking explicit agreement from the parties and thereby giving either side a veto. As Hannay usefully points out, the negotiations henceforth were to be based on a single negotiating text to which each side would react by agreeing, disagreeing or amending. This process was to replace the practice of each side tabling extensive drafts of their own approach to core issues (Hannay 2005: 129–140).

As the Annan process was about to kick off, an important aspect of the Greek Cypriot position was aired during the face-to-face talks between Clerides and Denktash. The Greek Cypriot leader clearly said that his attitude on Greek Cypriot returns to property in the north would be crucially affected by the scale of the territorial adjustment and that he could show flexibility on one if he got satisfaction on the other. In response, Denktash flatly declined to contemplate any discussion of the details of a territorial adjustment until the final stage. He continued to insist that the property issue must be dealt with in its entirety by compensation and by no return of the Greek Cypriots to the north (Hannay 2005: 155–160).

Subject to reservations by the parties, Annan sent his revised proposals – Annan Plan 2 – to Clerides and Denktash two days before the meeting of the European Council in Copenhagen (where the decision to admit Cyprus to the EU would be made). The major part of his first plan, its structure and most of the content were left untouched, but a number of modest changes were put forward (Hannay 2005: 188–189). Among the amendments were modifications in the cap on property restitution, although figures were declared to depend on the final territorial adjustment (Hannay 2005: 188–189). Turkish Cypriots declared that the proposals were unacceptable in too many ways and that there was nothing to negotiate about (Hannay 2005: 190–194). Meanwhile, the European Council made clear that it still hoped to welcome a reunited island by the time the Accession Treaty was signed in Athens in April. It called for a continuation and conclusion of negotiations on the Annan Plan by 28 February – which had always been the cut-off date in the plan for the end of negotiations – and repeated its commitment to 'accommodate' a UN settlement (Hannay 2005: 195).

Annan Plan 3 proposed a considerable number of changes that had emerged from the negotiations and the consultations that de Soto had had in the final six weeks. In this version of the plan, it was clear that the UN had adopted an approach that rather maximised the number of Greek Cypriots returning to their properties under the administration of the Greek Cypriot state. This was reflected in a precise proposal for territorial adjustment that considerably reduced the number of Greek Cypriot residencies that would remain in the territory administered by the Turkish Cypriot state. At the same time, in identifying the exact area of territorial adjustment, the UN also tried to avoid the inclusion of villages that historically had a substantial Turkish Cypriot population so as to minimise the effect on current inhabitants, thus bearing in mind not only restoring the rights of the dispossessed but also the ramifications of this restoration of rights. A distinction was then made regarding how property rights will be exercised in areas subject to territorial adjustment and how they will be exercised in other areas. Property rights in relation to property located in areas subject to territorial adjustment will generally be exercised by way of reinstatement. For affected properties located outside the areas subject to territorial adjustment, the agreement contains a more restrictive approach to reinstatement: a ceiling is placed on the number of residences and land located in the areas administered by a constituent state that would be reinstated to dispossessed owners who, on the day the agreement comes into force, reside in the other constituent state. In areas not subject to territorial adjustment, a claimant may seek to exercise their property rights by way of either reinstatement, compensation, sale, long-term lease or exchange. Each claimant will specify the manner in which they choose to exercise their property rights. The Property Board will then have to decide whether or not the specified option with the exception of compensation may be granted. If it is not possible for the Property Board to meet the requirement of the claimant, then compensation will be awarded in exchange for title to the affected property (The Property Regime in the Annan Plan 2003).

Annan states in his 2004 report what the last attempt to settle the Cypriot conflict – Annan Plan 5 – entailed and why it failed. The rights of the displaced and dispossessed was one of the issues subject to alterations in the last version of the Annan Plan, which, like its earlier versions, dealt with all property affected by events since 1963.[25] In comparison with its former version, the property scheme was revamped by removing all overall ceilings on property reinstatement, providing instead that most Greek Cypriots would have some property reinstated in the Turkish Cypriot state (usually their former home and one-third of the land) (Annan 2004).

Another key Turkish Cypriot concern taken into consideration by the plan was that concerning property-related cases filed before EU courts and the ECHR once a settlement took effect in the island. The finalised plan elaborated on this by incorporating draft letters by which the federal government would inform the President of the ECHR and the President of the Council of Europe that the settlement established a domestic mechanism for dealing with claims to affected property, and that to this end, the United Cyprus Republic would be the sole responsible state party concerning such matters and would request the Court to strike out any proceedings before it to allow the domestic mechanism to proceed (Annan 2004).

With those proposals, the UN had attempted to bridge the gap between the demands of the two parties. The parameters of a settlement, from a Greek Cypriot perspective, started off with demands for the new state to have a single voice internationally, a restoration for violated human rights, demilitaralisation of the island and that all displaced persons have the right to return to their properties. What the Turkish Cypriots called for, on the other hand, was separateness of the two communities, a relationship of political equality, few Greek Cypriots allowed to settle in the Turkish Cypriot state and limited reinstatement, if not a global exchange of properties. They also advocated compensation payments for the displaced persons and territorial adjustment to respect the bi-zonality. In response to both positions, the various UN efforts focused on the following: establishing a federal state with a single international personality and sovereignty, while giving maximum autonomy to the two federal states by minimising the powers of the federal state. The proposed settlement plan also acknowledged the right of return but simultaneously limited the number of Greek Cypriots that could settle in the north at any one time, allowing people to return or settle. By the same token, it acknowledged property rights but allowed for flexibility regarding the manner in which it may be exercised. This meant that property rights were not only exercised by full restitution but also by compensation.[26]

Despite its efforts to bridge the gaps between the two parties' positions and demands, the Annan Plan has nevertheless failed to withstand the vote it was subject to. During the referenda, the Greek Cypriots rejected the plan by 75.8 per cent of voters. The plan was, however, approved by 64.9 per cent of voters on the Turkish Cypriot side. A straightforward explanation of the voting results of both communities is difficult to put forward. Highlighting the EU factor within the politics of settlement in Cyprus does, however, help shed light both on the vote as well as the evolution of the Annan process. In fact, the latter was primarily prompted by the prospect of Cyprus's accession to the EU and Turkey's determination for a date to be given by the organisation for the start of its own accession negotiations. In his opening statement of the 2003 report, Annan states that:

> This effort was undertaken in the context of a unique opportunity which, had it been seized, would have allowed a reunited Cyprus to sign the Treaty of Accession to the EU on 16 April 2003.

The reason the SG advocates for renewing settlement efforts was a change in context. He mentions:

> A unique set of circumstances was emerging . . . the potential existed to make a true impact on the attitudes of the protagonists and bring about the required qualitative changes of positions.

Those new circumstances included the evolving Greek–Turkish rapprochement, the European Council's decision in 1999 that opened the door to Turkey's candidature accession and the prospects for enlargement of the EU. In fact, Annan went on to further state that 'the EU factor in particular offered a framework of incentives to reach a settlement as well as deadlines within which to reach it'. When the talks were suddenly revived in February 2004 after a year-long stalemate, it was also because of a renewed hope of Cyprus entering the EU on 1 May 2004 as a united country. The following section offers further explanations of how the EU accession process affected the settlement dynamics in Cyprus.

The European Union dimension

> The commitment given by the European Union in 1995 to open accession negotiations with Cyprus, divided or not, within six months of the end of the Inter-Governmental conference which was drawing up the Amsterdam Treaty [in 1997], meant that we were sliding towards the parting of the ways which might either consolidate the division of the island or lead to its entering reunited into the European Union.
>
> (Hannay 2005: vii–viii)

During the 1992 negotiations over the UN's Set of Ideas, the EU dimension did not gain front stage as it increasingly did afterwards. Although the Greek Cypriots had by then submitted an application to join the EU, the Commission had not yet delivered its formal opinion on it and accession negotiations had therefore not started. It was thus initially assumed that it would be a reunited Cyprus that would, in due course, conduct accession negotiations. In 1995, this application was, in principle, accepted as being valid by the EU. By the time negotiations between the Cypriot counterparts had resumed at the end of 1999, the prevailing situation had changed. The Greek Cypriot application had been endorsed by the Commission, accession negotiations had been opened with them in 1998 and the Turkish Cypriots had rejected all attempts to persuade them to associate themselves with these negotiations. Moreover, it was clear that Cyprus would be in the first wave of any accession package. Additionally, the Helsinki European Council had stated categorically that a settlement was not a precondition for membership, having previously fended off attempts by the Turks and Turkish Cypriots to argue that accession by a divided island was either illegal or should be stopped until there was a settlement. It was becoming evident, therefore, that the settlement and EU accession negotiations were no longer going to be sequential but rather more likely to be simultaneous.

This was not the only significance of the EU dimension in the Cyprus problem and the search for a solution. The EU accession factor cast its shadow over the procedures of the Annan Plan and the timeline of urgency adopted by the UN, with its eyes set on key dates concerning accession to the EU as mentioned above. Moreover, the EU factor also affected the Greek Cypriot position in the negotiations as well as the shift witnessed in the Turkish Cypriot stance, as apparent from their supportive vote to the last version of the Annan Plan subject to the 2004 referendum. Additionally, the EU accession dynamics in the case of

Cyprus demonstrated once again how the players of the game, namely the motherlands, can play a role in influencing the settlement perspectives.

From the Greek Cypriot perspective, one argument went that Clerides's desire to reach a settlement of the Cyprus problem before he quit the political scene in February 2003 played an important role in ensuring some flexibility in his negotiating position. An even stronger incentive was the need to avoid being seen as the obstructive party in the settlement negotiations. As the EU and its member states clearly signalled their preference for the accession of a reunited Cyprus rather than a divided one, this factor gained increasing weight. However, some analysts argue that the progress of the Republic of Cyprus towards accession has rather been at the cost of reaching a settlement. Brewin believes that the Greek Cypriot application did not run in parallel with a wish to unify the island. According to him, Vassiliou had several times resisted Greek Prime Minister Andrea Papandreou's pressure to follow Greece into the EU on the grounds that this would make a UN-brokered settlement with the Turkish Cypriots more difficult. Accordingly, the main purpose of eventually joining the EU was to enhance the Greek Cypriot position in negotiations by further internationalisation of the Cypriot problem (Brewin 2000: 3, Brewin 1999: 148–173).

The situation changed when Clerides defeated Vassiliou and denounced the Set of Ideas on the grounds that they violated basic human rights, international law and would 'block Cyprus' course towards Europe'. He stated at his investiture (28 February 1993) that his policy 'would take as its starting point the high level agreement of 77 and 79, the UN charter and the European convention on human rights'. He saw entry into the European Community as the guarantee of the security and prosperity of all Cypriots (Dodd 1988: 52). The solution of the Cyprus question, he further argued, had to be based on the principles of the EC. The Set of Ideas had to be revised in that direction. This was a strong new departure in Greek Cypriot rhetoric.

Moreover, while maintaining its official policy of its wish to see a political settlement before accession, the Greek Cypriot Government in effect adopted a few procedures not in line with its official policy. While working on aligning Cypriot law with the EU *acquis communautaire*, the Government did not request any derogation from the EU negotiators on the basis that derogations might delay the accession. Yet, it is thought that the compensation package for dispossessed property owners, essential to a political settlement, would have to be financed in large part by the EU. However, the Greek Cypriot Government seemed not to have wanted to invite delay by requesting large sums and allegedly chose to relegate the rights of dispossessed property owners to the back stage in favour of the accession procedures (Brewin 1999: 161–162). In addition, the following presidential election campaign in the south, in early 2003, did not focus much on the negotiations for a settlement, nor on the Annan Plan (Hannay 2005: 199–200). The newly elected Papadopoulos, in a broadcast speech on 7 April 2004, even called upon the people to reject the plan with a resounding 'No'. Among other things, the speech challenged the wisdom of doing away with:

> our internationally recognized state exactly at the very moment it strengthens its political weight, with its accession to the European Union.
>
> (Annan 2003)

In fact, in a 2005 Chatham House report on the political situation in Cyprus, Tim Potier predicts that the Cypriot Government will further seek to Europeanise the solution to the Cyprus problem via the EC, manoeuvring many vetoes regarding Turkey's accession to the EU[27] (Potier 2005).

The Turkish Cypriot leadership on its part accepted EU membership as an objective in theory but was highly sceptical of Cyprus's EU accession. Their support was conditional on first reaching a settlement protecting the political equalities of the Turkish Cypriots, as well as on Turkey's own membership, which would ensure the respect of the external balance of power. However, contrary to the leadership's stance, a large number of the Turkish Cypriot population was increasingly convinced that the EU accession negotiations presented an opportunity to reach a settlement on favourable terms, in addition to being a way out of their state of impoverishment, isolation and economic stagnation. These considerations were the background to the massive Turkish Cypriot public demonstrations at the end of 2002 and early in 2003 in favour of acceptance of the Annan Plan and of joining the EU (Hannay 2005: 47).[28] Moreover, opinion polls showed strong support for the Annan Plan – even in polls taken in Morphou, a town due to be handed back to the Greek Cypriots as a result of the territorial adjustment and whose inhabitants thus faced displacement once again (Hannay 2005: 196, Tocci 2004: 30). Left-wing Turkish Cypriot parties have protested against domination by Ankara and have urged for more emphasis on agreement with the south for a settlement that would allow the relatively impoverished north to benefit from entry into the European Union[29] (Dodd 1999b: 6).

While the previous paragraphs have illustrated the impact of the EU on the parties' positions as well as on the UN settlement process, the question often arises as to the extent of pressure the European Union may have exerted on the parties to settle the conflict prior to accession. Brewin believes that neither the Council nor the Commission showed interest in appointing a mediator, either directly or through the UN. Additionally, the author points out that the rhetoric of successive European summits expressed the contrast between EU commitment to eastern and central Europe on the one hand and its feeble interest in the status of Cyprus as it included it in the enlargement process. The decision to add Cyprus to the enlargement process was thought to be for two main reasons: first, the conviction that enlargement to 100 million central and eastern Europeans would be compromised if it were linked with the simultaneous accession of 60 million Turks. To compensate Turkey for the rebuff, the final stage of the Customs Union with Turkey had to surmount the obstacle of a Greek veto imposed in December 1994. The price for Greece lifting its veto was the setting for a date for opening negotiations with the Greek Cypriot Government without requiring a settlement of a dispute with the Turkish Cypriots. The second reason was also related to making a success of the unification of eastern with western Europe. The Greek Government and parliament would not agree to any treaty enlarging the EU unless Cyprus was included in the process (Brewin 2000: 14). Moreover, the fresh experience of Kosovo made the EU aware of the legal implications and complexities of engaging in a problem of conflict between two communities within the internationally recognised borders of one state (Brewin 2000: 3–15).[30]

In this section I have attempted to shed light on the various external players involved in the Cypriot conflict. The section has specifically focused on the role played by the UN in drafting proposals of a settlement. The evolution of the displacement and dispossession dossier within the various settlement proposals has been particularly traced. The final paragraphs have also pointed out some of the EU accession dynamics and how they influenced the positions of the parties and finally played a major role in the outcome of the referendum, which the Greek Cypriots voted against while the Turkish Cypriots voted in favour. The remainder of the chapter explores how these factors have shaped the nature of the reparations claim in both its basis and form.

The nature of the reparations claim

The evolution of the reparations claim through the various attempts to settle the Cypriot conflict, and the form it took in the final version of the

Annan Plan, call for an examination of the basis for reparations. In other words, was the reparation proposal in the case of Cyprus that of a legal remedy to a legal injury, or rather a political settlement addressing injustices defined by the dynamics of the conflict and balance of power? Or a mixture of both? Moreover, was there a moral contrition element in the search and formulation of reparations to Cypriot displacement and dispossession? Consequently, what were the factors influencing the form reparations finally took?

It is worth noting that inclusion of international law featured in this case of reparations. The legal dimension is not only present in the reparations proposals themselves, but also appears in the parties' initial demands and positions. Moreover, issues of legality were incorporated in the international resolutions related to the conflict and the UN position. This was evident in the evolution of the negotiations, the settlement proposals and finally in the form and basis of the reparations. But to what extent was international law the basis for provision of reparations?

As far as the Turkish Cypriots are concerned, the Turkish Army's operation in 1974 was a peace mission to protect their lives and was, therefore, consistent with the Treaty of Guarantees which made it legally correct. For the Greek Cypriots, Turkey illegally invaded the island, confiscating property and displacing a large proportion of the population in the process. The international community went along with the Greek Cypriot interpretation of events and the UN declared the Turkish military action in Cyprus illegal under international law. A counterargument to this claim is that the Cyprus problem in fact began in 1960 and the landing of Turkish troops was the consequence, not the cause, of the problem. Therefore, there were in fact two military actions in 1974: the first was by Greece, which caused the second by Turkey (Stephen 1997: 3).

According to their interpretation of events and the weight of the matching UN resolutions, the Greek Cypriots built their demands for rights of the displaced and the dispossessed on the illegality of the 1974 events. During the course of negotiations, Greek Cypriots maintained demands for the restoration of violated rights and an exercise of the Three Freedoms. This legal rhetoric not only illustrates the issue of the legal legitimacy of demands which Greek Cypriots ground on their interpretation of the Turkish intervention and the rights of displaced persons, but also the nature of the trade-offs between the various core contention issues of the conflict. The Greek part wants the territory and the property, whereas the Turkish side emphasised security, political equality and thus limited freedoms, therefore holding that a solution should emerge from the 'present realities' on the island rather than on rights (Tocci 2004: 29). The Greek Cypriots, citing international human rights law, the principles of the EU *acquis communautaire*, the realities of the modern world and the need for the settlement to be perceived as just if it is to be durable, wished to see a settlement based on freedom of movement, freedom of settlement and the right of displaced persons to return to their homes. The Turkish Cypriots argued that the distrust between the two sides, the need for security, the realities on the island, the numerical and economic disparities between the two sides and the principle of bi-zonality meant that property claims should be liquidated by a global exchange and compensation scheme and that freedom of movement and residence should be strictly controlled (Annan 2003).

The Greek Cypriots not only gained strength from the backing of the UN to their interpretation of the military action and the displacement that occurred in 1974, but had initiated international support for them earlier on. Greek Cypriots had in fact secured for themselves recognition as the government of all Cyprus and persuaded the world that they, and not the Turkish Cypriots, are the injured party.[31] The SC resolution, which established UNFICYP on 4 March 1964, provided the Greek Cypriot Government with legitimacy and therefore international recognition through its reference to the 'government of Cyprus'.[32] Thus, the resolution strengthened the hand of the Greek Cypriots and weakened that of the Turkish Cypriots until 1974 (Richmond 1998: xx, Tocci 2004: 60). Because of the international recognition of the Greek Cypriot Government as the legitimate authority on the island, it has been easy to sell to the international community that in 1974, Turkey invaded the sovereign state of Cyprus (Stephen 1997: 3, Dodd 1999a: 128). The lack of international approval for those *faits accomplis*, created by force in contradiction to UN principles and the expressed will of the world community, played a prominent role in preventing the legitimisation of the de facto partition of Cyprus (Joseph 1997: 232).

Nevertheless, while the GA and SC made frequent references to the continuing interference of Turkey in the island's affairs, the UN chose to continue negotiations on the basis of the new situation and to encourage the Greek Cypriots to move their positions closer to the new realities that now existed on the island (Richmond 1998: xxii). However, Tocci argues that since 1974, the Greek Cypriot public has been persuaded by its government of the moral and legal superiority of the Greek Cypriot cause. The political leadership never invested in arguing to the public the need, let alone the desirability, of a true compromise solution with the Turkish Cypriots. As such, the difference between the demands of the leaders and the public expectations have been stark, particularly when past leadership appeared to be more willing to make the necessary compromise to reach a negotiated agreement. The electoral defeats of moderate Vassiliou in 1993 to the then more hard-line Clerides, or the 2003 defeat of Clerides to the tougher Papadopoulos, are cases in point.

When analysed more closely, the illegality of the events of 1974 was not the only premise of the initial UN involvement illustrated in its GA resolution in response to the Turkish military operation in Cyprus. Another characteristic of the UN involvement was acknowledgement of the resulting displacement in addition to principal recognition of all property rights due as a result of inter-communal strife or military action between 1963 and 1974. Third, the GA resolution laid the ground for the organisation to undertake negotiation of a settlement between the parties. In the ensuing years, as the extent and nature of the UN's involvement increased and numerous settlements have been put forward, several other characteristics of the organisation's proposals in relation to the displacement and dispossession dossier could be discerned. These characteristics have ultimately led to the form of the final reparations claim featuring in the last version of the Annan Plan.

From this starting point, the journey to a solution and the evolution of reparations to the displacement and dispossession developed through several phases. The inter-communal talks in 1977, resulting from 'efforts' by the SG, recognised since the very beginning the property question as well as the priority of the federal solution in the hierarchy of importance of issues to be solved in the search for a settlement to the conflict. The subsequent 1979 inter-communal talks reaffirmed the principle of building on previous settlement attempts and UN resolutions, and also introduced the first links between displacement and territorial adjustment in a potential settlement. With the shift from proximity talks to summit meetings in 1985 came the first draft of a framework agreement which formalised bi-zonality and bi-communality in settling the Cypriot issue. In comparison, the Ghali Set of Ideas in 1992 was much more comprehensive in the issues it covered. The document further demonstrated the clear link between territorial adjustment and displacement. Moreover, it tackled the property issue in detail for the first time, recognising claims of both Turkish and Greek dispossessed Cypriots. The Set of Ideas initiated the principle that property rights, although honoured in principle, are not to be exercised by full restitution of property and proceeds to link between the extent and nature of territorial adjustment and property restitution. And in order to complement the limitations set on restitution of property, compensation was introduced. In other words, the form of reparations here was subject to the trade-offs between the issue of territorial adjustment and property rights. The Annan Plans put on the table a few years later were more extensive and covered all areas of contention in great detail. They reflected the UN stepping in more forcibly and built on all previous settlement attempts. As explained in detail in the previous section, the Annan Plan confirmed the principle of treating loss of property by restitution, compensation and exchange and link with territorial adjustment. They also confirmed the principle of inclusiveness and conclusiveness and marked a shift from talks to negotiations.

It is of importance here to clarify the philosophy behind the Annan Plan and how it ultimately came to formulate the reparations part of the settlement the way it did. This essence of Annan's thinking can be traced through the premises the SG based himself upon as guidelines to his proposed settlement. In his identical statement to Clerides and Denktash prior to the first version of the Annan Plan, the SG lay down the foundations of his philosophy as follows:

> Concerning property, we must recognize that there are considerations of international law to which we must give weight. The solution must withstand legal challenge. The legal rights which people have to their property must be respected. At the same time, I believe that a solution should carefully regulate the exercise of these rights so as to safeguard the character of the 'component states'. Meeting these principles will require an appropriate combination of reinstatement, exchange and compensation. For a period of time to be established by agreement, there may be limits on the number of Greek Cypriots establishing residence in the north and Turkish Cypriots establishing residence in the south. It is worth mentioning in this context that the criteria, form and nature of regulation of property rights will also have a bearing on the extent of territorial adjustment, and vice-versa.
> (quoted in Hannay 2005: 139)

In his detailed report to the SC after the failure of the third version of the plan in 2003, the SG further elucidated the UN's approach to the property issue as one seeking to find a balance between competing legitimate interests and individual human rights for both dispossessed owners and current users. And that the provisions relating to property rest on respect for international law and the principle of bi-zonality, which is enshrined in the plan. They also address some important political concerns of the two sides, including the need for a substantial majority of refugees to return to their homes, the need to minimise the dislocation of current users and other security, humanitarian and human rights concerns. In addition, in keeping with these principles, the property regime respects the right of persons to their property whilst limiting and regulating the way in which persons may exercise their rights in certain cases. While it is possible to differ on details, this approach, particularly when married to the territorial adjustment, strikes a fair balance between competing legitimate interests and individual human rights and respects the principle of bi-zonality and international law (including international human rights law and the fourth Geneva Convention) (Annan 2004). Moreover, Annan expressed how he also had to bear in mind 'international developments since the Second World War', both those related to Cyprus and others (Annan 2004). Such past practice in the SG's view favours a settlement based on respect for individual property rights, such as the ECHR's decision recognising the property rights of Greek Cypriots in the northern part of the island and allocating damages at the expense of Turkey, especially since thousands of similar cases are pending before the Court:

> In making any suggestions I took into account these developments and the positions adopted recently by the United Nations and the international community in the former Yugoslavia, but also the fact that the events in Cyprus happened 30 to 40 years ago and that the displaced people have had to rebuild their lives and their economies during this time.
>
> (Annan 2004)

Since the referendum of 2004, no further UN-brokered negotiations have been held. At present, the Cyprus problem is at a total stalemate.[33]

Conclusion

This chapter has tackled attempts to repair the displacement and dispossession elements of the Cypriot conflict. The main purpose of the chapter was to discuss how Greek and Turkish Cypriot positions, in addition to UN settlement proposals, interact in addressing reparations to Cypriot displacement and dispossession.

In this present case, proposals for reparations – in conjunction with the other core issues of the conflict – were incorporated into the various settlement proposals put forward by the UN. The inclusiveness of the search for a solution to the entire conflict, as well as the evident involvement of the international organisation as a third party putting proposals on the table, are two of the main characteristics of the Cypriot case.

Annan Plan 5, drafted in 2004, represents the final efforts of settlement on behalf of the UN. As the chapter has demonstrated, such efforts have expanded since they started in the aftermath of the events of 1974. Negotiation rounds and settlement proposals have moved along a steady line, building on details of the core issues without reneging on previous proposals. In sum, it may be concluded that in formulating his philosophy, as reflected in the final settlement plan in relation to reparations, Annan took account of a number of considerations. In the broader context of dispossession, the Annan Plan covers property loss only as the damage to be remedied and addresses it by means of restitution, compensation and exchange. Such a form of reparations reflects the various factors Annan had to bear in mind while formulating his proposals. The plan indeed contained considerations of international law that originally stemmed from the illegality of the events of 1974 and acknowledgements of property rights of all dispossessed since 1963. However, while a full acknowledgment of rights implies full restitution of property, introducing the element of compensation as a form of remedy reflects the political concerns Annan has had to bear in mind while proposing reparations.

As the chapter has proceeded to illustrate, such political considerations emanate from the wider context of the conflict, the link with the other core issues dealt with, as well as the disparate positions of the Greek and Turkish Cypriot sides. Since displacement and property loss have inescapably followed the track of the other elements of the conflict, reparations to dispossessed and displaced Cypriots were conspicuously subject to the trade-offs with the other issues that settlement plans have addressed.

A close look at those trade-offs has indicated a hierarchy of importance regarding elements of solving the conflict. In its unpacking of the various settlement proposals, the chapter analysis has revealed that the most directly linked issue with displacement and dispossession proved to be territorial adjustment and the issue of the Three Freedoms. It was not possible to treat displacement and dispossession without linking the proposals to the extent of territorial exchange, nor addressing the freedoms Greek Cypriots demanded. Higher on the echelon of priority in the search for a solution was the centrality of the federal solution as the main core issue to be dealt with within an overall settlement. The bi-zonal, bi-communal intrinsic characteristics of the coveted state-to-be cast their shadows on the extent of territorial adjustments and, by consequence, on the type of reparations offered to the displaced and dispossessed Cypriots. Therefore, the main outcome of accommodating the matrix of trade-offs was setting limitations on the exercise of property rights by means of full restitution.

Incorporating this hierarchy of trade-offs in settlement proposals put forward by the UN reflects the substance and influence of each party's declared position towards reparations. Greek Cypriots derived the legitimacy and power of their demands from the illegal stamp the UN sealed on the events of 1974 and thus advocated rights in their demands for settling property and displacement issues. Turkish Cypriots, on the other hand, played on the chords of the right to self-determination and therefore called for global compensation as their preferred solution as a correlation of treating the conflict on the basis of 'realities on the ground'. Such perceptions of the conflict with eyes set on the overarching issue of power-sharing on the island led to relegating the property issue – while central to a solution – to the status of a pawn on the chess board.

Another pertinent observation drawn from analysing the Cypriot reparations case is the absence of apology as a form of reparations. Such an absence pulls the moral contrition element out of the equation and further emphasises that the struggle for reparations was a mixture of political as well as legal considerations. In fact, the final goal proved to be a political settlement based on a number of legal considerations. In other words, the legal rights here were politicised for the sake of an overall settlement. In sum, the search for settling the Cypriot conflict meant that within the process of operationalising justice, there was no room for moral contrition.

A multitude of explanatory reasons are advocated for the hitherto elusive solution to the Cypriot conflict and the extent of the protagonists' agreement or disagreement over the core issues. Singling out one main contentious point would be an oversimplification of a complex situation. Indicative indeed was Annan's evocation of the concept of a zero-sum game to describe the conundrum:

> One of the obstacles to solving the Cyprus problem has been the perception on both sides that this was a zero-sum game: one side's gain was the other side's loss. I am strongly convinced that, had it been accepted, my proposal would have created a win-win situation.
> (Annan 2004, Hannay 2005: 229–230)

However, it may be concluded that the displacement/dispossession factor, while being a core issue, is not the deal-breaker in the context of the Cyprus problem and the search for a settlement.

Within this context, the chapter also demonstrated how the EU accession factor vigorously entered the scene of the search for a solution to the Cypriot problem. Notwithstanding that the issue of accession was the main trigger for the launch of the Annan process itself, the failure to make accession conditional to commitment to the Annan peace plan has been a blow to the 'opportunity' created by such an incentive. The carrot represented by imminent membership to the European Union was not accompanied by the necessary stick of signing the deal. By rejecting the Annan Plan in the 2004 referendum six days prior to official accession, Greek Cypriots indicated they felt they could live without the compromises a settlement inevitably entailed. The opportunity was indeed missed.

5 Prospects of reparations to Palestinian refugees

This book has embarked on a search for insights into the failure to reach a reparations agreement to Palestinian refugees in spite of the numerous attempts over the past six decades. Pondering the issue, the study wondered if the answer could lie in the presence of a model of reparations whose component elements are lacking from the Israeli–Palestinian case. By consequence, if such a model were to be outlined, would its application to the case of Palestine finally lead to reaching a reparations agreement dealing with Palestinian displacement and dispossession?

The introductory chapter explained how the objective of the book is to focus on what precedes the concrete reparations agreement, the factors conducive to it and influencing it. Accordingly, the focus of the comparison has been to analyse the position of each of the conflict's protagonists and third party players in their effect on the basis and form of the reparations claim. In that sense, the pattern and emerging themes derived from analysing the reparations process within the German–Jewish Reparations Agreement of 1952 and Cyprus are intended to shed light on the Palestinian refugees reparations case.

A pertinent concern was to define what reparations are. A notion widely deliberated among various disciplines, the study has previously delineated in Chapter 2 how international law scholars, political scientists, historians and philosophers have made contributions in this regard. This overview of traditional and modern approaches to reparations has led to an important observation. In spite of the diversity of opinions and disciplines focusing on reparations, several main broad lines seem to run along the various lines of thought. How a wrongful act is identified and perceived, the form of the remedy to that wrongful act as well as the final aim of reparations are issues pertinently present in all the literature concerned with reparations. The difference, however, lies in the breaking-down of those broad lines and the weight given to each matter. Nevertheless, the shared parameters of a definition of reparations were found to be two basic elements: the determination of a wrongful act and how to redress the wrongful act.

The legal, moral, historical or political standpoints of the protagonists influence the identification of the nature of an injustice and thus the basis of the reparations claim. Reparations then may be perceived as a right in itself, conducive to the end of a conflict, or a means of restoring a previous condition. Once this question is addressed, another one arises: whether the determination of a wrongful act implies a model reparations form. In light of the fact that reparations take several forms, does the nature of the harm necessarily lead to adopting a certain form of remedy as most adequate? Those sets of questions are also linked to the final objective of the reparations process. Overall, the debate over reparations has suggested the concept to be composed of four main elements, as presented at the end of Chapter 2: the identification of an injustice, the establishment of a responsibility, the form of remedy and the final aim of the reparations process. In other words, reparations consist of a set of questions: what is the wrong done? Who is responsible? What is the form of redress? And what is the aim?

Yet, outlining those elements of reparations is not sufficient for the process to go a full circle. Which of those elements should come first? Does the comparison shed light on a preferred order of sequence among those elements of reparations? Does the comparison suggest a model for reparations?

Both cases looked at – the German–Jewish case and Cyprus – have led to several observations relating to reparations. In light of that, this last chapter aims to push the argument one step further by exploring the following: what are the prospects for a reparations agreement in the Palestinian case? The following pages thus elaborate on the issue of a reparations model distilled from the two comparative cases and the extent to which the case of Palestine relates to such a model. Additionally, the chapter concludes with a final section outlining the main themes derived from the comparison. Those themes act as a contribution towards enhancing Palestinian prospects for reparations to their displacement and dispossession predicament.

However, weaving together observations drawn from two diverse cases, each with a different set of characteristics, calls for doubts over the possibility of such a matter. Linking such observations to yet a third case complicates the matter further. 'Uniqueness' and 'exceptionalism' are adjectives often connected with the case of Palestinian refugees. Does the

Palestinian case thus evade the possibility of being compared with other cases?

Confronting this concern in his attempts to apply comparison of global refugee repatriation programmes to the Palestinian case, Dumper pinpoints that 'by studying a number of similar cases scholars can both avoid an ethnocentric bias and place events and patterns within a broader perspective so one can derive the essential elements that can be found in all cases' (Dumper 2006: 289). He then proceeds to outline some aspects of uniqueness of the Palestinian refugee case, such as longevity, lack of protection and demography – to name but a few. While central issues to repatriation options are worthy of discussion in the context of Dumper's endeavour, the reader is kindly reminded that the departing point in this study, as a rationale for the comparative analysis, is the existence of a common denominator running through the cases. This common thread, stated in the introduction, is twofold: all the cases looked at in this study share two features acting as a departing point. In all three of them there has been an occurrence of displacement and dispossession resulting from a violent conflict or incidence. The wrongful act is thus an occurrence of displacement and dispossession. In addition, the three cases share a quest for a remedy. Therefore, from the outset, common ground could be built upon in order to construct a comparison regardless of the diversity of characteristics of each particular case. Consequently, while acknowledging the differences in characteristics between the three cases, it is nevertheless possible to link observations drawn from each of them.

The following section focuses on the broad outcome of the comparison conducted between the cases of the German–Jewish Reparations and Cyprus. More precisely, the next pages examine whether the comparison has indicated the presence of a model for reparations in the two case studies.

A model for reparations?

In the quest for an answer to the overarching question of the study about the philosophy behind the search for reparations, three elements have been analysed in their approach to reparations. The interaction of the positions of the parties and the external involvement has shed light on the nature of reparations as a general act of redress. Has the interaction of those in relation to reparations in the two case studies indicated the presence of a model for reparations?

Irrespective of the details and particularities of each case study, the general outcome of the comparative analysis has revealed two main findings. The first is that both case studies spell out the conclusion that there is no reparations model derived from the comparison of the two cases. Reparations as deconstructed into its four main elements – identifying an injustice; establishing a responsibility; the form of remedy; and the aim – do not suggest a model form of occurrence in both cases. Both of them do not share the same form, do not perceive the process as fulfilling a similar aim and have not perceived the wrongful act in the same manner.

However, the comparative analysis also reveals that the differences between the reparations process in both cases proved to stem from each party's perception of the aim of reparations. Throughout the relevant chapters covering the case studies, analysis has uncovered that the aim of reparations was reflected on how each protagonist, as well as the external party, perceived the wrongful act. Furthermore, it was the approach to the wrongful act that led to the type of redress deemed adequate to remedy the injustice. Hence, such was the chain leading to the form of reparations proposed in each case. In sum, the journey towards reparations started with a delineation of the aim of reparation ending with the form it finally took. This refutes the widespread notion that agreement between the parties over form of reparations should be the departing point for a reparations process.

Yet, while a model for reparations could not be discerned from the present comparison, the preceding paragraphs suggest that a certain pattern of reparations could nevertheless be detected. Figure 5.1 illustrates this pattern.

The chapter covering the German–Jewish Reparations Agreement of 1952 has illustrated how the position of each party towards reparations, and the factors influencing their perception of the wrongful act, have ultimately shaped the basis and form of reparations. A set of external as well as internal circumstances have acted as incentives motivating each party to seek a conclusion of a reparations agreement. Such incentives have prompted each party to define its objective: did it seek reparations as a goal in itself or reparations as a step leading to another, larger aim? Defining this objective has subsequently shaped the strategy adopted by each party. This is discernable in the indirect vs. direct policy of contact and negotiations, in addition to the moral glove so evident in each party's policy moves. The analysis of the Israeli position revealed how the Jewish state perceived a reparations treaty as a financial rescue to its empty coffers. As for Germany, reparations to Jewish victims of Nazism were deemed a winning card for admission into the post-war international club.

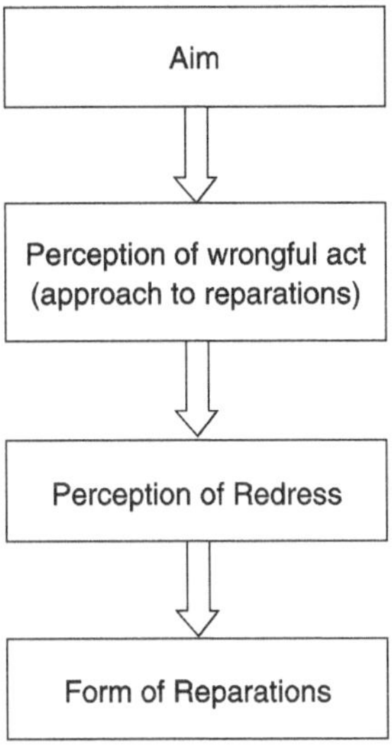

Figure 5.1 Pattern of reparations.

The declared objective of reparations, though, was not as pragmatically stated as it really was. Instead, negotiating a reparations agreement was presented by both protagonists as an act of moral contrition for the historical injustice perpetrated by the Nazi regime against the Jews, displacing them and expropriating their property. As the chapter has unveiled, moral guilt was not the motivator for the search for reparations on behalf of the claimants. By the same token, this case of reparations was not one aimed at claiming rights for the displaced and the dispossessed. The remedy was thus not based on a legal remedy for a breach of legally defined rights. Moreover, the drive for reparations in this case was not to achieve reconciliation between the parties. Significant enough was the name the Claims Conference chose for itself as being confined to 'material claims'. Teitel presents an interesting exploration of the question by looking at the terms used by each party in its own language in relation to reparations. In the German language, '*Wiedergutmachung*' literally means 'to make good again', to return to former conditions. This, in Teitel's analysis, matches reparations drawing political support in Germany as a way to regain credibility in the eyes of the international community in the aftermath of de-Nazification. By contrast, rejecting the notion that reparations could ever make anything 'good' again, the Jewish side called reparations by a Hebrew term, '*Shilumim*', meaning 'to make amends'. For the latter, reparations were a matter of economic necessity. Therefore, the point of departure in negotiations was the refugees' cost of resettlement. Teitel thus proceeds to explain that for perpetrators and victims alike, reparations were about settling accounts, but for each in a different way. Nevertheless, despite completely different understandings of the nature and purposes of the reparations scheme, negotiations over the varying concepts culminated in a political agreement (Teitel 2000: 124).

Defining this goal has subsequently shaped the form of reparations as decided upon during the negotiations process. Hence, discussing the form of reparations was not the contentious point, as much as agreeing to negotiate reparations was. The objectives behind reparations shaping the perception of the wrongful act were manifest in the final agreement. Reparations to the Jews took the form of a global compensation claim, indemnification and restitution laws. Reparations to the Jewish world as represented by the state of Israel and the Claims Conference also took the form of a recognition statement on behalf of the German Government for the historical injustices the Nazi regime inflicted on the Jews. This recognition denoted that the wrongful act was acknowledged by the perpetrators of the injustice.

Similar to the German–Jewish case, Cyprus was also a case whose form of reparations was subject to the nature of the overall aim of reparations. As analysed in the relevant chapter, reparations to displacement and dispossession in Cyprus was part of the package deal of the entire settlement to the conflict. Therefore, this all-inclusive nature of settlement proposals affected the perception of the parties of the wrongful act and hence the form of redress. While the affected party – the Greek Cypriots – called for full implementation of rights in relation to expropriated property and return of the displaced, the legal rights were nevertheless politicised for the sake of an overall settlement. Whereas an optimal implementation of rights calls for full restitution of property, introducing the element of compensation as a form of remedy reflects the nature of the remedy sought. International law considerations were taken into account, yet had to be adjusted according to the needs of the overall settlement of the conflict and the trade-offs with the core issues. By the same token, morality was not advocated in the context similar to the moral contrition element so characteristic of the German–Jewish case. The parties clearly agreed on the essence of what they were negotiating: a power-sharing formula for a state-to-be.

This section has outlined the main findings of the comparative study, namely the absence of a model for reparations yet the presence of a certain pattern revealed by each case study. This pattern, broadly outlined, is that the form of reparations is a function of the aim of reparations as perceived by each party. Such an approach to reparations defines the perception of the injustice or the wrongful act and thus the nature of adequate redress to that wrongful act. In other words, the negotiations process of reparations defines the form of the latter based on the aim of each party and the perception of the harm. The following section seeks to shed light on the case of Palestine in relation to the pattern suggested by the two case studies. To what extent is that pattern present in the case of Palestine?

The Palestinian refugee case

The reader may recall from the overview of the Taba negotiations in Chapter 1 that they were described as the most detailed negotiations round regarding the refugee file. However, comparing Taba with the pattern outlined above, this section demonstrates that the reparations process in Taba evolved differently.

An important point to make relates to why the focus is on Taba rather than the Road Map presented by the Quartet – the US, the EU, Russia and the UN – in 2003. The last of these proposals within the context of the Middle East Peace Process, as mentioned in Chapter 1, hasn't put forward any vision for the refugee issue. Therefore, a focus on Taba, as the last round of official negotiations between Israelis and Palestinians, better serves the purpose of the present analysis.

Taba produced what many analysts deemed to be the most comprehensive discussions of the refugee file, although a concrete agreement failed to materialise. Tactically different from the negotiations at Camp David, the talks between the delegations at Taba dealt at first with a general presentation of the method of solving the refugee problem as both parties saw it, and ended up addressing rehabilitation and compensation mechanisms (Beilin 2004: 235). In his assessment of the Taba negotiations, Yossi Beilin, chief Israeli negotiator for the refugee file, wrote the following:

> the lack of an agreement was due to lack of practicality on the Palestinian side . . . I was beginning to believe that the problem was much more easily resolved than had been imagined, and that on the majority of questions it was possible, immediately or in the near future, to come to terms. The stronger this sense became, the greater – for me, and perhaps the other Israelis – my anger at the Palestinian leadership. For so many years they had prevented a

> solution to the refugee problem, had perpetuated the camps, encouraged the countries of the world not to offer immigration quotas for refugees . . . enable them to live better lives. . . .
>
> (Beilin 2004: 245)

In this quote lies the essence of what went wrong in Taba. Putting the blame on the Palestinian side, Beilin accused it of lack of practicality, 'preventing a solution', halting resettlement and failing to improve on humanitarian needs. Those remarks are some of the indicators of the disparate perceptions of the wrongful act between both parties. Israel – as it always had – considered the refugee issue as a humanitarian problem whose address would be through welfare and resettlement. Palestinians, on the other hand, considered it a legal and historical injustice that called for implementation of relevant legal rights. The fact that the perception of the harm was not agreed upon – and by consequence neither was the adequate remedy – was the most pertinent feature of negotiations at Taba.

Yet, Taba was hailed as the most advanced negotiations round due to its elaboration on issues of the form of reparations. Compared with the pattern outlined in the previous section, Taba in fact put the cart before the horse. By virtue of focusing on form, rather than working on a common perception of the harm, Taba talks reversed the order of the reparations pattern detected in the two case studies. The issue of consensus over the broad contours of the past is something that has preoccupied scholars. Taking the case of Northern Ireland as an example, Bell argues that such consensus does not exist. She describes such an anomaly as 'a conflict-about-the-conflict' or 'a meta-conflict', a situation whereby no agreement exists as to what the conflict is about, nor as to what caused it (Bell et al. 2004: 316). Bell's concept of meta-conflict resembles Brynen's notion of 'quasi-negotiations' mentioned in Chapter 1 in the context of his analysis of the proceedings of the RWG.

Further elaboration on the reparations process in relation to the Taba talks is of merit. The most significant contribution on the refugee file in Taba was the form of reparations and the negotiations in that context. The Moratinos Document covered many technical details of the compensation package and the question of what compensation ought to cover. A deeper look at the discussion of such details reveals that, while they may have gained depth and details, they did in fact demonstrate the disparate perceptions of the wrongful act and the means to redress the wrongful act. Article 3.6 of the Moratinos Document states that: 'The Palestinian side raised the issue of restitution of refugee property.

The Israeli side rejected this.' In his non-paper, Beilin had initially rejected the idea of restitution, emphasising instead compensation programmes addressing financial and in-kind compensation for displacement and material loss, as well as the economic growth of the relevant communities. According to the Israeli negotiator, the dual objectives of individual historic justice and communal economic development are to guide the elaboration of these programmes (Private Response on Palestinian Refugees 2001). Thus, the preferred form of reparations according to each party reflected its perception of the nature of the injustice and the adequate redress in its point of view. Anchoring their demands on a rights-based approach, Palestinians deemed restitution of property an ideal form of remedy. Israelis, on the other hand, focused on the compensation angle and economic welfare as a reflection of their perception of the displacement and dispossession being a humanitarian problem necessitating a solution similar in nature.

The Israeli reaction in response to the Palestinian demands for restitution of property calls for similarities with the case of Cyprus. The latter also featured the situation of the victimised side denied its demands for full restitution, compensation stepping in instead as the compromise solution. In the case of Cyprus, though, responsibility for the wrongful act was not denied by the perpetrator. Rights were thus acknowledged, yet 'adjusted', so as to pave the way for a settlement. In the case of Israeli–Palestinian deliberations over reparations for displacement and dispossession, responsibility still remained an un-bridged gap. Compensation was presented as a welfare solution to the humanitarian aspects of the Palestinian refugee problem as seen by the Israeli side. In fact, delving further into details concerning the mechanism and modalities of compensation payment, Article 3.3 of the Moratinos Document states that both sides agreed to the establishment of an international commission and an international fund as a mechanism for dealing with compensation in all its aspects. Such a structure could be interpreted as an attempt to circumvent the issue of Israel's direct responsibility in relation to the refugee question.

The relation between establishing a responsibility and the perception of the nature of the injustice is further illustrated in the Israeli and Palestinian position regarding 194 as a basis for a solution. According to Article 3 of the Moratinos Document, both parties suggested in their non-papers that, as a basis, the parties should agree that a just settlement of the refugee problem in accordance with SC Resolution 242 must lead to the implementation of GA Resolution 194. The Palestinian non-paper had initially demanded that:

> Israel recognizes its moral and legal responsibility for the forced displacement and dispossession of the Palestinian civilian population during the 1948 war and for preventing the refugees from returning to their homes in accordance with United Nations General Assembly Resolution 194.

Moreover, Article 3 of the same paper had also demanded that 'Israel shall bear responsibility for the resolution of the refugee problem'. By contrast, the Israeli paper did not contain an explicit acceptance of 194 but rather accepted responsibility for being 'a partner' in finding a solution. It is thought that the two Palestinian principles of the right of return and Resolution 194 were put in the Israeli paper in connection with Palestinian demands that Israel had already accepted the establishment of an independent Palestinian state and 242 (Klein 2006: 101). In fact, Article 3.7 of the Moratinos Document in particular stated that:

> . . . it was suggested that the implementation of the agreement shall constitute a complete and final implementation of UNGAR 194 and therefore ends all claims.

In a subsequent interview, Beilin declared that:

> 194 was not just a basis upon which the solution will be established, but that the solution we suggested is already the implementation of 194 and from then on there would be no more claims.
>
> (Eldar and Tamari 2002)

In the book he published a few years later, Beilin explained that the pending issues were to address 'what the Palestinians call Right of Return' and the question of the responsibility for the creation of the refugee problem. Beilin states that the agreement would include a concise history of events in the eyes of each party, recognition of the suffering and distress of the refugees and separate interpretations of 194 while agreeing that 194 would be implemented commensurate with the Clinton plan (Beilin 2004: 230). Overall, Israel was not accepting legal responsibility. What it offered was a joint historical narrative in collaboration with the Palestinians although no agreement was reached on that front (Article 3.1).

Failure to trigger an acknowledgement of the legal responsibility of Israel towards the creation and solution of the Palestinian refugee problem has been a regular feature of the history of the conflict. As outlined in Chapter 1, the question of responsibility, closely linked with the interpretation of 194, has caused steady disagreement over basing the claims on 194. Recapitulating the previous analysis, it is worthy to remember that during the two decades following the events of 1948, 194 remained the basis for most international efforts to achieve a settlement to the conflict. As previously noted, though, the relevance of 194 as a basis for a solution gradually diminished. Whether it has in effect legally and politically superseded 242 is subject to conflicting legal interpretation.

Israel's refusal to accept 194 as a basis for a solution denies the refugee problem from being treated as a legal issue implying legal responsibility. This leads Israel to present its arguments in terms of practical solutions and advocating the humanitarian dimension of the refugee problem. Indicative of this is Barak's speech in the opening of the Knesset winter session on 4 October 1999, stating that:

> We regret the heavy suffering that the conflict caused not only us, but all of the Arab nations that fought against us, including the Palestinian people . . . In the time of peace Israel will be ready to take part in the efforts to heal the wounds of the war out of goodwill, friendship and good neighbourliness, and under no circumstances out of feelings of guilt or responsibility for causing the conflict and its results.
>
> (quoted in Ma'oz 2001: 110)

The Palestinian side, on the other hand, views the refugee problem as a wrongful act requiring a remedy and thus steadily demanding its claims to be based on 194 and advocating the rights of refugees.

Such were characteristics of reparations in the Palestinian case. By discussing details of form of reparations prior to agreeing on a common perception of what reparations are for and about, the chain was broken and the pattern distorted. The following section discusses how the issue of reparations to Palestinian displacement and dispossession could be advanced in light of the comparison conducted by this study.

Towards enhancing Palestinian prospects

Within the scope of the findings of the comparison between the two case studies, Taba has gone down a different alley in tackling reparations to Palestinian displacement and dispossession. More progress ought to be made on meeting over a common concept of the wrongful act, which will unlock problems regarding redressing that wrongful act. Such a matter relates to what each party is looking for when seeking to discuss the refugee issue and search for a solution to it. Needless to say, the international and regional environments constitute a factor of utmost importance in facilitating such a matter, or perhaps – more accurately – complicating it.

However, the comparison does not only shed light on the core pattern outlined in this chapter. Throughout the study, certain issues, themes and characteristics seem to have been of importance in the reparations story told by each case. Some of those themes were particular to one specific case, while others were shared in both, although perhaps with different significances. Such themes have influenced the path to reparations and have contributed towards the positions of the parties and the aims and final structure of reparations. Highlighting those issues serves as a contribution towards the enhancement of prospects of reparations in the case of Palestinian displacement and dispossession. The remainder of the chapter discusses issues such as opportunity, the trade-offs with other core components of a conflict, responsibility, the aim of reparations and lobbying efforts as revealed by the comparison.

Emerging themes

The concept of opportunity

The chapter covering the path to the Luxembourg agreement reveals that the success of the German–Jewish reparations case was first and foremost a product of a seized opportunity, which both sides perceived as a reparations agreement to fulfil. In the case of Cyprus, Annan succinctly described accession to the EU as 'a unique opportunity' to settle the conflict. Failing to link this opportunity with committing the parties to sign a settlement agreement has markedly distorted opportunity in the Cypriot context from *seized* to *missed*.

Unlike the German–Jewish case, where both parties shared parallel motivation to seek reparations, opportunity was lost in Cyprus for lack of a solid incentive to settle. The two Cypriot parties did not share the same sense of urgency about settlement during the various phases of negotiations. Hence, a meeting point has so far never materialised. At early stages, Greek Cypriots believed that continued division of the island favoured the separation option preferred by Turkish Cypriots. Greek Cypriots thus felt a greater sense of urgency than Turkish Cypriots, who were more satisfied with the status quo. In the last years, in conjunction with the EU accession dynamics, the situation reversed. As Annan describes in his report, the prospect of accession of Cyprus to the EU, and the opening of Turkey's path towards that goal, provided a context of balanced incentives. The leadership of the Turkish Cypriots and Turkey did not initially seize this opportunity while it existed. By the time they were willing and able to seek a compromise solution, the incentives for compromise on the Greek Cypriot side had substantially weakened (Annan 2003).[1] As Hannay accounts, 'This [EU accession] was seen by many Greek Cypriots as a tactical stroke of genius enabling them to gain points painlessly without the concessions that would be required of them at the UN's negotiating table' (Hannay 2005: 229–230).

Within the limits of the comparison conducted by this study, opportunity may be viewed from two aspects. The first aspect of opportunity relates to a set of favourable external circumstances acting as incentives to parties of the conflict to seek settlement. Such a favourable systemic environment facilitates reaching a point of balance at which parties meet in order to marry their interests. In the German–Jewish case, none of the parties considered what would be achieved through reparations as a painful compromise. Instead, reparations and their final form were perceived as common interests and a condition heralding gains.

Yet, analysis of the case studies also suggests that to fulfil criteria for an opportunity-to-be-seized, external factors must be matched with a common acknowledgement of the nature of the injustice itself, in addition to a mutual desire to address – not to mention redress – the wrongful act.

According to such an understanding of opportunity, was there a likelihood of an opportunity-to-be-seized in the history of the Israeli–Palestinian deliberations over reparations? Could Taba, for example, be compared with Cyprus's loss of a 'unique opportunity'?

In fact, neither Taba nor Camp David nor any of the former rounds of negotiations has satisfied the outlined criteria for an opportunity-to-be-seized. As discussed in the previous section, a consensus over the nature of the harm in the case of Palestinian refugees was never achieved. Such a lack of consensus is reinforced by the absence of an external systemic environment conducive to conditions allowing Palestinians and Israelis to agree over a common narrative of the wrongful act. So far, international pressure has rather been in favour of the Israeli narrative rather than the Palestinian demands for redress. Nonetheless, Salim Tamari, for example, explains why in his view it is possible to achieve an equitable resolution for the refugee problem despite inequitable power relations between the protagonists. According to the Palestinian former negotiator, Israel is likely to respond to Palestinian demands of accountability with regard to the refugee problem despite the lack of equity in power relations. Such likelihood stems from the Israeli desire to achieve closure of the refugee file. Additionally, Israel's search for 'ultimate legitimacy' and its acceptance as a state within the Arab world, a solution of the refugee problem steps in as necessary (Tamari 2005: 256).

Whether the regional and international setting will eventually put pressure on Israel to reverse its standard policy of denying responsibility for the creation, and therefore solution, of the Palestinian refugee problem is a question open to the unfolding of future events.

Establishment of responsibility

As a common perception of the wrongful act is lacking between Israelis and Palestinians, so is an interpretation of the nature of justice. However, the term 'just', as far as this comparison of reparations cases is concerned, not only relates to the perception of the harm but also to the establishment of responsibility. As patently detectable in Taba and the history of the negotiations between Palestinians and Israelis over the refugee issue, establishing responsibility has been conspicuously absent from all rounds of talks.

The modern literature on reparations, discussed in Chapter 2, illustrates how the issue of responsibility can come in a number of versions. First, there is the legal responsibility of the state of Israel in the creation of the refugee problem, as well as the legal implications of such a responsibility. In addition to legal dimensions, historical responsibility covering causes for the creation of the refugee problem, as highlighted in Chapter 1, is another aspect of responsibility. Moral responsibility as an act of contrition symbolising a step towards reconciliation and paving the way for a solution is yet another version. Finally, political responsibility is suggested by the present study as a commitment on the side of parties to the conflict in forging a solution addressing a historical injustice.

In the German–Jewish case, responsibility for the wrongful act and perception of that act was never a point of contention once the need for reparations was perceived on both sides. Responsibility in this case took the form of moral responsibility and was thus dealt with mostly with an act of moral contrition: acknowledgement of the wrongful act, in addition to compensation and legal codification to complement the act of redress. Cyprus shares the consensus over the nature of the harm, yet parties disagree over the redress mode. This disagreement, as the analysis has revealed, is caused by the overarching perception of the conflict as a power-sharing and state-building one rather than over remedying displacement and dispossession in the first place. However, declaring who was responsible for the displacement and dispossession in the context of the Cypriot conflict was not presented as the legal principle for addressing displacement and dispossession. The case of Cyprus was thus closer to political responsibility for finding a solution to the injustice within the contours of the overall conflict.

Therefore, there emerges a necessity to establish responsibility in the case of Palestinian reparations. Is there a way to narrow the gap between Palestinian demands for an acknowledgement of responsibility and a denial of the latter by the Israeli side? Working out a compromise formula is ultimately left to negotiators and legal scholars. The *sine qua non*, though, seems to establish one aspect or the other of responsibility.

The legal establishment of responsibility would trigger applying state responsibility, as outlined in Chapter 1, the implications of which would have to be addressed by international law scholars.

In this regard, pondering the issue of what the elements of a fair and just solution to the refugee question are, Rashid Khalidi contends that an absolute justice is an elusive notion. Instead, he proposes '... justice within the limits of what is realistically attainable in current and future circumstances' (Khalidi 1995: 72). Since historic responsibility is essential to the Palestinian side '... because this issue is so central to the national narrative and the self-view of the Palestinian people that any approach which tries to sweep history under the rug will fail utterly ...' (Khalidi 1995: 73), Israel will have to take responsibility for its conduct in the past. However, accepting unlimited liability will be seen as a step to an avalanche of returnees, an issue Khalidi deems politically unacceptable to the Israeli side. Thus, unlimited responsibility is unrealistic in the historian's view. This means Khalidi stresses on an acknowledgement of the wrongful act while working out legal implications.

From another perspective, the modern literature on reparations has demonstrated the centrality of apology as a symbol of moral responsibility. Irrespective of the laws of state responsibility, mere acknowledgement of an injustice requires an apology that is lacking in the Palestinian case. In spite of covering many aspects of the Palestinian refugee problem, the Geneva Accords, for example, adopt no statement of moral regret or responsibility. Instead, in the context of Article 7 on refugees, the document proposes a series of 'reconciliation programs' between the two sides. These programmes would be intended to exchange historical narratives, foster educational contacts and promote cross-community programmes. Also envisaged are 'appropriate ways of commemorating those villages and communities that existed prior to 1949' (Article 7.14.iv). Steps are thus to be found regarding a common view of the nature of the injustice and the official acknowledgement of the narrative in the guise of an apology. What legal implications this may have is subject to the legal advisers of both sides. As I pointed out in the conclusion to Chapter 1, a significant observation related to 194 is the fact that the resolution most referred to in relation to demands for Palestinian refugee rights, neither mentioned satisfaction, admission of liability nor apology as components of a solution to the Palestinian refugees problem.

The trade-offs

One of the main characteristics of the German–Jewish case is the sole focus on reparations to displacement and dispossession, with no wider conflict to consider. Could this be the leading factor in the success of this reparations case? While not possible to answer assertively, it is safe enough to state that the lack of other contentious issues in need of settlement may have contributed towards the overall progress and finalisation of the reparations agreement between the two parties.

Cyprus, on the other hand, proved to be a reparations case at the other extreme. A steady feature of settlement plans for the Cypriot conflict included parallel proposals for reparations in conjunction with the other core issues of the conflict. The dynamics of the trade-offs between those core issues played a significant role in the nature of proposals put forward. Redressing displacement and dispossession was not the main priority of this conflict primarily concerned with power-sharing. While an important element, a deal-breaker it was not. The bi-zonal, bi-communal intrinsic characteristics of the proposed overall solutions cast their shadows on the extent of territorial adjustments and, by consequence, on the type of reparations offered to the displaced and dispossessed Cypriots. Therefore, accommodation of the hierarchy of trade-offs had its effect on the final form of reparations and the full exercise of property rights.

With the German–Jewish agreement representing reparations free of trade-offs on the one hand, Cyprus comprising a matrix of interlinked conflict elements on the other hand, where does the case of Palestinian refugees fit? As a key element to the Israeli–Palestinian conflict, Palestinian refugee displacement and dispossession – similar to the case of Cyprus – is closely associated with other core issues. On the broader level comes the link with the thorny issues of the status of Jerusalem, a Palestinian state-to-be and borders, for example. On a narrower level, the files of host states and Jewish migration from Arab states prove to be cards played on the negotiation table of Palestinian displacement and dispossession. Such a web of trade-offs has been a characteristic of the politics of the conflict since its inception in the late 1940s. The discussion over the matter in Chapter 1 highlighted that the creation of a specific UN body in the guise of the UNCCP to deal with the Palestinian refugee issue on a legal basis was not in light of the problem being a refugee displacement one in the first instance, but by virtue of it being a part of the overall Arab–Israeli conflict. The rationale was that solving the refugee issue would be conducive to an overall solution to the conflict. From another perspective, one argument goes that by concentrating on the question of autonomy, as well as keeping the PLO out of the Palestinian delegation, Camp David I in 1978 kept the refugee question at bay. A couple of decades later, Camp David II stumbled over the issue of Jerusalem. Some analysts believe that concentration on Jerusalem led to a failure to make progress on a solution to the refugee problem (Fried 2002: 28–31, Hanieh 2001, Gresh 2001). This was also the case in the Geneva Accords despite its unofficial character. According to Beilin:

> the heart of the agreement is the concession of sovereignty over the Temple Mount to the Palestinians in exchange for Israeli sovereign discretion over the number of refugees admitted to Israel with the rest free to settle in the Palestinian state . . . Geneva is perhaps the last opportunity to realise the Zionist dream.
>
> (Beilin 2004: 264–265)

The Road Map also follows the same trend in treating the refugee file as part of an overall conflict. As a vision for an overall solution to the Israeli–Palestinian conflict, the Road Map is strikingly thin on the refugee issue in comparison with the question of Palestinian statehood.

Moving to the more specific issues of host countries and Jewish migration from Arab countries proves to have found some common ground among the Israeli and Palestinian sides. In relation to the issue of compensation to host countries, the Palestinian non-paper at Taba demanded that host countries receive compensation for the significant costs they bore in hosting the refugees. Similarly, Article 11 of the Israeli private response states that: 'The refugees' host countries shall receive compensation for the significant costs they bore in hosting the refugees. Future rehabilitation costs and investments shall be addressed according to the details of this agreement, via bilateral arrangements between the host countries and the International Commission.' Resettlement being the most favourable option in the Israeli view, facilitating refugee integration in the host countries is encouraged by the Government.

From another perspective, the issue of compensation to Jews from Arab states often featured in the negotiations over settling the Palestinian refugee problem. Israel's refusal to pay any compensation to Palestinians is often attributed to the Israeli argument that it was obliged to absorb almost all of the Jews 'forced to flee' Arab countries in the late 1940s and early 1950s, leaving behind most of their property. Israel welcomed and rehabilitated Arab Jews without any official compensation. Therefore, Israel saw no reason to pay any compensation to Palestinian refugees without a precise accounting of the numbers absorbed by Israel and the value of their properties left behind (see Fischbach 2008 and Gazit 1995: 67).

However, the issue of Jewish migrants from Arab states seems to be more of a bargaining card on behalf of the Israelis and gives signs of being accommodated in the negotiations between the two sides. In fact, Article 3.5 of the Moratinos Document states that:

> The Israeli side requested that the issue of compensation to former Jewish refugees from Arab countries be recognized, while accepting that it was not a Palestinian responsibility or a bilateral issue. The Palestinian side maintained that this is not a subject for a bilateral Palestinian–Israeli agreement.

Tamari argues that in spite of the fact that this matter has acquired recent weight by virtue of being officially adopted by Netanyahu and Sharon, it has sufficiently been challenged during the multilateral peace talks. The broad outcome was that Palestinian restitution claims cannot be reduced to the status of generic Arab claims and pertain to Israeli actions during the war and its aftermath. Therefore, Jewish property claims belong to the arena of bilateral negotiations between Israel, or individual claimants, and the concerned Arab states (Tamari 2005: 256).

Tamari also brings in an interesting observation in relation to the Israeli argument in this regard. If the refugee settlement will be part of a wider process of negotiating the Arab–Israeli conflict, then Jewish property in Arab countries is a matter the Israeli state wants to address. If this is the case, Tamari argues, then it makes sense to bring in the issue of German–Israeli reparations – not only because they set precedence but also because Palestinian refugees were themselves the indirect victims of the German displacement of Jews (Tamari 2005: 252).

While compelling as a case of displacement triggering related rights as in all refugee cases, the Palestinian refugees' status as a function of the politics and the dynamics of the whole conflict is inescapable.

Defining the aim of reparations

The reader may recall that the discussion of reparations in Chapter 2 pinpointed the possibility of approaching reparations as a backward-looking process or a future-oriented one. Recapitulating the essence of the discussion, backwards-looking was meant to designate a reparations process as being rather concerned with the nature of the harm, the type of violation and ascertaining a right. Future-oriented, on the other hand, casts an eye on reconciliation. In that sense, backwards-looking and future-oriented may be viewed as different ways of expressing the 'just' vs. the 'adequate' or the 'right' vs. the 'practical' debate previously invoked. Interpretation of justice within the realm of international law is realised by addressing the commitment of a wrongful act through various legal specified forms. However, international law obligations, devoid of the power of enforcement, are constantly subject to the friction between the legal and the political. As Cyprus has clearly demonstrated, settlement of a conflict in the international system does not necessarily imply full implementation of relevant international law principles.

In his reflections on the Cyprus conflict, Gobbi touches on this issue. He poses the question as to whether the *status quo ante bellum* should be the determinant principle for settlement, or if to the contrary, whether we must understand the *status quo post bellum* to be the base point. The first approach, in his opinion, illustrates how 'excessive emphasis on the law' can reach 'partial conclusions on international reality'. What is needed, according to Gobbi, is 'a less perfect legality which may acquire formal validity but not factual validity'. In other words, 'this is not a problem of *eleganta juris*, where the concepts must answer solely to technical criteria because they may collapse at the first confrontation with social reality' (Gobbi (no date): 33–35).

Such an issue reflects a duality characterising approaches to the Palestinian refugee problem. The political as well as scholarly history covering Palestinian displacement suggests an ongoing debate between two schools of thought and policy/diplomacy strategies: a drift between the concept of compromise and absolutism or maximalist demands. Do we proceed from where we stand today and move forward or do we go back to the origins? This relates to the desired aim. What kind of a solution do we want to reach? And therefore, what is the consensus that could be reached about what exactly constitutes a plausible solution?

As previously mentioned, the reparations process, although leading to reconciliation in the German–Jewish case, was not as far-looking. The shorter gains such as economic recovery and an entry into the international club were the immediate gains triggering motivation. In that sense, the German–Jewish case is a case of a futuristic motivation. Both parties were guided by an eye on the future using the past as a tool.

Annan's philosophy was also future-oriented in the sense that it went beyond a sole focus on an implementation of full rights to remedy a past injustice. This was achieved by means of curtailing implementation of full rights on the one hand, as well as taking into consideration implications of the remedy. The case of Cyprus is complicated by the fact that expropriated Greek Cypriot property in the north is inhabited by Turkish Cypriots. In the event that full restitution of property is exercised, a new displacement would occur. This in fact means that restoring justice in this context would trigger a new injustice.

Such an issue is very much relevant to the Palestinian case. Tamari brings out this point when he mentions that one major argument used against restitution of property is that such an act would dispossess current Israeli occupants. Hence, the need for lessons learnt from precedent cases such as Germany and Bosnia to shed light on the mechanisms facilitating owners' repossession of their former properties while not triggering a new injustice to current owners (Tamari 2005: 254). The case of Cyprus is another case worthy of consideration for that particular angle.

The issue of the 'just' vs. the 'adequate' or the 'right' vs. the 'practical' is also very much related to the debate over collective vs. individual compensation often brought up within the context of Palestinian refugees, as highlighted in Chapter 1. The development of international law, progressing from being state-centric towards incorporating individual human rights, established the norm that an international wrongful act, for which a state is held responsible, includes violations of human rights. In more concrete terms, this has accordingly put forward an increase in importance of the entitlement of refugees in particular – as victims of human rights violations – for compensation for their displacement and lost property. In their formulation of the aim for reparations and thus the relevant notion of the adequate redress, parties take into consideration the implications of advocating remedy for the victimised group as a whole or rather an individualised type of remedy. This issue is worthy of thorough examination by international law experts.

Identifying an aim of reparations in that sense is very much related to the idea of legitimising the reparations process. Would demands for reparations be based on moral contrition, political settlement or legal obligations? This issue is subject to further elaboration below.

Legitimising demands for reparations

Observations drawn from the analysis of the two case studies call for attention as to the importance of the basis of the reparations claim. The lack of legal rhetoric in the reparations process was a major characteristic of the German–Jewish case. Legal connotations were rather derived from the signing of the treaty, which set a precedent in terms of property restitution in international legal and diplomatic history. As noted in the analysis, legal instruments and a quest for rights were not the tools employed by the claimants to advance their demands for reparations. Instead, legitimacy of the claim was derived from the moral contrition the victims wished to extract from the perpetrator of the wrongful act. This absence of the language of rights, and calls for legal responsibility on behalf of the Jewish side, came as a result of the prevailing circumstances. Absence of international practice as well as the lack of legal precedence in this sphere are crucial factors to be noted. Instead, the moral element surfaced as the suitable means for reinforcing the claims for reparations.

Finding the suitable means for backing claims for reparations is also present in the case of Cyprus. In the Cypriot context, though, legitimacy came through legality. Analysis of the Cypriot case highlighted how Greek Cypriots derived the legitimacy and power of their demands from the international backing they gained to their interpretation of events in 1974 as a military occupation of Cyprus on behalf of Turkey. The declaration by the UN that the events of 1974 were illegal geared the position of Greek Cypriots towards demanding for remedies to displacement and dispossession as lost rights to be restored. Likewise, Turkish Cypriots, relying on the military strength of Turkey as their winning card, called for global compensation as their preferred solution. Both stances were correlations of treating the conflict on the basis of 'realities on the ground'.

Such observations call for the kind of legitimacy Palestinians are to invoke in their quest for reparations. Despite the very unfavourable balance of power between the two parties, in addition to the unsuccessful negotiation attempts, the Palestinian side holds an important card in its hands. Israeli persistence in dismissing 194 as a basis for a solution to the refugee problem is but an evident indicator to the empowering legitimacy engendered by legal instruments and UN resolutions. Rights, in the Palestinian context, come on two levels: on the one hand, further use of relevant UN resolutions and international law instruments directly related to their particular case as Palestinian refugees, such as 194. In parallel comes the use of international forums to further strengthen the international legitimacy of the Palestinian refugee cause. On the other hand, additional efforts dedicated to their rights as refugees in the body of legal instruments covering displacement are called for. Yet, while rights are insufficient on their own, banking on rights, further spreading of awareness of those rights and lobbying efforts make it more difficult to give up rightful demands under pressure during negotiations. We have seen how the Jewish claimants banked on moral contrition in their demands for reparations from Germany. Likewise, Cypriots banked on the illegitimacy of the events of 1974 to demand for lost rights of the displaced and dispossessed. Similarly, Palestinians ought to legitimise their demands for reparations.

Lobbying and preparation

A striking feature of the German–Jewish case lies in the evolution of the negotiations track with the Claims Conference. Significant indeed are the efforts of the Diaspora Jewish organisations, scattered in the four corners of the world, in their path towards uniting under the umbrella of one organisation. Small communities of Jews, acting as claimants for reparations, succeeded in forming one entity to speak in their name. This was a significant precedent of a non-state actor negotiating a reparations agreement with a state. Similarities with the Palestinian case are striking. This also brings into the limelight the issue of whether negotiating reparations or an agreement over the refugee issue should precede the establishment of a state or follow it. This also blends with the issue of the trade-offs with other components of the conflict.

Another matter worthy of observation in this context is the significant amount of effort undertaken by the Jewish side in preparation for their eventual demands for reparations from Germany. When the negotiations took off, a considerable amount of effort had been exerted on the Jewish side preparing data on property seized, damages suffered and restitution legislation. In the body of literature over the history of the German–Jewish negotiations of the reparations claims, several studies are mentioned as prominent in the efforts exerted on this track. The scholarly contribution in this regard constituted the basis of the Jewish claims against Germany formulated a few years later. Worth mentioning is Siegfried Moses, a pioneer in researching the question of war reparations in peace treaties, especially in the Treaty of Versailles, and how to draw conclusions in support of the Jewish cause (Sagi 1980: 17). Moses's booklet was the basis of Weizmann's important note to the Allied Powers in May 1945, launching the beginnings of the calls for reparations (Sagi 1980: 20). In parallel came Nehemiah Robinson's veteran study entitled *Indemnification and Reparations – Jewish Aspects*. Robinson, who later was the person to draft the Claims Conference claim, was one of the first to document the process of dispossession and persecution of the Jews, classified the kind of damage inflicted and estimated the value of property seized and presented his own detailed proposal of principles to be adopted in the demand for reparation (Pease 1976: 13–16).

As detailed in Chapter 1, archiving property losses, evaluation and identification of damages in the Palestinian context have been the main preoccupations of many Palestinian scholars. The early efforts of the UNCCP were also of great relevance and reliability despite the shortcomings. Such evaluations were of political relevance such as in the Taba talks calling for the use of the UNCCP and the Custodian for Absentee Property for assessment of losses. In his thorough discussion of the matter, Tamari explains that the gradual opening of important data archives that delineate the nature of property and land claims, as well as the social composition and distribution of the Palestinian refugee population, has made the issue of documenting refugee claims much more feasible than at any previous time. According to him, 'we can say without exaggeration that these data bases and UNRWA and UNCCP files contain the most extensive and reasonably reliable information about the social attributes as well as socioeconomic and property claims of the Palestinian refugees' (Tamari 2005: 248–252, Tamari and Zureik 2001). Therefore, there is a further need to make more use of available archives and advance expertise on identification and evaluation of losses in preparation for the resumption of negotiations over Palestinian refugee reparations.

This chapter has presented the main observations derived from the comparison of the case studies. It argues that examination of the two case studies does not suggest the presence of a model for reparations. Nevertheless, while a model remains elusive, a reparations pattern was discerned from the comparison. Such a pattern indicated that the aim of reparations was the factor influencing the perception of the wrongful act and thus the nature of redress to that wrongful act. Form of reparations was, therefore, the last in the chain of a reparations process. Such a pattern thus refutes the notion that agreement between the concerned parties over the form of reparations is the first step towards a successful reparations process. When compared with this pattern, the Taba talks – the round of negotiations covering the refugee file the most – proved to be a distorted version of the pattern detected by the comparative analysis. The chapter has demonstrated how the process of reparations in Taba went through a discussion of form without agreeing on a perception of the wrongful act and thus on the way to address it and redress it. Nonetheless, the final section of the chapter has further synthesised the observations brought out by the comparison. Drawing on those observations, a number of themes present an attempt to enhance prospects of reparations to Palestinian refugees. Highlighting issues such as opportunity, establishing a responsibility, trade-offs with other conflict components, identifying the aim of reparations, legitimisation of demands for reparations and the importance of preparation and lobbying efforts are all tracks open for further enhancement of Palestinian refugee efforts in their ongoing search for reparations to their displacement and dispossession predicament.

Conclusion

In its issue of 22 November 2007, *The Economist* dedicated its front cover to George W. Bush, stating that 'Mr Palestine [was] the only man who could make it happen.' The occasion was the Annapolis summit about to take place a few days later in the frantic attempt by the outgoing US president to 'make it happen' before he kissed the White House goodbye. After years of dormant diplomacy, the Bush Administration hosted a resonating event inviting top Israeli and Palestinian leaders, together with a wide range of high-profile Arab and international heads of state and diplomats. The optimistic note underlying *The Economist*'s hopes for peace in Palestine turned rather sour. The end of 2008 came and went with neither an independent Palestinian state, nor a peace agreement as promised by Bush in his opening speech at Annapolis.[1] Instead, the beginning of 2009 ushered in a full-scale Israeli war on Gaza, a newly elected right-wing Israeli Government and a political rift between the leaders of the Hamas movement and the Palestinian Authority led by Mahmoud Abbas (Abu Mazen).

On its own, Annapolis may be dismissed as much ado about nothing, having brought no life to the peace process it sought to resurrect. Limited to the fanfare and an exchange of speeches, Annapolis wasn't even a negotiations round. Yet, when it comes to tracing policy strategies on the fate of the Palestinian refugee issue, George Bush's last year in office laid a renewed indication of the American approach to settling the Israeli–Palestinian conflict.

Bush's speech, as well as the joint statement, included many references to the nature of the Palestinian state-to-be, denunciation of terror, security and peace. That these were the primary concerns of the peace dilemma preoccupying Bush is no new revelation. From here, unpacking his understanding of peace, ending the conflict and how to achieve a settlement, add perspective to his vision of settling the refugee issue. Would this conform to a process of reparations?

According to the US president, 'the parties further commit to continue the implementation of the ongoing obligations of the road map until they reach a peace treaty. The United States will monitor and judge the fulfilment of the commitment of both sides of the road map.' To the American administration, the basis for a solution was as vague as the Road Map was. Significantly, when it comes to negotiating peace and contentious conflict issues, there is no reference either to acknowledgement of injustices, clear basis for a solution, nor an attempt to bring narratives of the two parties together. The refugee issue was not even mentioned in Bush's speech. Moreover, the only reference to the notion of 'responsibility' appeared in reference to the Palestinian side, when Bush said, 'They [the Palestinians] must show that a Palestinian state will accept its responsibility and have the capability to be a source of stability and peace for its own citizens, for the people of Israel and for the whole region.' On the other hand, Israel's part in the peace-seeking game went as follows: 'Israel must demonstrate its support for the creation of a prosperous and successful Palestinian state by removing unauthorized outposts, ending settlement expansion, and finding other ways for the Palestinian Authority to exercise its responsibilities without compromising Israel's security.'

The Israeli speech went in line with the previous position maintained by successive Israeli governments. Prime Minister Ehud Olmert declared he was at Annapolis 'to extend a hand in peace, a hand which marks the beginning of historic reconciliation between us and you, the Palestinians, and all of the Arab nations'. Yet, Olmert's understanding of historic reconciliation departed from ignoring history: 'we came here today not in order to settle historical accounts between us and you about what caused the confrontations and the hatred, and what for many years has prevented a compromise, a settlement of peace.' When he added, 'I know that this pain [living in camps] and this humiliation are the deepest foundations which fomented the ethos of hatred toward us. We are not indifferent to this suffering. We are not oblivious to the tragedies that you have experienced,' he maintained the Israeli view of the perpetuation of the refugee presence in the camps.

Olmert went on expressing views on the refugee issue with a statement whose contents can be traced in public statements made by Bush two months later, as we shall see below.

> I believe that, in the course of negotiations between us, we will find

> the right way, as part of an international effort, in which we will participate, to assist these Palestinians [refugees] in finding a proper framework for their future, in the Palestinian state that will be established in the territories agreed upon between us. Israel will be part of an international mechanism that will assist in finding a solution to this problem.
>
> (Olmert in his Annapolis speech)

Abbas, on his part, also maintained the Palestinian position, which was reiterated as an all-encompassing Arab–Israeli peace process. The Palestinian leader called for:

> a reciprocal strategic willingness that would basically lead to ending the occupation of all Palestinian occupied territories in 1967, including East Jerusalem, as well as the Syrian Golan and what remains occupied from Lebanese territories, and to resolve all other issues relating to the conflict, especially the Palestinian refugees question in all its political, humanitarian, individual and common aspects, consistent with Resolution 194, as emphasized by the Arab peace initiative and the participation of sister states that host refugees and carry huge burdens in this regard.

Such was the position of both parties, a position which conforms to the evolution of diplomatic efforts to reparations, as we have seen throughout this book. Over the years and throughout the history of the conflict, Palestinians and Israelis have had divergent positions over the issue of refugees. Palestinians were demanding lost rights of the displaced and dispossessed, while Israel maintained a no-rights policy towards the injustice at the heart of the conflict. The Israeli position was to treat the Palestinian refugee problem as a humanitarian issue requiring a humanitarian solution. Therefore, we have seen in the last chapter how the absence of a common perception of the wrongful act between the two parties has distorted the search for reparations, as we have learnt from the Cypriot and German–Jewish experiences. Annapolis was no exception to the evolution of reparations in the diplomacy of peace-making between Israelis and Palestinians.

In the eleventh hour of his presidency, Bush made two visits to Jerusalem in which he further weaved the vision for a settlement he had outlined at Annapolis. Upon his arrival in Jerusalem in January 2008, Bush said he 'detected a new opportunity for peace', adding in his detailed press statement delivered at the King David Hotel that 'we have to look forward to the creation of a Palestinian state and new international mechanisms, including compensation, to resolve the refugee issue.'[2] With such a statement, Bush had clearly gone one step further by invoking the issue of compensation to Palestinian refugees in the Jerusalem press conference. From a reparations perspective, the good news about this inclusion is that Bush acknowledged that a notion of peace had to address the Palestinian refugee issue as an element of the Arab–Israeli conflict. The good news is not limited to 'addressing' the refugee issue, though, but also extends to invoking a form of redress in the form of compensation. On the other hand, the bad news associated with these declarations is that Bush's notion of reparations is problematic for a number of reasons. First, it confines reparations to financial compensation and dismisses any other form of reparations. Also absent from Bush's notion of reparations is any mention of repairing an injustice and acknowledging a wrongful act. Bush's stance was still ignoring how proceeding with reparations requires recognition of the injustice at the heart of the conflict.

Dismissing the narrative of the party seeking reparations was further pursued on Bush's subsequent visit to Jerusalem in May 2008:

> We gather to mark a momentous occasion. Sixty years ago in Tel Aviv, David Ben-Gurion proclaimed Israel's independence, founded on the 'natural right of the Jewish people to be masters of their own fate'. What followed was more than the establishment of a new country. It was the redemption of an ancient promise given to Abraham and Moses and David – a homeland for the chosen people Eretz Yisrael.[3]

Bush's address to the Knesset on the occasion of the sixtieth birthday of the state of Israel was a celebration of the victory of one side and a denial of the catastrophe suffered by the other side. The past was far from being acknowledged. The envisioned future is thus standing on an unsteady basis.

With George Bush gone and a new administration now in power, Palestinians, Israelis and the whole world turn hopeful eyes to the president in the White House. The story of reparations to Palestinian refugees is still ongoing.

Notes

Introduction

1 The full text of Rudd's speech is available on the Australian Government's website: http://www.australia.gov.au/about-australia/our-country/video-national-apology-to-the-stolen-generations
2 Additional details on the examples invoked in this introduction are provided in Chapter 2.
3 'normal place of residence was Palestine during the period 1 June 1946 to 15 May 1948 and who lost both home and means of livelihood as a result of the 1948 conflict' and their descendants
4 For example, even within the terms of UNRWA's definition, its statistics may not be fully representative. Some refugees have never registered with the organisation, for example. In other instances – particularly refugees in Lebanon – UNRWA figures are significantly inflated because many refugees have left Lebanon but are still included in UNRWA's records. For a discussion on the scope and limitations of UNRWA's definition and figures, see Takkenberg (1998: 68–83).
5 For an account of why Palestinian refugees fall under the mandate of UNRWA rather than UNHCR, see Takkenberg (1998: 28–32).
6 For a detailed overview of the status and aspects of livelihood of Palestinian refugees in the Arab host states (Jordan, Syria, Lebanon and Egypt) see for example El-Abed (2009), Shafie (2003) and Shafie (2007). For the situation of Palestinian refugees in the Gaza Strip and the West Bank, see Rempel (2006).
7 This issue is further discussed in Chapter 5.

1 Reparations in the Palestinian context

1 Some of the most significant contributions of the Israeli New Historians are found in the following sources: Segev (1986), Flapan (1987), Morris (1987), Shlaim (1998), Pappe (1992) and Pappe (2006).
2 See for example Masalha (1991), Morris (1991) and Finkelstein (1992).
3 All these materials are on hard copy and on microfilm.
4 Hadawi states that apart from the political considerations involved, the

revised survey shows that the Arab indigenous inhabitants of Palestine still own about 92 per cent of the total territory of Palestine, which they regard as their homeland, against a Jewish land ownership of roughly 8 per cent (Hadawi 1988: 114).

5 According to Kubursi, a list of Arab losses in Palestine should include the following items: immovable property, movable property, lost opportunities and psychological damage (Kubursi 1988: 121).

6 For a thorough discussion of Jewish property claims against Arab countries and their implications on the Israeli–Palestinian negotiations, see Michael Fischbach's latest study on the issue (Fischbach 2008).

7 For more details see Brynen and Tansley (1995).

8 The other working groups are: Arms Control and Regional Security, Regional Economic Development, Water and Environment.

9 For details see Peters (1996), Brynen and Tansley (1995) and Brynen et al. (2003).

10 Altogether, the RWG held eight official meetings between May 1992 and May 1996.

11 The Declaration of Principles on Interim Self-Government Arrangements (13 September 1993) can be found at: http://www.nad-plo.org/inner.php?view=nego_nego_SiAgreem_nsigned1p

12 The other final status issues are settlements, security arrangements, borders and Jerusalem.

13 For a detailed account of the negotiations preceding the signing of the DoP, see Abbas (1995). See also Shlomo Ben-Ami's account of the Oslo process (Ben-Ami 2005: 201–239). See also (Agha et al. 2003: 29–6).

14 For a general detailed account of the Camp David negotiations see Swisher (2004), Beilin (2004: 147–173), Abdul Rahman (2003), Hanieh (2001), Agha and Malley (2001) and Morris and Barak (2002).

15 The Moratinos Document was published in *Hdaretz* on 14 February 2002 (Eldar 2002).

16 The International Commission shall consist of the Palestinian state, host countries, Israel and members of the international community, including the United Nations, the World Bank, The European Union and the G8, as well as other relevant international institutions. The International Commission shall have full and exclusive responsibility for implementing the resolution of the refugee issue in all its aspects.

17 The text of the Road Map can be found at: http://www.nad-plo.org/inner.php?view=nego_peace_road_Primary_ciroadm2p

18 For full details on the implications on the refugee issue, see Brynen (2003).

19 The text of the Arab League's Beirut Declaration of 28 March 2002 can be found at: http://www.nad-plo.org/inner.php?view=nego_peace_saudi-int_Primary%20Documents_cisaudip

20 These programmes would be intended to exchange historical narratives, foster educational contacts, and promote cross-community programmes. They could also include 'appropriate ways of commemorating those villages and communities that existed prior to 1949' (Article 7.14.iv). The international commission is to form a series of technical committees: determination of refugee status, a compensation committee, a committee for

remuneration of host countries, a rehabilitation and development committee, a committee to administer the 'refugeehood fund', and a 'permanent place of residence' (PPR) committee.

21 According to Brynen, although the agreement does not spell this out, its implication seems to be that Israel will finance all or most property claims, while other aspects of compensation (to host countries and to a proposed 'refugeehood' fund) will be financed by the international community (Brynen 2004).

22 See Ottawa Workshop (1997). Final Report (1999).

23 These activities were intended to facilitate Palestinian–Israeli dialogue, expert analysis, joint problem-solving and limited pre-negotiation of the refugee issue. For full details, see Brynen et al. (2003).

24 Except for a brief initiative in the early years of the conflict when restitution was considered (Masalha 2001).

2 Reparations: in search of a definition

1 The ILC Articles on State Responsibility can be found at: http://untreaty.un.org/ilc/texts/instruments/english/commentaries/9_6_2001.pdf
The Draft Principles on reparations can be found at: http://www2.ohchr.org/english/law/remedy.htm

2 Report available at: http://www2.ohchr.org/english/law/remedy.htm

3 Historically, the Palestine refugee compensation issue was first raised by the UN mediator, Count Folke Bernadotte, in his September 1948 recommendations to the UN proposing 'payment of adequate compensation for the property of those [refugees] choosing not to return [to their homes in Israel].' His proposals received international backing by virtue of UNGA 194, which incorporated, with slight modifications, many of Bernadotte's recommendations, including payment of compensation (Peretz 1995: 2).

4 According to Lynk, 194 spoke to several primary features of the compensation question, all of which flowed directly from the Bernadotte report: 1) First it stated that those refugees willing to live at peace with their neighbours were entitled to the restitution of their homes at the earliest practicable time; 2) Those refugees not returning home should be entitled to compensation for their lost property; 3) Those refugees who do return and find their property damaged or destroyed should be compensated for their losses.

5 For a detailed discussion of Fischbach's arguments, see Fischbach (2005: 75–81).

6 'The right of the Arab refugees to return to their homes in Jewish-controlled territory at the earliest possible date . . . and their repatriation, resettlement and economic and social rehabilitation, and payment of *adequate* compensation for the property of those choosing not to return . . .' (Progress Report of the United Nations Mediator on Palestine, UN Doc. A/648 (18 September 1948)).

7 The notions of full compensation and adequate compensation are discussed later in this chapter.

8 Other recent contributions to the literature on reparations are, for

example, De Greiff (2006), Miller and Kumar (2007), Brophy (2006), Torpey (2006), Lenzerini (2008) and Berg and Schaefer (2008).
9 Brooks' key study is outlined in Brooks (1999a). For an abridged version of Brooks' theory of redress, see Brooks (2003).
10 For a detailed comprehensive analysis of the Black Redress Movement, see Brooks (2004).
11 Such as amnesty, affirmative action and municipal services.
12 For a detailed analysis on the TRC in South Africa, see for example Minow (1998) and Brooks (1999a).
13 In Barkan's mapping of the restitution phenomena, another sphere of restitution cases resulted from the post-colonial condition and the expansion of civil rights and indigenous minorities as entities. Since the 1980s, a widespread expansion of indigenous rights has occurred negotiating property rights (land, economic resources and cultural property), native Americans, Australia, New Zealand, Canada (Barkan 2003: 96).
14 Minow particularly discusses trials, truth commissions and reparations.
15 This point highlighted by Minow is observed in the case of Northern Cyprus, where Turkish settlers have occupied property belonging to displaced Greek Cypriots. This matter has been taken into consideration by the Annan Peace Plan, as discussed in Chapter 4. The same issue is also valid in the case of Palestinian property confiscated by the Israeli Custodian for Absentee Property in the aftermath of the exodus of 1948.
16 Example of landowners vs. non-landowners in Palestine.
17 This was an issue present in the debates over reparations and privatisation after Communism. See for example the arguments put forward by Teitel (2000: 129–138).
18 For a thorough discussion of the significance of apology in international practice, see for example Marrus (2006).
19 For more on the Australian reparations case, see Barkan (2000), Thompson (2007) and Samy (2008).
20 Under the comfort women system, an estimated 200,000 women were held as sex slaves for the Japanese Imperial Army during the Second World War.
21 Atif Kubursi's research on Palestinian refugee compensation is presented in Chapter 1 of this volume.

3 The German–Jewish Reparations Agreements of 1952

1 In the past decades, new compensation agreements have been negotiated with Germany as well as with other European governments. The number and characteristics of those agreements falls beyond the scope of the present study, as does the issue of the proper/improper allocation of compensation funds. For information on other subsequent reparations agreements, see for example Finkelstein (2001), Finkelstein (2003), Timm (1997), Sieradzka and Lerman (1994).
2 Early in the negotiations, Israel announced that of its overall claim of $1.5 billion, it would demand one-third from East Germany so that the amount claimed from West Germany was finally reduced to $1 billion. The $715 million Israel finally agreed upon represented 71 per cent of its claim; the

Claims Conference settled for 21 per cent of its original $500 million demand. Thirty per cent of the total sum was paid in cash for Israeli oil purchases from Britain. The remainder was paid in the form of goods, machinery and equipment in accordance with a schedule of delivery, which was part of the agreement (Rubinstein 1962: 34–38).

3 The number of payments to Israel in the agreement was fixed at 12. There were, however, in fact 14 payments (between 1 April 1953 and 31 March 1966) since Germany utilised its rights to reduce the payments yearly.

4 On 18 March 1953, the Bundestag approved the Reparations Agreement by a two-thirds majority. Two days later, representatives of the *Lander* in the Bundestag unanimously voted in favour. On 22 March 1953, the Government of Israel approved the agreement, with implementation completed in 1965.

5 The Jewish Agency was one of the major Jewish organisations catering for the Jewish community in Palestine, prior to the establishment of the state of Israel in 1948.

6 Throughout its first years, Israel's foreign policy was formulated against a backdrop of chronic economic stress, the primary reason for which was massive immigration (Bialer 1991: 237–238, Ginor 1972/73).

7 For more information on the Israeli public opposition, see for example Lustick (2005: 116–117).

8 Israel's representative in Paris, Maurice Fischer, proposed a solution. A non-Israeli Jewish figure would organise an informal, secret meeting between senior-echelon Israeli and German participants. Fischer suggested that the meeting be held in a neutral country and stressed that the initiative for the meeting had to come from the Germans (Auerbach 1991: 279).

9 The role Goldmann played in convening the Diaspora organisations in preparation for the birth of one single organisation, and in formulating the separate reparations claim, is crucial to the history of the reparations treaty and is elaborated upon later in the chapter.

10 Nineteen organisations ultimately endorsed negotiations and two abstained. Only Agudat Yisrael opposed direct negotiations on the basis of Adenauer's September 1951 statement to the Bundestag. Although the Agudat supported Israel's claim for reparations through the Allied Powers, it rejected the German attempt to raise reparations as a means for making 'moral and material amends'. In its view, Germany must be compelled to return what had been stolen, but it should be granted no measure of moral rehabilitation by reparations (Zweig 2001: 29).

11 Prof. Carlo Schimd, spokesman for the Social Democratic Party, suggested that a unified federal bill be enacted that would grant all heirless Jewish property and indemnification claims to the state of Israel. On 30 August 1951, Erich Luth, director of the Hamburg State Press Office, and Rudolf Kustermeier, editor-in-chief of *Die Welt*, published articles under the title 'we beg Israel for peace' (Vogel 1968/69).

12 Lustick (2005: 107–115) presents a thorough analysis of the political expediency of Adenauer's speech.

13 Even Dr Kurt Schumacher, chairman of the Social Democratic Party and

Adenauer's outspoken political opponent on most major issues, was of like mind on the question of reparation (P.G. 1954: 256).

14 The nature of the legal status of the CC prevented the Federal Republic from signing a 'treaty' with it.

15 As mentioned earlier, many of those Jewish organisations had acquired a considerable amount of expertise and experience in the general area of restitution, in the work of the successor organisations and in the rehabilitation of displaced persons. See for example Bentwick (1965).

16 Of this 33.3 per cent, 15 per cent was to be spent outside of Israel and the balance (18.3 per cent) was to be spent in Israel by the organisations on their own welfare programmes within the new state.

17 The German delegation's initial proposal was a sum of $750 million in settlement. Certain German banking interests were seeking to link the German–Israeli negotiations in The Hague with the settlement of Germany's pre-war commercial debts, which were being negotiated in London at the same time. When the debt conference was resumed in London, Hermann Abs, chief of the German delegation, insisted that any financial obligations to Israel would depend on the outcome of the conference (P.G. 1954: 262). At that time Germany was negotiating in London to obtain a clarification of all her foreign debts and was trying to obtain an overall reduction. The reparations to Israel should therefore, in its view, have been reduced in the same proportion as the German commercial debts – a proportion still unknown when the proposal was made (Sagi 1980: 108).

18 These 125,000 people were the remnant of the massive post-war refugee problem and were largely persons who could not be resettled because they represented problems of health, age, family composition or occupational category.

4 Cyprus

1 Details of the historical background of the Cyprus conflict may be found in Dodd (1988), Richmond (1998), Tocci (2004), Joseph (1997), Hannay (2005), Scherer (1997) and Mallinson (2005).

2 British rule began in Cyprus in 1878 when the island was leased to Britain by the Ottomans. Britain unilaterally annexed it in 1914 and declared it a crown colony on 1 May 1925. After the independence of Cyprus in 1960, Britain retained two military sovereign bases on the island covering 99 square miles.

3 When it gained independence, Cyprus comprised a Greek Cypriot majority of roughly 80 per cent of the population, while the Turkish Cypriots composed about 18 per cent. Recent statistics in 2001 placed the Greek Cypriots at 77 per cent of the total population of the island and Turkish Cypriots at 18 per cent (CIA online world factbook on Cyprus available at http://www.cia.gov/ last accessed in March 2009).

4 It is widely agreed that the Cypriot constitution required a high degree of cooperation between the two communities in order to function adequately and smoothly (for details on the constitution see, for example, Hannay 2005).

5 On the events of 1963, see for example Stephen (1997: 10–13). For details on the early period of the conflict, see Sonyel (1999: 16–53).
6 In 1963, the Turkish Cypriots withdrew from participation in the institutional structures of the state. A major cause of this withdrawal was a dispute over fiscal matters. From this time on the security situation deteriorated steadily, with extensive harassment, particularly of Turkish Cypriots by Greek Cypriots and of Greek Cypriots by paramilitary nationalists, with numerous atrocities committed by both sides. The much less numerous Turkish Cypriots tended to abandon their houses scattered in villages and towns where Greek Cypriots were in majority and to group themselves together in enclaves where they could better defend themselves (Hannay 2005: 4).
7 On Greek and Turkish rivalry over Cyprus, see for example Richmond (1998: xv). This matter is discussed further in the section on external intervention later in the chapter.
8 For details on the events of 1974, see for example Joseph (1985: 103–111), Scherer (1997: 35–46) and Stephen (1997: 23–28).
9 In 1983, the Turkish-held area declared itself the 'Turkish Republic of Northern Cyprus', recognised only by Turkey.
10 For an account of the Turkish Cypriot perspective, see Ertekun (1999).
11 For a detailed account of the overall Greek Cypriot perspective and the domestic politics, see Stavrinides (1999).
12 For a general overview of the substance of those core issues, see Hannay (2005: 27–47) and Ediz and Tsatsas (2002).
13 Refusing to contemplate any right of return, Turkish Cypriots placed great weight on the precedent of the population transfer between Greece and Turkey in 1923–24, which had been conducted on this basis (Hannay 2005: 38–39).
14 For a detailed account of Greek perspectives of the Cypriot conflict, see Zambouras (1999).
15 For a detailed analysis of the Turkish perspective, see Dodd (1999b).
16 For details on American and Soviet superpower nature of involvement, see Joseph (1985: 117–158).
17 For details on NATO, see Joseph (1997: 163–192).
18 For a detailed account of the politics of UN involvement at early stages of the Cypriot conflict, see for example Joseph (1997: 195–233) and Richmond (1998: 87–131).
19 For details on the Vienna Talks, see Richmond (1998: 139–147).
20 For details on the 1977 High-Level Agreement, see Richmond (1998: 147–153).
21 For details on the second High-Level Agreement of 1979, see Richmond (1998: 153–157).
22 Proximity talks are talks in which the parties do not meet directly, but communicate through an intermediary.
23 The UN Secretary-General Boutros Boutros-Ghali's 'Set of Ideas' were at a stage of preparation during 1990–91 on the basis of consultations by UN officers with both sides of the conflict, including discussions in Athens and Ankara.
24 For a discussion of the Set of Ideas, see for example Dodd (1988: 44–51).

25 The complete version of Annan Plan 5 can be found on the UN website: www.un.org
26 I wish to acknowledge the insightful comments provided by Dr Yiouli Taki regarding this issue during my visit to Cyprus in November 2004.
27 For further details on the matter, see Chatham House's briefing paper on Cyprus (Potier 2005).
28 Estimates of their size varied, but 80,000, a remarkably high proportion of the total population of north Cyprus of fewer than 200,000, was generally regarded as closer to the mark.
29 For further analysis of the impact of the politics of the EU accession, see Brewin (2000).
30 For another discussion of the Cyprus problem from an EU perspective while considering accession, see Axt (1999).
31 Turkish Cypriots maintain that the government in Cyprus is unconstitutional and thus should not be recognised as the legitimate government of Cyprus.
32 According to Richmond, the SC did so partly because of the need to find a responsible party to deal with in order to help stop the bloodshed in Cyprus, partly because of pressure from the UK and the US, which wanted to prevent a wider escalation of the conflict, and also because of U'Thant's sympathy towards newly independent states. Richmond believes an examination of the period indicates that the resolution was a hasty response that gave the need to deal with a responsible party a higher priority than the local constitutional aspect because the international ramifications of an escalation in the dispute were deemed far more serious by Western powers than the situation of the Cypriots (Richmond 1998: xx).
33 For a detailed update on the recent diplomatic developments between Greek and Turkish Cypriots over the various elements of the conflict, see the most recent International Crisis Group (ICG) reports (23 June 2008 and 10 January 2008).

5 Prospects of reparations to Palestinian refugees

1 An analysis of the shift in urgency can be found in the International Crisis Group report (2006: 5–8).

Conclusion

1 The full text of all the speeches delivered at Annapolis can be found on the Ha'aretz website at: http://www.haaretz.com/hasen/objects/pages/PrintArticleEn.jhtml?itemNo=928652
2 Full transcript of Bush's press statement is available on the BBC website at: http://news.bbc.co.uk/1/hi/world/middle_east/7182041.stm
3 Full text of Bush's speech to the Knesset on 15 May 2008 is available on the White House website at: http://georgewbush-whitehouse.archives.gov/news/releases/2008/05/print/20080515-1.html

Bibliography

Abbas, M. (Abu Mazen) (1995) *Through Secret Channels: the Road to Oslo: Senior PLO Leader Abu Mazen's Revealing Story of the Negotiations with Israel* (Reading: Garnett Publishing).

Abdul Rahman, A. (2003) *Revisiting Israeli–Palestinian Peace Negotiations on the Palestinian Refugee Problem: 1991–2000*. Badil Expert Forum: The Role of International Law in Peacemaking and Crafting Durable Solutions for Palestinian Refugees, 22–23 May.

Abowd, T. and Tamari, S. (1999) Palestinian Refugees and the Palestinian Israeli negotiations. *Journal of Palestine Studies*, 29 (1) Fall, pp.81–89.

Abu-Sitta, S. (1999) *Restitution and Compensation*. Paper presented at the Workshop on Compensation for Palestinian Refugees, International Development Research Centre, Ottawa, 14–15 July.

Agha, H. et al (2003) *Track II Diplomacy: Lessons from the Middle East* (Cambridge, Massachusetts: The MIT Press).

Agha, H. and Malley, R. (2001) Camp David: The Tragedy of Errors. *New York Review of Books*, 48 (13) 9 August.

Akram, S., Dajani, S. and Thiele, B. (2005) *Re-claiming Palestine: The Legal Basis for Rights of Return and Restitution*. For the Record, no. 230/2 August (Washington, DC: The Palestine Center).

Al-Husseini, J. (1999) *Observations on Compensation in the Palestinian Refugees' Case*. Paper presented at the Workshop on Compensation for Palestinian Refugees, International Development Research Centre, Ottawa, 14–15 July.

Annan, K. (2004) *Report of the Secretary-General on his Mission of Good Offices in Cyprus*. S/2004/437, 28 May.

Annan, K, (2003) *Report of the Secretary-General on his Mission of Good Offices in Cyprus*. S/2003/398, 1 April.

Arzt, D. (1999) *The Right to Compensation: Basic Principles under International Law*. Paper presented at the Workshop on Compensation for Palestinian Refugees, International Development Research Centre, Ottawa, 14–15 July.

Auerbach, Y. (1991) 'Ben-Gurion and Reparations from Germany', in R. Zweig (ed.) *David Ben-Gurion: Politics and Leadership in Israel* (London: Frank Cass).

Axt, H-J. (1999) 'The Island of Cyprus and the European Union', in C. Dodd (ed.) *The Need for New Perspectives* (Huntingdon, UK: The Eothen Press).

Badil Resource Centre (1999) *The Impact of Return on Compensation for Palestinian Refugees*. Paper presented at the Workshop on Compensation for Palestinian Refugees, International Development Research Centre, Ottawa, 14–15 July.

Balabkins, N. (1971) *West German Reparations to Israel* (New Brunswick, NJ: Rutgers University Press).

Balabkins, N. (1967) The Birth of Restitution: The Making of the Shilumim Agreement. *Wiener Library Bulletin*, 21 (4) new series 9, pp.8–16.

Barkan, E. (2005a) History on the Line: Engaging History, Managing Conflict and Reconciliation. *History Workshop Journal*, 59, pp.229–236.

Barkan, E. (2005b) 'Considerations Toward Accepting Historical Responsibility', in A. Lesch and I. Lustick (eds) *Exile and Return: Predicaments of Palestinians and Jews* (Philadelphia: University of Pennsylvania Press).

Barkan, E. (2003) 'Restitution and Amending Historical Injustices in International Morality', in J. Torpey (ed.) *Politics and the Past: On Repairing Historical Injustices* (Lanham: Rowman & Littlefield Publishers, Inc.).

Barkan, E. (2000) *The Guilt of Nations: Restitution and Negotiating Historical Injustices* (Baltimore: The Johns Hopkins University Press).

Beilin, Y. (2004) *The Path to Geneva: The Quest for a Permanent Agreement 1996–2004* (New York: RDV Books).

Bell, C., Campbell, C. and Aolain, F. (2004) Justice Discourses in Transition. *Social and Legal Studies*, 13 (3), pp.305–328.

Ben-Ami, S. (2005) *Scars of War Wounds of Peace: The Israeli–Arab Tragedy* (London: Weidenfeld & Nicolson).

Bentwick, N. (1965) Nazi Spoliation and German Restitution: The Work of the United Restitution Office. *Leo Baeck Institute Yearbook*, 10, pp.204–224.

Benvenisti, E. (2003) *Modalities for Processing Refugee Claims for Compensation*. Paper presented at the International Conference on Israel and the Palestinian Refugees, Max Planck Institute for Comparative Public and International Law, Heidelberg, 11–13 July.

Benvenisti, E. (1999) *Principles and Procedures for Compensating Palestinian Refugees: International Legal Perspectives*. Paper presented at the Workshop on Compensation for Palestinian Refugees, International Development Research Centre, Ottawa, 14–15 July.

Berg, M. and Schaefer, B. (eds) (2008) *Historical Justice in International Perspective: How Societies are Trying to Right the Wrongs of the Past* (Cambridge: Cambridge University Press).

Bialer, U. (1991) 'Israel's Global Foreign Policy: 1948–1956', in L. Silberstein (ed.) *New Perspectives on Israeli History: The Early Years of the State* (New York: New York University Press).

Blondel, J. (1995) *Comparative Government: An Introduction* (New York: Harvester Wheatsheaf).

Bradley, M. (2005) The Conditions of Just Return: State Responsibility and Restitution for Refugees. *RSC Working Paper*, (21).

Brewin, C. (2000) *The European Union and Cyprus* (Huntingdon, UK: The Eothen Press).

Brewin, C. (1999) 'Turkey, Greece and the European Union', in C. Dodd (ed.) *The Need for New Perspectives* (Huntingdon, UK: The Eothen Press).

Brooks, R. (2004) *Atonement and Forgiveness: A New Model for Black Reparations* (Berkeley: University of California Press).

Brooks, R. (2003) 'Reflections on Reparations', in J. Torpey (ed.) *Politics and the Past: On Repairing Historical Injustices* (Lanham, MD: Rowman & Littlefield Publishers, Inc.).

Brooks, R. (1999a) 'The Age of Apology', in R. Brooks (ed.) *When Sorry Isn't Enough: The Controversy over Apologies and Reparations for Human Injustice* (New York: New York University Press).

Brooks, R. (1999b) 'Japanese American Redress and the American Political Process: a Unique Achievement', in R. Brooks (ed.) *When Sorry Isn't Enough: The Controversy over Apologies and Reparations for Human Injustice* (New York: New York University Press).

Brophy, A. (2006) *Reparations: Pro & Con* (Oxford: Oxford University Press).

Brynen, R. (2004) *The Geneva Accord and the Palestinian Refugee Issue*. Department of Political Science, McGill University, available at http://www.arts.mcgill.ca/mepp/new_prrn/research/research_papers.htm#articles

Brynen, R. (2003) *The Roadmap and the Refugees*. Paper presented at the IDRC Stocktaking II Conference on Palestinian Refugee Research, Ottawa, 17–20 June.

Brynen, R. (1999) *Financing Palestinian Refugee Compensation*. Paper presented at the Workshop on Compensation for Palestinian Refugees, International Development Research Centre, Ottawa, 14–15 July.

Brynen, R. (1998) *Palestinian Refugees and the Middle East Peace Process*. New Hampshire International Seminar/Yale-Maria Lecture in Middle East Studies, University of New Hampshire, 3 April.

Brynen, R. (1997) Much ado about Nothing? The Refugee Working Group and the Perils of Multilateral Quasi-negotiation. *International Negotiation*, 2 (2) November.

Brynen, R. and Tansley, J. (1995) The Refugee Working Group of the Middle East Multilateral Peace Negotiations. *Palestine–Israel Journal*, 2 (4).

Brynen, R. et al. (2003) *The 'Ottawa Process': An examination of Canada's Track Two Involvement in the Palestinian Refugee Issue*. Paper presented at the IDRC Stocktaking II Conference on Palestinian Refugee Research, Ottawa, 17–20 June.

Caplan, N. (1993) *The Lausanne Conference, 1949: A Case Study in Middle*

East Peacemaking (Tel Aviv: Moshe Dayan Center for Middle Eastern and African Studies, Tel Aviv University).

Cattan, H. (1969) *Palestine, the Arabs & Israel: The Search for Justice* (London: Longman).

Central Intelligence Agency (2009) *World Fact Book: Cyprus* (Washington, DC: CIA). Available at https://www.cia.gov/library/publications/the-world-factbook/geos/cy.html

Clinton, W. (2001) *Transcript of Clinton Remarks at Israel Policy Forum Gala, January 7th, 2001*. U.S. Newswire, Washington, 8 January.

Collier, D. (1991) 'The Comparative Method: Two Decades of Change', in D. Rustow and K. Erickson (eds) *Comparative Political Dynamics: Global Research Perspectives* (New York: Harper Collins).

Compensation (1997) A Stocktaking Conference on Palestinian Refugee Research, Ottawa, 8–9 December.

Crawford, J. (2002) *The International Law Commission's Articles on State Responsibility* (Cambridge: Cambridge University Press).

De Greiff, P. (ed.) (2006) *The Handbook of Reparations* (Oxford: Oxford University Press).

Deutschkron, I. (1970) *Bonn and Jerusalem: The Strange Coalition* (Philadelphia: Chilton Book Company).

Dodd, C. (1999a) 'A Historical Overview', in C. Dodd (ed.) *The Need for New Perspectives* (Huntingdon, UK: The Eothen Press).

Dodd, C. (1999b) 'Cyprus in Turkish Politics and Foreign Policy', in C. Dodd (ed.) *The Need for New Perspectives* (Huntingdon, UK: The Eothen Press).

Dodd, C. (1988) *The Cyprus Imbroglio* (Huntingdon, UK: The Eothen Press).

Dogan, M. and Pelassy D. (1990) *How to Compare Nations: Strategies in Comparative Politics* (London: Chatham House Publishers).

Dumper, M. (2006) 'Global Perspectives on Palestinian Refugee Repatriation', in M. Dumper (ed.) *Palestinian Refugee Repatriation: Global Perspectives* (London: Routledge).

Ediz, T. and Tsatsas, M. (2002) *Cyprus: Defying History*. Chatham House Report, 10 December.

El-Abed, O. (2009) *Unprotected: Palestinians in Egypt since 1948* (Washington, DC & Ottawa: Institute for Palestine Studies & International Development Research Centre).

El-Abed, O. (2004b) *Palestinian Refugees in Egypt*. Forced Migration Online Research Guide. Available at http://www.forcedmigration.org/guides/fmo028/

El-Abed, O. (2004a) *Palestinian Refugees in Jordan*. Forced Migration Online Research Guide. Available at http://www.forcedmigration.org/guides/fmo025/

Eldar, A. (2002) 'Moratinos Document' – The Peace that nearly was at Taba. *Ha'aretz*, 14 February.

Eldar, A. and Tamari, S. (2002) The Refugee Problem at Taba: Interview with Yossi Beilin. *Palestine–Israel Journal*, 9 (2). pp.12–17.

El-Malak, L. (2004) *Israel's State Responsibility vis-à-vis Palestinian Refugees.* Paper presented at the International Symposium: A Just Solution for Palestinian Refugees? Organised by the Aïdun Group in cooperation with the University of Damascus, Damascus, 6–7 September.

Encyclopaedia Judaica (1971) *Reparations, German.* Volume 14, Jerusalem.

Ertekun, N. (1999) 'The Turkish Cypriot Outlook', in C. Dodd (ed.) *The Need for New Perspectives* (Huntingdon, UK: The Eothen Press).

Final Report (1999) Workshop on Compensation for Palestinian Refugees, International Development Research Centre, Ottawa, 14–15 July.

Finkelstein, N. (2003) *The Holocaust Industry: Reflections on the Exploitation of Jewish Suffering* (London: Verso).

Finkelstein, N. (2001) 'Lessons of Holocaust Compensation', in N. Aruri (ed.) *Palestinian Refugees: The Right of Return* (London: Pluto Press).

Finkelstein, N. (1992) Rejoinder to Benny Morris. *Journal of Palestine Studies*, 21 (2) Winter, pp.61–71.

Fischbach, M. (2008) *Jewish Property Claims against Arab Countries* (New York: Columbia University Press).

Fischbach, M. (2005) *The Peace Process and Palestinian Refugee Claims: Addressing Claims for Property Compensation and Restitution* (Washington, DC: United States Institute of Peace Press).

Fischbach, M. (2003a) *Records of Dispossession: Palestinian Refugee Property and the Arab–Israeli Conflict* (New York: Columbia University Press).

Fischbach, M. (2003b) *The Usefulness of the UNCCP Archives for Palestinian Refugee Compensation/Restitution Claims.* Paper presented at the IDRC Stocktaking II Conference on Palestinian Refugee Research, Ottawa, 17–20 June.

Fischbach, M. (2002) The UN and Palestinian Refugee Property Compensation. *Journal of Palestine Studies*, 31 (2) Winter, pp.34–50.

Flapan, S. (1987) *The Birth of Israel: Myths and Realities* (London: Croom Helm).

Frei, N. (2002) *Adenauer's Germany and the Nazi Past: The Politics of Amnesty and Integration* (New York: Columbia University Press).

Fried, S. (2002) The Refugee Issue at the Peace Conferences: 1949–2000. *Palestine–Israel Journal*, 9 (2), pp.24–34.

Gaps, Problems and Priorities in Palestinian Refugee Research (1997) A Stocktaking Conference on Palestinian Refugee Research, Ottawa, 8–9 December.

Garlick, M. (2003) *The UN Peace Plan for Cyprus: Property, Displacement and Proposed Solutions.* Paper presented to Badil Expert Forum for a Rights Based Approach to the Palestinian Refugee Question, Geneva, 2–5 October.

Gazit, S. (1995) Solving the Refugee Problem: A Prerequisite for Peace. *Palestine–Israel Journal*, 2 (4), pp.65–70.

Geddes, B. (1990) How the Cases You Choose Affect the Answers You Get: Selection Bias in Comparative Politics. *Political Analysis*, 2, pp.131–150.

Gelber, Y. (2001) 'The Historical Background', in J. Ginat and E. Perkins (eds) *The Palestinian Refugees: Old Problems – New Solutions* (Brighton: Sussex Academic Press).

George, A. (1979) 'Case Studies and Theory Development: The Method of Structured Focused Comparison', in P. Lauren (ed.) *Diplomacy: New Approaches in History, Theory, and Policy* (London: The Free Press).

Giniewski, P. (1959) Germany and Israel: The Reparations Treaty of September 10, 1952. *World Affairs Quarterly*, July, pp.169–185.

Ginor, F. (1972/73) The Impact of German Reparations and Restitution Payments on the Israeli Economy. *Wiener Library Bulletin*, 26 (3–4), pp.38–45.

Gobbi, H. (no date) *Rethinking Cyprus* (Tel Aviv: HaDfus Hejadash).

Goldmann, N. (1969) *The Autobiography of Nahum Goldmann: Sixty Years of Jewish Life* (New York: Holt Rinehart and Winston).

Goldmann, N. (1952) Why I Favour Direct Israel–German Negotiations. *Jewish Observer and Middle East Review*, 22 February.

Goodwin-Gill, G. (2000) 'Return and Compensation', in Palestine Liberation Organization, Department of Refugee Affairs, *The Final Status Negotiations on the Refugee Issue: Positions and Strategies* (Ramallah: PLO Department of Refugee Affairs).

Gresh, A. (2001) Proche-Orient, la paix manquée. *Le Monde Diplomatique*, Septembre. http://www.monde-diplomatique.fr/2001/09/GRESH/15632

Hadawi, S. (1988) *Palestinian Rights and Losses in 1948: A Comprehensive Study* (London: Saqi Books).

Hague, R., Harrop, M. and Breslin, S. (1992) *Political Science: A Comparative Introduction* (New York: St Martin's Press).

Hanieh, A. (2001) The Camp David Papers. *Journal of Palestine Studies*, 30 (2) Winter, pp.75–97.

Hannay, D. (2005) *Cyprus: The Search for a Solution* (London: I.B. Tauris).

Henley, J. (2005) The Plight of the Island Children. *Guardian*, 13 September.

Hicks, G. (1999) 'The Comfort Women Redress Movement', in R. Brooks (ed.) *When Sorry Isn't Enough* (New York: New York University Press).

Holt, R. and Richardson, J. (1970) 'Competing Paradigms in Comparative Politics', in R. Holt and J. Turner (eds) *The Methodology of Comparative Research* (New York: The Free Press).

Hopkin, J. (2002) 'Comparative Methods', in D. Marsh and G. Sroker (eds) *Theory and Methods in Political Science* (New York: Palgrave Macmillan).

International Crisis Group (2006) *The Cyprus Stalemate: What Next?* Europe report no. 171, 8 March.

International Organization for Migration (2008) *Property Restitution and Compensation: Practices and Experiences of Claims Programmes* (International Organization for Migration).

International Peace Research Institute (2003a) *The Annan Plan for Cyprus: A Citizen's Guide* (Oslo: PRIO).
International Peace Research Institute (2003b) *The Property Regime in the Annan Plan: A Citizen's Guide* (Oslo: PRIO).
Joseph, J. (1997) *Cyprus: Ethnic Conflict and International Politics* (Great Britain: Macmillan Press Ltd).
Joseph, J. (1985) *Cyprus: Ethnic Conflict and International Concern* (New York: Peter Lang Publishing, Inc.).
Khalidi, R. (1995) The Palestinian Refugee Problem: A Possible Solution. *Palestine–Israel Journal*, 2 (4), pp.72–78.
Klein, M. (2006) 'The Palestinian 1948 Refugees – Models of Allowed and Refused Return', in M. Dumper (ed.) *Palestinian Refugee Repatriation: Global Perspectives* (London: Routledge).
Kubursi, A. (1996) *Palestinian Losses in 1948: The Quest for Precision* (Washington, DC: Center for Policy Analysis on Palestine).
Kubursi, A. (1988) 'An Economic Assessment of Total Palestinian Losses in 1948', in S. Hadawi (ed.) *Palestinian Rights and Losses in 1948: A Comprehensive Study* (London: Saqi Books).
Landman, T. (2003) *Issues and Methods in Comparative Politics: An Introduction* (London: Routledge).
Lapidoth, R. (2002) *Legal Aspects of the Palestinian Refugee Question.* Jerusalem Letter, Viewpoints, no. 485, 1 September. Jerusalem Center for Public Affairs, available at http://www.jcpa.org/jl/vp485.htm, last visited on 26/01/2005
Lee, L. (1999) *The Issue of Compensation for Palestinian Refugees.* Paper presented at the Workshop on Compensation for Palestinian Refugees, International Development Research Centre, Ottawa, 14–15 July.
Lee, L. (1986) The Right to Compensation: Refugees and Countries of Asylum. *American Journal of International Law*, 80 (3) July, pp.532–567.
Lenzerini, F. (ed.) (2008) *Reparations for Indigenous Peoples: International and Comparative Perspectives* (Oxford: Oxford University Press).
Lustick, I. (2005) 'Negotiating Truth: The Holocaust, Lehavdil, and Al-Nakba', in A. Lesch and I. Lustick (eds) *Exile and Return: Predicaments of Palestinians and Jews* (Philadelphia: University of Pennsylvania Press).
Lynk, M. (2003) The Right to Restitution and Compensation in International Law and the Displaced Palestinians. *Refuge*, 21 (2) February, pp.96–113.
Mallinson, W. (2005) *Cyprus: A Modern History* (London: I.B. Tauris).
Ma'oz, M. (2001) 'Traditional Positions and New Solutions', in J. Ginat and E. Perkins (eds) *The Palestinian Refugees: Old Problems – New Solutions* (Brighton: Sussex Academic Press).
Marrus, M. (2006) *Official Apologies and the Quest for Historical Justice.* Occasional paper no. 111 (Toronto: Center for International Studies, University of Toronto).
Marx, E. (2001) 'Refugee Compensation: Why the Parties Have Been Unable to

Agree and Why It Is Important to Compensate Refugees for Losses', in J. Ginat and E. Perkins (eds) *The Palestinian Refugees: Old Problems – New Solutions* (Brighton: Sussex Academic Press).
Masalha, N. (2003) *The Politics of Denial: Israel and the Palestinian Refugee Problem* (London: Pluto Press).
Masalha, N. (2001) 'The Historical Roots of the Palestinian Refugee Question', in N. Aruri (ed.) *Palestinian Refugees: The Right of Return* (London: Pluto Press).
Masalha, N. (1991) A Critique of Benny Morris. *Journal of Palestine Studies*, 21 (1) Autumn, pp. 90–97.
McCurry, J. (2005) Discomfit women. *Guardian*, 14 June.
Miller, J. and Kumar, R. (eds) (2007) *Reparations: Interdisciplinary Inquiries* (Oxford: Oxford University Press).
Minow, M. (1998) *Between Vengeance and Forgiveness* (Boston: Beacon Press Books).
Morris, B. (1991) Response to Finkelstein and Masalha. *Journal of Palestine Studies*, 21 (1) Autumn, pp.98–114.
Morris, B. (1987) *The Birth of the Palestinian Refugee Problem 1947–1949* (Cambridge: Cambridge University Press).
Morris, B. and Barak, E. (2002) Camp David and After: An exchange (1. An Interview with Ehud Barak). *New York Review of Books*, 49 (10) 13 June.
Nasser, M. (2003) *Palestine Refugee Records Project*. Paper presented at the IDRC Stocktaking II Conference on Palestinian Refugee Research, Ottawa, 17–20 June.
Nathanson, R. (2003) *Survey of Palestinian Refugee Real Estate Holdings in Israel: Legal Mechanisms after 1948 which Enable Accurate Identification of Real Estate Owned by Palestinian Refugees and a Proposed Compensation Model Accordingly*. Paper presented at the IDRC Stocktaking II Conference on Palestinian Refugee Research, Ottawa, 17–20 June.
New Encyclopedia of Zionism and Israel (1994) *German–Israel agreement* (A Herzl Press Publication, Associated University Presses).
Office of the United Nations High Commissioner for Human Rights (2008) *Rule-of-law Tools for Post-conflict States: Reparations Programmes*. (New York and Geneva: United Nations).
O'Malley, B. and Craig, I. (1999) *The Cyprus Conspiracy: America, Espionage and the Turkish Invasion* (London: I.B. Tauris).
Ottawa Workshop (1997) *Plenary Session*. A stocktaking conference on Palestinian Refugee Research, Ottawa, 8–9 December.
Palestinian Refugees (2001) 22 January. Available at http://www.monde-diplomatique.fr/cahier/proche-orient/refugeespal-en
Palestinian Refugee ResearchNet (2008a) *Palestinian Refugees: An Overview*. Available at http://www.arts.mcgill.ca/mepp/new_prrn/background/index.htm
Palestinian Refugee ResearchNet (2008b) *Palestinian Refugees and Final*

Status: Key Issues. Available at http://www.arts.mcgill.ca/mepp/new_prrn/background/background_resolving.htm

Palestinian Refugee ResearchNet (2009) http://prrn.mcgill.ca/

Pappe, I. (2006) *The Ethnic Cleansing of Palestine* (London: Oneworld Publications).

Pappe, I. (2001) *The Making of the Arab–Israeli Conflict: 1947–1951* (London: I.B. Tauris).

Pappe, I. (1994) *The Making of the Arab-Israeli Conflict 1947–51* (London: I.B. Tauris).

Pappe, I. (1988) *Britain and the Arab–Israeli Conflict: 1948–51* (Basingstoke: Palgrave Macmillan).

Patel, V. (2003) *Comparative Analysis of Mass Claims Mechanisms*. Paper presented at the IDRC Stocktaking II Conference on Palestinian Refugee Research, Ottawa, 17–20 June.

Pease, L-E. (1976) *After the Holocaust: West Germany and Material Reparation to the Jews, from the Allied Occupation to the Luxembourg Agreements*. Ph.D thesis. (Florida State University College of Arts and Sciences).

Penguin Dictionary of International Relations (1998a) *Jus Cogens* (London: Penguin Books).

Penguin Dictionary of International Relations (1998b) *Justice* (London: Penguin Books).

Penguin Dictionary of International Relations (1998c) *Reparations* (London: Penguin Books).

Peretz, D. (2001) 'Refugee Compensation: Responsibility, Recipients, and Forms and Sources', in J. Ginat and E. Perkins (eds) *The Palestinian Refugees: Old Problems – New Solutions* (Brighton: Sussex Academic Press).

Peretz, D. (1999) *Palestinian Refugee Compensation*. Paper presented at the Workshop on Compensation for Palestinian Refugees, International Development Research Centre, Ottawa, 14–15 July.

Peretz, D. (1995) *Palestinian Refugee Compensation*. Information Paper Number 3, May (Washington, DC: The Center for Policy Analysis on Palestine).

Peretz, D. (1993) *Palestinian Refugees and the Middle East Peace Process* (Washington, DC: United States Institute of Peace Press).

Peters, B. (1998) *Comparative Politics: Theory and Methods* (Basingsoke: Palgrave).

Peters, J. (1996) *Pathways to Peace: The Multilateral Arab–Israeli Peace Talks* (London: Royal Institute of International Affairs).

P.G. (1954) German Reparations to Israel: The 1952 Treaty and its Effects. *The World Today*, 10 (6) June, pp.258–274.

Plenary Session (1997) A Stocktaking Conference on Palestinian Refugee Research, Ottawa, 8–9 December.

PLO Negotiations Support Unit (2006) *Return and Compensation*. PLO Negotiations Affairs Department, available at www.nad-plo.org/hrreturncomp.php

Potier, T. (2005) *Cyprus: Entering Another Stalemate?* Briefing paper, European Programme, EP BP 05/03 November, Chatham House.

Private Response on Palestinian Refugees (2001) 23 January. Available at http://www.monde-diplomatique.fr/cahier/proche-orient/israelrefugees-en

Quigley, J. (1999) *Compensation for Palestinian Refugees: Initial Comments.* Paper presented at the Workshop on Compensation for Palestinian Refugees, International Development Research Centre, Ottawa, 14–15 July.

Rempel, T. (2006) *Palestinian Refugees in the West Bank and Gaza Strip.* Forced Migration Online Research Guide. Available at http://www.forcedmigration.org/guides/fmo043/

Rempel, T. (2000) *The United Nations Conciliation Commission for Palestine and a Durable Solution for Palestinian Refugees.* Badil Information and Discussion Brief, issue no. 5, June.

Rempel, T. (1999) Compensation and Palestinian Refugees. *Journal of Palestine Studies*, 29 (1) Autumn, pp.36–49.

Richmond, O. (1998) *Mediating in Cyprus: The Cypriot Communities and the United Nations* (London: Frank Cass).

Roth, S. (1982) *West German Recompense for Nazi Wrongs: Thirty Years of the Luxembourg Agreements.* Research Report, nos. 16 & 17, November, Institute of Jewish Affairs, London.

Rubinstein, A. (1962) German Reparations in Retrospect. *Midstream*, 8 (1), pp.29–42.

Sagi, N. (1980) *German Reparations: A History of the Negotiations* (Jerusalem: The Hebrew University Magnes Press).

Samy, S. (2008) When Australia Said Sorry. *Al-Ahram Weekly*, 6–12 March.

Sanders, D. (1994) Methodological Considerations in Comparative Cross-national Research. *International Social Science Journal*, December, pp.513–521.

Sayigh, Y. (1964) *The Israeli Economy* (al-Qāhirah: Mahad al-Dirāsāt al-Arabīyah al-Ālīyah).

Scherer, J. (1997) *Blocking the Sun: The Cyprus Conflict* (Minneapolis: Mediterranean and East European Monographs, number 5, University of Minnesota).

Segev, T. (1986) *1949: The first Israelis* (London: Collier Macmillan).

Shafie, S. (2007) *Palestinian Refugees in Lebanon.* Forced Migration Online Research Guide. Available at http://www.forcedmigration.org/guides/fmo018/

Shafie, S. (2003) *Palestinian Refugees in Syria.* Forced Migration Online Research Guide. Available at http://www.forcedmigration.org/guides/fmo017/

Shelton, D. (2005) *Remedies in International Human Rights Law* (Oxford: Oxford University Press).

Shlaim, A. (1998) *The Politics of Partition: King Abdullah, the Zionists and Palestine 1921–1951* (Oxford: Oxford University Press).

Sieradzka, K. and Lerman, A. (1994) *Jewish Property in Central and Eastern Europe: New Developments in Restitution and Compensation Claims*. Research reports, no. 5 March, Institute of Jewish Affairs.

Smith, D. (2004) 200 years on, the Queen is told to say sorry for Britain's role in slave trade. *Observer*, 5 December.

Sonyel, S. (1999) 'New Light on the Genesis of the Conflict: British Documents 1960–1967', in C. Dodd (ed.) *The Need for New Perspectives* (Huntingdon, UK: The Eothen Press).

Sozen, A. and Ozersay, K. (2006) The Annan Plan: State Succession or Continuity. *Middle Eastern Studies (forthcoming)*, available at http://cpc.emu.edu.tr/ (last accessed February 2006).

Stavrinides, Z. (1999) 'Greek Cypriot Perceptions', in C. Dodd (ed.) *The Need for New Perspectives* (Huntingdon, UK: The Eothen Press).

Stephen, M. (1997) *The Cyprus Question* (London: The British–Northern Cyprus Parliamentary Group).

Swisher, C. (2004) *The Truth about Camp David: the Untold Story about the Collapse of the Middle East Peace Process* (New York: Nation Books).

Takkenberg, L. (1998) *The Status of Palestinian Refugees in International Law* (Oxford: Clarendon Press).

Talhami, G. (2003) *Palestinian Refugees: Pawns to Political Actors* (New York: Nova Science Publishers, Inc.).

Tamari, S. (2005) 'Palestinian Refugee Property Claims: Compensation and Restitution', in A. Lesch and I. Lustick (eds) *Exile and Return: Predicaments of Palestinians and Jews* (Philadelphia: University of Pennsylvania Press).

Tamari, S. (1995) The Future of Palestinian Refugees in the Peace Negotiations. *Palestine–Israel Journal*, 2 (4) pp.8–14.

Tamari, S. and Zureik, E. (eds) (2001) *Reinterpreting the Historical Record: The Uses of Palestinian Refugee Archives for Social Science Research and Policy Analysis* (Jerusalem: Institute of Jerusalem Studies).

Teitel, R. (2000) *Transitional Justice* (Oxford: Oxford University Press).

Thompson, J. (2007) 'Coming to Terms with the Past in Australia', in J. Miller and R. Kumar (eds) *Reparations: Interdisciplinary Inquiries* (Oxford: Oxford University Press).

Timm, A. (1997) *Jewish Claims against East Germany: Moral Obligations and Pragmatic Policy* (Budapest: Central European University Press).

Tisdall, S. (2005) Sino-Japanese 'cold War' Stirs New Tensions. *Guardian*, 18 January.

Tocci, N. (2004) *EU Accession Dynamics and Conflict Resolution: Catalysing Peace or Consolidating Partition in Cyprus?* (Aldershot: Ashgate Publishing).

Torpey, J. (2006) *Making Whole what has been Smashed: on Reparations Politics* (Cambridge, MA: Harvard University Press).

Tovy, J. (2003) Negotiating the Palestinian Refugees. *Middle East Quarterly*, Spring.

UNRWA. (2009) United Nations Relief and Works Agency for Palestine Refugees. Available at www.unrwa.org

Vidal, D. (2002) *Le Peche Originel d'Israel: l'Expulsion des Palestiniens Revisitee par les Nouveaux Historiens Israeliens* (Paris: Les Editions de l'Atelier).

Vogel, R., (1969) *The German Path to Israel: A Documentation* (London: Oswald Wolff).

Vogel, R. (1968/1969) Voices in the German–Israeli dialogue: Adenauer, Strauss and Others. *The Wiener Library Bulletin*, 23 (1) new series 14 winter, pp.6–12.

Waldron, J. (1992) Superseding Historic Injustice. *Ethics*, 103 (1) October, pp.4–28.

Wolffsohn, M. (1993) *Eternal Guilt? Forty Years of German–Jewish–Israeli Relations* (New York: Columbia University Press).

Yamamoto, E. and Ebesgugawa, L. (2006) 'Report on Redress: The Japanese American Internment', in P. De Greiff (ed.) *The Handbook of Reparations* (Oxford: Oxford University Press).

Zambouras, S. (1999) 'Current Greek Attitudes and Policy', in C. Dodd (ed.) *The Need for New Perspectives* (Huntingdon, UK: The Eothen Press).

Zweig, R. (2001) *German Reparations and the Jewish World: A History of the Claims Conference* (London: Frank Cass).

Index

In this index figures and tables are indicated in bold. Notes are indicated by n.